THE LIFE
OF
JUNE
COLEBANK
BLANSHAN

By June Colebank Blanshan

Edited by Rebecca Blanshan Colebank

Table of Contents

Little Log Cabin in Woodside Township

I was born in the downstairs bedroom of a farmhouse in Woodside Township, Polk County, Minnesota. The house was just across the road and a little west of the Maple Lake Lutheran Church. I made my debut in the dead of winter on January 29th, 1926. Dr. Griffin was called to come from Fertile, about 14 miles away. Nellie (Mrs. Helmer) Kittleson, a nearby neighbor, was called to be midwife and nurse. She stayed overnight a few days to help while my mother recuperated. My mother and dad were both 32 at the time, and my brother Warren was five.

My mother and dad had just moved to Woodside Township a couple years before that from Madelia, a small town in the farming country of southwestern Minnesota. My dad had been laid off from his job at the cement factory there. My dad's brother John Colebank and his family were already up there and wrote glowing letters about how good the farms were up there and how they got so many bushels to the acre of grain, so my parents packed up and moved up there. At first they rented a farm belonging to my mother's half-brother, John (Jack) Nasman, where we lived until they bought an 80-acre farm about three miles away.

When I was born my skin was white, not red like a lot of babies. I had a little button nose that everyone called a pug nose. My brother Warren said his little sister had a "plug nose." Warren had been the center of attention for five years and didn't like it when baby sister took over.

My mother had to help my dad milk the cows. She tried leaving me in the house with my brother, but when she checked on us Warren had the poker out of the hot ash pan of the heating stove and said he was going to hit me because I wouldn't stop crying. So that was the end of that. My dad built a pen in the barn and I spent my time in there while they milked. My first word was "cow-Mahuh." I walked when I was 14 months old. We weren't encouraged to walk because they thought we might get bowlegged if we walked too early. That was probably due to lack of vitamins rather than the walking, however.

One day my mother sat me in my high chair near the kitchen stove to keep warm. I started rocking the chair and it fell against the stove. The back of my right hand was burned and I still have a scar there. My mother must have caught me before I got burned worse.

Grandma Oleson and baby June

Grandma Oleson, my mother's mother, came to visit, and she was holding me on her lap when I kept grabbing for her food. She said "Why, this child is hungry!" and proceeded to feed me mashed potatoes from her plate. My mother changed me to a bottle with cow's milk then.

At one time I had a breaking out on my head and my mother took me to the doctor. He said it was eczema and not to wash my head with water, just clean it with oil. Aunt Clara (Uncle John's wife) came over, took one look at it and said "That's nothing but cradle cap!" She took me and washed my head with soapy water until my head was raw and oozing. Then she said, "I guess the doctor was right."

The year 1926 was a year for babies among our relatives: Uncle John and Aunt Clara Colebank had John Francis on February 18th; Uncle Ernest and Aunt Mary (mother's sister) Cambronne had Rodney on January 20th; Uncle Victor (mother's brother) and Aunt Manie Nasman had Viola on October 25th; Aunt Clara (Dad's sister) and Uncle Doan (John) Strean had Kenneth on March 10th, and Henry (Dad's brother) and Ruth Colebank had Henry Jr. on June 11th of that year.

Cousin Ann Colebank holding brother John and baby June

Sometime after I learned to walk I was still sucking my thumb, mostly at night when I was going to sleep. My mother decided to try to break me of the habit, so she tied mittens on my hands. The first night I cried a long time. The second night I cried for a while and the third night I went to my mother and held up my hands to have the mittens put on. I quit sucking my thumb.

3

In May of 1929 my Grandma Oleson died in St. James, a town near Madelia. My mother took me and went down for the funeral. I was three years and four months old. I was not shy at all on the train. I was friendly with everyone and sat on their laps. Later on I became very shy. I would run and hide when we got company. Mama was worried about how I would do in school so she took me to visit school in the spring of the year before the fall I was to start. She sat down at a desk, and I immediately crawled under it and wouldn't come out until school was over.

When I was 2 my parents moved to the 80-acre farm they had bought about 3 miles from their present farm. There weren't many buildings on the farm – just an old log cabin with a lean-to on each side and a very small barn. No water or electricity, of course. I think mama was very disappointed in the house but thought it would be nice for us to own our own farm. My dad promised he

would build her a new house as soon as he could afford it. Dad had borrowed money from his dad to buy the farm but wouldn't go in debt anymore after that. The new house didn't come until about 12 years later.

At this time my parents owned three cows, two horses, one pig, and 24 chickens. The barn on the farm was open on one side and would only hold a few animals, so the first thing my dad did was

4

build a barn. The new barn had a haymow and room for four horses and eight cows.

Dad built a lean-to on the north side which housed the red Delaval cream separator and pump with gasoline engine. Behind it was a room for his pigs.

The present well was no good so Dad had to have a new well drilled. It ended up being quite far from the house because that was the only spot they could find water. The well was 100 feet deep. The water was very nice and clear and oh, so cold. It tasted very good. Dad ran a pipe through a good-sized wooden tank that he had placed near the pump house. From there, another pipe ran to the other side of the barn to the cow's water tank. The water in the tank was always cold so that's where we kept the cream cans until they could be taken to the creamery. We also kept our milk for drinking in there.

In 1930 Dad built a chicken house that could house 100 chickens. He later admitted that the chickens were what kept them in groceries during the depression years.

At first they had an assorted variety of chickens but later Mama had leghorns. They were good layers but very flighty and would

The chicken coop

get scared too easily. When she heard about a chicken breed named Austra Whites she ordered them. They were a little heavier and tamer. They were white with a few black feathers and were good layers. I helped my mother feed them, carry water to them, gather eggs, etc. I enjoyed the chickens. They always talked to me when I was in the chicken house.

The chicks were ordered to come in the spring. When they arrived at the post office they would call and say the mailman was bringing them out so we should meet him at the mailbox. In the fall Mama would sell the older hens. They would be replaced by the new chicks who were fully grown by fall. If we accidentally got some roosters we ate them. Mama had a large egg crate that she filled with eggs and sent to the store to be exchanged for groceries. The store man, Ed Ness, would always insert a sack of candy in the groceries sent back in the egg crate which we kids looked forward to. We took our cream and eggs to Maple Bay to sell. Maple Bay consisted of a grocery store, a creamery, two Lutheran churches, a blacksmith shop and a few houses.

My hair was blonde and curly when I was little. It was fine and easily got tangled. I made such a big fuss when Mama tried to comb it she cut my hair. It didn't curl so much after that. When I was about four years old Grandpa L S and Grandma Martha

Grandparents LS and Martha with baby June

Colebank come up from Madelia to visit. Grandma brushed my hair into curls.

Various relatives came to visit us. Once Dad's sister Jennie and her husband Friday (Enoch Howard Holmes, but he didn't like to be called that) came from southern Minnesota. They had a daughter who was several years older than I. Aunt Jennie brought a coat and bonnet set that their daughter had outgrown that was very pretty. It was red taffeta and had some shirring on it. I remember them putting the coat and bonnet on me, holding me and saying how pretty I looked.

Another time my dad's cousin Pearl Colebank and his wife Wynafred came. We were sitting at the table eating a meal when I suddenly held out my arm and said "See, I've got an elbow!" Everyone laughed and I didn't know what they were laughing at so I was very embarrassed.

My dad made some changes to the log cabin we lived in, and I remember the exact layout of the cabin to this day. He closed up the door on the west and put one in on the other side because he wanted the driveway on the other side of the house. Later he built a porch there too. Although there was only room for a few, he put cupboards in the kitchen along with a sink. The sink had a drainpipe going outside so we didn't have to carry out dishwater. He also made a window just above the sink. There was a Monarch wood range that had a reservoir for warm water, and what they called a warming oven up above where you could keep your food warm. It had little doors on it. The wood box stood to the left of the stove. It was my brother's job to keep that full.

There was a tall metal can painted green to the right of the cupboard in which my mother kept flour. We always bought it by the 100-pound bag. A square oak table that could be made larger by adding leaves was on the east side of the room. We had five chairs. Three of the chairs we got from Grandma Oleson's when she died. They had actually belonged to Adam Oleson's first wife. Mom never cared much for them and called them "Adam Oleson's chairs." They must have gotten the other two when they got married.

Before we had the porch, the washing machine had to be in the northeast corner of the kitchen which made the kitchen very crowded. There was a window on the north and two windows close together on the east. They were all small and had about four panes each. On the floor was linoleum. The walls were one thickness of boards with wallpaper over that. Seems like there was a layer of tar paper too. There were some hooks on the south wall which were used to hang up coats.

The door to the living room was in the middle of that wall and the high chair stood to the right of that. We used the same wooden high chair for all three of us. Warren got it when he was older because he was the first to sit in it. The living room had log beams on the ceiling. The heating stove was on the north wall to the left of the door to the kitchen.

In the northwest corner was my dad's rocking chair. My mother's rocking chair was by the piano. In the southwest corner was the secretary (bookcase desk.) There was a shelf by my dad's chair for the radio and whatever papers he had. Next to that was the piano with a piano bench. On the north wall to the right of the bedroom door were some orange crates which served for a table for plants. On the east wall on the north end was the stairway which was a ladder type and very steep. There was also some sort of table on that wall because I remember studying there. When Vickie was a baby the crib was in that spot.

The bedroom was in the north end of the house. It was very small and there was room only for a bed and dresser. It had one window on the north. To the left of that were hooks for clothes. There was a big framed picture on the wall that always fascinated me. My mother said her mother had traded a peddler a chicken or two for it. It was of a big black dog lying down and a little girl in a red dress lying beside him. I believe it was by a seashore. The dog seemed to be protecting the little girl who seemed to be sleeping.

Our upstairs was like an attic. The ceiling was not very high. My dad partitioned it into two rooms. Warren's was on the west. He had a cot and a dresser and my mother's big trunk. On the east was a double bed and a dresser. On the north wall by the stairway was my mother's big red wooden box. We called it the "red box." It contained my mother's schoolteacher clothes. She taught school for eight years before she got married.

Student souvenir with Linda's picture from District 22, Nelson Township, Watonwan County in 1914

The cabin had one four-pane window on each end – no storm windows. Jack Frost painted the most beautiful pictures on those in the winter. When the wind was in the east or northwest and it snowed, fine snow would drift in on our beds.

The outside of the house was white-washed. Vines grew up in the summer and covered a lot of the log part. On the roof was an aerial for the radio and a small windmill to charge the battery for the radio. There was also a lightning rod on the aerial going down to a rod in the ground below the window on the East. Many trees surrounded the house so we were somewhat protected from the wind.

There was a trap door on the living room floor not far from the stairway with a ladder which went down into the dirt cellar. It was only under the main part of the cabin. It had shelves for canned goods, a bin for potatoes and a big crock to make sauerkraut in. The potatoes had to last a year. There was also something filled with sand to put carrots in. Surprising how long they kept.

One day my mother was down in the cellar and Vickie was watching her. I think Vickie was less than two years old. Vickie said "I'm coming right down," and she stepped right off the ladder and fell down on the floor, barely missing the big stone crock. She didn't seem to be hurt.

Linda, Lester and kids in front of John and Clara's house

Animals

We always had a dog. The earliest one I remember was Jackie. He was a long-haired black and white dog about the size of a lab. He would howl when my Dad played the harmonica. The next one was similar but we had to get rid of him because he started eating chickens. The next one was a cross between rat terrier and bull dog. He was brown and white and short-haired. We had him the longest of all our dogs. His name was Arky after Arkie, the Arkansas Woodchopper who was on "WLS Barn Dance" on the radio.

Warren, June and Vickie with Arky.

Arky was death on any stray animals that came around, especially woodchucks. He would get one up a tree and sit and bark at it until my Dad came and shot it. He would shake it and make sure it was dead, then go and bury it. He didn't want me to see where he was putting it, so I had to hide and watch until he was gone. I wanted the front feet because there was a bounty on them.

I used to trap gophers too. I got five cents for each gopher (had to cut off the front feet) and ten cents for each woodchuck. Arky got in a dog fight when he was ten years old and died of the injuries. He managed to crawl home before he died. We all thought a lot of him and hated to lose him.

The next dog we had was Poochie. He was a small dog but had long hair and looked somewhat like a shepherd. He was white with brown spots. He had a certain chair he liked to be in and we put a rug in it just for him. If we took the rug off the chair he would try to drag it back up there.

We always had cats too. They were barn cats. Wild tom cats would roam around in the woods behind the house and yowl loudly at night. My brother told me they were as big as lions and would eat you up. I believed him and would not go outside at

June and cat

13

night alone. Those toms always mated with our cats and we got all manner of kittens.

Once we got a kitten with six toes on each foot. We called her "Toeser." Another time one of the kittens was black angora. It was so pretty but it was male and they always left. Mama even had him neutered but he still left. She called him Tack.

Those same tomcats would come around later and kill the kittens. The mama would grab one and run. I guess that was nature's way of keeping the population down. One night a gray cat whom we called Daisy was determined that she wanted to be in the house. She yowled and yowled and finally crawled up on the roof under the eaves and stayed all night. It was 40 below and by morning she was frozen stiff but still alive. My mother brought her in the house and warmed her up by rubbing her. She survived but she never tried that again. Sometimes Vickie and I would pretend the cats were babies and dress them up.

Other animals out in the woods were skunks, porcupines, red squirrels, gray squirrels, flying squirrels, weasels, raccoons, minks, deer, and wolves. We even heard a lynx screaming out in the woods but it never came where we could see it.

We usually kept about eight cows. They were Holstein cows. Our favorite was old Pet. She was always so gentle and would let anyone milk her. When it was cold the cows had to be kept in the barn. That made a lot of work for my dad as he had to clean out the manure every day with a scoop shovel. He put it in a manure spreader and when it was full he would hitch up the horses to it and spread it out on the fields for fertilizer. He fed the cows hay from the haymow and mixed grain that he had ground up himself.

I don't remember how he gave them water when they were kept inside. Whenever he could he would let them out in the cow lot by the barn to get a drink and a little exercise. They were so happy to get out they would jump around. When the weather warmed up they were turned out in the pasture. We had two pastures.

One was across the road. They were rotated as the grass was eaten up. The cows were milked twice a day at the same time. My dad was fussy about that. He said they gave more milk that way. Pet gave the most.

Cow yard in Woodside

When the haymow got empty my dad would go out in the field where he had haystacks and get some more. In the winter the deer found the haystack and liked to have a snack now and then. One day they were so intent on eating that they didn't notice my dad sneaking up on them with a board. He got close enough to hit one of them on the rump and they all took off. You couldn't shoot the deer because there was no deer season during the Depression. There were a lot of them around. My dad counted 40 one day out in the field by the big woods.

We also kept one or two sows which would have piglets in the spring. They usually each had 10 or 15. We sold them in the fall but kept one for us to eat. When the little pigs were born I could hardly wait to see them. My Dad didn't let me see them for a few days because he was afraid it would excite the sow and she would lay on some of her pigs.

We always had two horses and sometimes three. My Dad loved his horses and took good care of them. They worked hard, hauling manure out to the field, plowing, cultivating, raking, putting up hay, and in winter they were our only means of getting out since the road by us was never plowed.

My dad built an enclosed sled. He put a little heater in it and a car seat across the back and a chair for the driver. Twice a week he had to make the three-mile drive in winter to carry the cream cans to the creamery. Our neighbor Ingbret Akre took turns with my dad. In fact, the horses took us wherever we wanted to go. We didn't ride them much although we could have. My mother was a good horseback rider when she was growing up and herding cows, but I never saw her on a horse.

Vickie with the enclosed sled

It was a catastrophe to lose a horse and we lost several. One of them ate something that made him bloat up and die. The other one got "sleeping sickness" (encephalitis.) That was Nellie. There was an epidemic of it that year and many farmers lost horses. My dad made slings attached to the ceiling which went around their bellies so when they passed out they wouldn't get hurt.

Nellie was a smart horse. She discovered how to unlatch the door to the chicken house and go in and eat the chicken feed. Chickens would be squawking and flying everywhere. When we heard that, we knew Nellie was in the chicken house again.

Nellie also couldn't stand to see a fire. When my mother tried to burn trash she would paw it out. She liked to scratch her back by going under the clothesline when there were clean clothes on it. They would get all dirty and make my mother mad. Nellie would also get in the rain barrels containing the rainwater we were saving to wash our hair with and mess it all up.

My dad kept his horses even after he got a tractor. They kept our yard mowed very nicely and would do winter jobs that the tractor

Lester and his beloved horses

wasn't much good at. They also helped dig out the basement for the new house my dad built. He used what he called a scraper. It looked like a big scoop with handles with which my dad guided it. My dad was very sad when he had to give the horses up. He was so happy when he found some Norwegian bachelors that bought old horses just because they didn't want to see them killed. They had a life of leisure and didn't have to work anymore.

One time when I was wandering around in the pasture I saw the horses were standing still with their heads and ears up. I looked where they were looking and there was a deer grazing among the cattle. The cattle were ignoring it but the horses didn't know what to think of it.

Lester, Linda, Esther and Robert with their children L to R: Warren, Vickie, June, Dale, Carroll and George. Esther was Linda's twin and Robert was Lester's cousin.

Entertainment

There was always something to do on the farm. My favorite thing was to run through the woods observing the many kinds of trees, berry bushes, wild flowers, etc. Sometimes I pretended I was an Indian. There was a culvert under the road past our driveway and I liked to crawl through it. It was only about a foot and a half in diameter. I pulled myself through on my elbows. The last time I tried it I could barely get through because I had grown. That gave me a little scare because my folks didn't know I did that and wouldn't know where to look.

There was a big woods bordering our farm on the north. Our neighbors, the Ganzhorns, had one of their little girls, Beulah, get lost in there for four days and nights. They couldn't find her. Then they noticed the dog would be gone at times so they followed him. He led them to her. She was bitten up by mosquitoes but otherwise unharmed. They thought she had eaten berries for food. She was only three years old.

Beulah Ganzhorn

I went and explored in that same woods. I found an old woodcutter's cabin that was falling down. I didn't go there much because it was too big. I did go there and pick juneberries, though.

There was an interesting pond between the barn and the house. Lots of frogs, dragonflies, and other creatures lived in it. Once, Vickie, our neighbor girl and I decided to go swimming in there. It was more or less a mud hole. We had fun for a while until we started itching. We itched so badly my mother had to give us baths. We were allergic to something in there.

There was a lake on part of our farm that was interesting, too. There were muskrats living on one end of it but not on our property. There was a small sandpit near the lake where my dad got sand for cement-making. Sometimes it was fun to play in that sand. One summer when we had a dry year the lake almost dried up. The cows would wade out there and get stuck in the mire and have to be pulled out.

Minnow Lake

We belonged to 4-H and had meetings once a month at some of the members' homes. We had to have a project and keep records

about it. I took cake and bread-baking and sewing. We could exhibit our things at the fair and get some money if we won a prize. My mother belonged to an extension club which was like an adult 4-H. They did mostly sewing. There was also the Community Club that met occasionally in the town hall. Anyone could attend that. At one of the meetings my mother got first prize for being the fastest one to peel a potato with a paring knife.

My cousin Ann used to come and get me and take me to some parties. The entertainment was ring games which were a sort of folk dance. We played until midnight and then had lunch. Usually we were celebrating someone's birthday. After lunch we played some more games. Some of them were: "There is Somebody Waiting," "Two in the Boat," "Skip to My Lou," "Four Little Girls went Skating on the Ice," "Please, Oh Please, Oh Do Not Let Me Fall," and two games which were all in Norwegian. I didn't know the words but I knew the actions. After that the girls hoped some boy would ask to take them home.

We had games we played at home too. I remember Chinese checkers, which was actually a marble game on a board with holes large enough for marbles. We also had "Authors," "Old Maid," and regular cards with which we were allowed to play solitaire. We didn't play cards with them otherwise because some of the Lutherans didn't believe in playing cards.

We had a wind-up phonograph which we kids had a lot of fun with. We had a black box full of records. Some of them were songs by a tenor and a Scottish singer by the name of Harry Lauder. There were some comical ones, I remember. One dialog was "Sister Sorrowful Entertains the Minister." Another record had an etiquette song in it. Some of the words were "Always mix your peas with your potatoes. That makes eating with your knife a cinch. Take two helpings on your plate, eat so fast you won't be late. Thank you for your very kind attention."

Vickie, June, Afhild Akre and cousin Grace Colebank

Our closest neighbors were Ingbret and Lily Akre. They had a little girl a little younger than I whose name was Alfhild. I loved going over to Akre's to play. Alfhild and I would go back and forth to each other's homes and play with our dolls, etc. Our enclosed sled made a good doll house in the summer. We also played school, using Vickie for our pupil. Because of that she could read when she went to school and they put her a grade ahead.

Alfhild Akre

Mrs. Akre made the best peanut butter cookies and rosettes. One day I asked my mother if I could go over to Akre's. She said no. I tried to persuade her but she didn't give in. She said if I went over there I would get a spanking when I got back.

I went anyway. When I came home I very reluctantly made my appearance. I knew what was coming. My mother was true to her word and gave me a spanking with her boiler stick (part of an old broom handle used to stir clothes when boiling them). I learned my lesson and never did that again. That's the only spanking I remember getting from her. My dad never spanked me.

On holidays we got together with the relatives. If we ate at Uncle John and Aunt Clara's we got goose; if we ate at Uncle Rob and Aunt Esther's we got turkey, and if we ate at our place, we got chicken, because that's what we raised.

On the Fourth of July we rented or borrowed a big five-gallon freezer. The ice had been cut from the lake and hidden down in the sawdust pile. It kept very well there. We had to crank the freezer by hand, and we had plenty of boys to do that. One family would bring the cream, one the eggs and one the sugar, all on a rotating basis. The ice cream was so delicious and we could eat our fill. The boys and men would usually have a game of ball.

Listening to the radio was another amusement. Warren would rush home and fill the wood box so he would be in time to listen to "Jack Armstrong." My mother enjoyed the soap operas while she worked – "Ma Perkins," "The Guiding Light," "Mary Martin," "Vic and Sade," and others. My dad listened to the news, weather reports, boxing and the WLS barn dance. We also listened to "Fibber McGee and Molly," "Jack Benny," "The Burns and Allen Show," and sometimes to "The Shadow," "Gangbusters" and "Kaltenburg's Kindergarten." I liked a show called "Let's Pretend," which aired on Saturdays. We always discussed these programs the next day at school, repeating the jokes and giving our opinions on them.

The new Woodside house dining room with the radio in corner

My dad always took a day off for each county fair. One fair was in Fertile (Polk) and one in Fosston (East Polk). We would leave early and take a lunch. We were anxious to see if we had won a prize on our 4-H stuff. If you took an animal to exhibit you had to stay overnight and take care of it. There were lots of exhibits, a show in the grandstand and lots of rides. Daddy gave us each a little money and we could spend it as we liked. Boys who had cars liked to take their girlfriends for a night at the fair.

We could always visit our neighbors, but it was kind of hard for us because we had to get the chores done first. One New Year's Eve we were invited to Selmer and Helen Johnson's. Warren and Harlan went upstairs in Harlan's room. They had a cot in the living room where I slept.

Warren would get together with his friends and they would play their instruments. Warren taught several of them to play guitar. They performed once for the Hillside School PTA. They met at each other's houses.

Sometimes on a Sunday afternoon we would go to Uncle Rob and Aunt Esther's. Uncle Rob could play a lot of instruments. His favorite seemed to be the mandolin. He would play that and my dad would accompany him on the guitar. He inspired my brother to play guitar and violin. My mother enjoyed visiting with her twin sister while they played.

I remember my mother having some ladies over to help her tie a quilt. She had it all set up on chairs in the living room. The ladies could visit while they worked and there was always lunch.

The school PTA meetings were a social event too. They met once a month. They elected officers, had a business meeting, and lunch. Sometimes the desks were pushed back after lunch so the young people could play games. There was always a lunch committee and a program committee. My dad was often asked to sing and play his guitar. Hartvig Folvig was asked to play his accordion and Ted Austinson his violin, although Ted always played the same tune. I think it was "Snow Deer." Uncle Rob would play his various instruments and my mother and Aunt Esther would give humorous monologues.

Mr. and Mrs. Ganzhorn with daughter and husband

One time they asked Jake Ganzhorn to give a talk. He was from Ohio and they thought he might have something to tell. Well, he started talking – more like rambling on and on – and didn't know when to quit. So the people started talking to each other thinking he would take the hint but he didn't. Finally the gas lantern started to get dim. Nobody got up to pump it up. He finally quit when the light got really dim. Immediately, someone got up and pumped up the light.

Another time Warren sent a note to Aunt Esther (she was on the program committee) asking if he could sing for PTA. Aunt Esther called my mother up and asked her if he could sing and if she should let him be on the program. My mother said, "Let him try." He was probably about 11 or 12 and had gotten a ukelele for Christmas. He wanted to play and sing with that. We didn't know if he could do it or not as we had never heard him. Well, he got up there and did a good job. I think the song was "Where is My Wandering Boy Tonight."

Warren and ukulele and harmonica

Once or twice during the summer, usually on a Sunday, my dad would take us to Union Lake. It was six or seven miles from us. My Dad didn't believe in working on Sundays so he could get away. My mother got a real nice bathing suit for me, probably out of the catalog. It was aqua blue and made out of some stretchy, satiny material. I liked to be in the water but was afraid to put my head under. I never learned to swim and no one tried to teach me. My parents could swim. I probably was too scared to learn.

26

Grandma Anna Greta Oleson, Uncle Berndt's daughter holding June, Linda's twin Esther and her husband Rob, Warren in front of Lester Colebank

Grandma Anna Greta Oleson with Warren and June

Country School

District 156 School

I started school when I was six years old. My birthday came in January so I had to wait until the next fall to start. The law said you had to be six by January 1st and my birthday was January 29th. I had gotten over being shy about going and always enjoyed school. My first grade teacher was Miss Lang. We had the "Little Red Hen" reading book. She also taught us phonics and had flash cards. We had a workbook called "Read and Do." I loved to do the workbook and asked the teacher if I could work ahead in it, but she said no.

I got in trouble for the first and last time while Miss Lang was teaching. One of the big boys, Norman (Pitts was his nickname) Broske, motioned for me to shake my fist at the teacher. I didn't know what that meant so I did it. Miss Lang was at the blackboard with her back to me but she turned around and saw me. My punishment was to stand by the blackboard with my nose touching a circle that she had drawn there.

When I was in first grade we had a kind of a "show and tell." I had no idea what to say. It was "Did you know?" day. So, when it was my turn I stood up and said "Did you know girls aren't "fosed" to wear overalls?"

The school was about a mile from us if we cut across the neighbor's pasture and fields. If we walked the road it was two miles. The school was fairly new at the time, I think. In the main room were four rows of desks, with smaller ones by the windows. Blackboards were on the walls in front and back. Teacher's desk was in front of the pupils' desks. On the front wall were pictures of Washington and Lincoln and a flag. A big black stove was on the right up in front and right by it was the wood box. The boys had to keep that filled. On the right side of the main room were 3 small rooms. At the front was the boys cloakroom with a toilet and the middle room was the girl's cloakroom with a toilet. There were a lot of hooks in them to hang up coats, etc. The third room was our little library. There were several shelves with a curtain going across below. Behind that curtain were stored things like the tin cups for PTA and the big gray enamel coffee pot, also for PTA. The basement stairway door was off the boy's cloakroom, and that is where we stacked the wood in neat piles along the walls. The tanks for the chemical toilets were down there too.

Every fall the parents would come and bring a saw and saw up wood for the winter. There was a small woods on the school yard where I suppose they got the wood. We always took some time from school to carry the wood down to the basement and stack it up.

The big stove had a jacket around it so we wouldn't get burned. It had a pan of water on top for humidity. We used to bring jars of soup from home and set them atop the stove. They would be nice and warm by noon. We also brought potatoes sometimes and put them in the ash pan. They would be done by noon and would be very tasty.

Our school was District 156, also called the Prompt Band School. We usually had 15 to 20 students. The school board hired the teachers. My dad was on the school board and when he quit they elected my mother. I think they thought she was well-qualified having taught school herself for eight years.

Miss McKinnon was our next teacher for two years. She came from Crookston and it was rumored she came from a well-to-do family. She had very nice clothes and often wore a pretty smock over them.

Our teacher wanted us to know something about art. She brought pictures of famous paintings. She gave us each a small picture of each painting and we made a little book out of them.

Every Friday from 1:00 p.m. to 2:00 p.m. we had music. Miss Lang brought her record player and played classical music for us. She had us learn the names of the songs and who wrote it. Some of the other teachers didn't spend that much time on music or art. I think Miss Lang thought it was important.

Other teachers that followed were Miss Woelk, Kordula Holmvik and Miss Howe. Mrs. Holmvik thought we were very talented in music and had us sing in a music contest in Crookston. We had two eighth grade boys who could sing tenor and bass. We had all four parts. I can't remember the song or if we rated well or not.

Mrs. Holmvik offered to give us group piano lessons for 25 cents each if we were brought to her house, which was over near Fertile. I think six or eight kids signed up. The parents took turns driving us over there. I think I got about 10 lessons. That was all the lessons I ever had.

Mrs. Holmvik also read to us every day out of Richard Haliburton adventure books. We thought they were very exciting.

Kordula Holmvik ran a variety store in later years (1964)

School started at 8:30 a.m. and continued until 4 p.m. We had a 15-minute recess in both the afternoon and the morning. At noon we had an hour. We bolted down our food in order to get the most use out of that hour. In winter we took our skis and went to a nearby hill to slide down. In the spring we went to a nearby pond and played on the ice. We especially liked it when the ice got thinner. We called it "rubbery ice." Of course we played on it until it broke and we fell in and got our feet wet. Luckily it wasn't very deep. When we got back to school the teacher made us take off our shoes and stockings and sit up by the stove until we were dry. I think she hung the socks up on the stove jacket. The teacher always rang the bell five minutes early so we could get back on time if we were off the school ground.

Other games we played were pom-pom-pullaway, tag, wolf and dog, drop the handkerchief, last couple out, nib stick, freeze tag,

31

jump rope and kitten ball. If it was rainy or stormy we stayed inside and played games like clap in and clap out, Simon says, bird, beast or fish and hangman on the blackboard.

Our lunch boxes were usually a lard or syrup pail. Later on Warren and I got metallic lunch boxes. Mine was green and his was blue. They had little vacuum bottles in them for a drink. They got broken in no time. We usually put our lunch boxes on top of the wood box in plain sight. (Sometimes food would disappear out of them if we left them in the cloakroom.) My lunch usually consisted of an apple or orange, cookies or cake, two sandwiches (peanut butter and jelly, cheese or potted meat.) The other kids sometimes had lefse. I wished I could have that but my mother didn't make it. She tried it once but my dad didn't care for it so she didn't make it again.

Every day we said the Pledge of Allegiance. We had a flag pole outside that also had a flag. Someone was chosen each week to have the privilege of raising it up and taking it down at the end of the school day. We had to be very careful not to let it touch the ground. If it rained or snowed we had to take it down.

When it was cold out we always dressed warm. I remember my mother knitted a big long maroon scarf for me and a green one for Warren. They were wrapped around our heads but we could see through them. Our hands and feet always got cold when we skied. My mother made us cloth book bags with straps over our shoulders so our hands were free.

We had to cut across the neighbor's pasture. He always kept a Holstein bull that was huge. I was deathly afraid of him. Whenever I saw him I would go way around him. He used to stand by the fence between our pasture and theirs and growl and paw the ground. We had to have about five strings of barb wire to keep him out of our pasture. We were also afraid of their dog. He bit Warren right through his overshoe. The rest of the way was all fields. Warren had to go first through snow and break a track. I followed. He always complained that I was slow.

Field in Woodside

One time a blizzard came up right after we left. My dad got worried and put on his skis and followed our tracks all the way to school to see if we got there okay. When he saw our skis propped up on the entryway he knew we had made it.

We never had any snow days. I had perfect attendance in 3rd grade. A lot of kids missed school on real cold days if they had a long way to go. The teacher boarded at a home right across from the school so she was always there with the fire started.

There was a pump in the school yard. We had to keep the ceramic fountain filled. It had a spigot on it so we didn't have to use cups or glasses.

We always had to walk home from school as did the other children. One day a boy named T. (Trygve) Ardell Hauge asked to carry my books for me after school. That was fine with me. When we got to the spot where we had to part, he gave me my books, gave me a kiss on the cheek and took off running. I was so surprised that I think I just stood there with my mouth open. I did have a crush on him but didn't admit it. We must have been 5th or 6th graders.

The highlight of the year was the Christmas program. We practiced for weeks. We usually performed the manger scene and sang songs from the "Golden Book of Favorite Songs" to go along with it. Several times I got to be Mary.

There were also recitations, skits and more Christmas songs from the Golden Book. We took up a collection of dimes and one of the parents was commissioned to get the gift for the teacher. The teacher gave each one a little gift like a pencil. The pupils also exchanged names so we each got a gift. The program was first and then the opening of gifts, followed by lunch. We all had to get to the program with horses and sleds. It must have been quite a sight to see all those horses tied up in the schoolyard.

We had a little party in school for Valentine's Day. We brought shoe boxes and covered them with tissue paper and red hearts, etc., and we took our valentines home in those.

Another fun time was our "last day of school" picnic. It was pot luck. I don't remember any program for this — I think the parents just visited. I believe we got our report cards on that day.

My ambition was to read all the books in the library. I missed it by one and that was "The Deerslayer." I tried but it didn't interest me. One of my favorite books was a big book about a Norwegian child named Ola. It had lots of pictures in color. I thought it looked like a fun place to live with the fjords, etc. It had some great pictures of the northern lights too.

When I was about ten years old the students were each given a pen pal from another country school in the Mojave Desert. I was given a girl my age named Sylvia Reynolds. We exchanged letters and liked each other so well we have been exchanging letters for more than 80 years! Sylvia married Orville Skirven and we met a couple of times over the years, once in Bemidji and once in Florida. Sylvia is now also in assisted living.

When we finished seventh grade we had to take a state exam. We got little booklets to study from. The exam usually took place in June and the teacher had to supervise it. If you didn't pass you had to repeat seventh grade. When we finished eighth grade we had to take four exams: English, math, history and geography, I think. Our graduation was held in Crookston. I believe my 7th and 8th grade teacher's name was Clara Howe.

Clothes

It was during the Great Depression so none of us had many clothes. My mother made a lot of mine out of her old schoolteacher clothes from the big red box. In winter we had to wear long underwear under stockings that were held up by garters. There was usually a tab on each side of our underwear on which to fasten our garters. The stockings were cotton and were brown or black. It was hard to get them on over the underwear. I hated the way they got baggy after a couple hours of wear. In winter we wore snow pants, mostly made of wool. There were no pants for girls yet. We had to take the snow pants off when we got to school. The boys wore overalls. We wore overshoes of rubber when the weather was wet or snowy. They went up over our ankles and had buckles on them.

My mother made most of my clothes. I remember once she sent for a little cotton dress with apples on it. I was so proud of my "boughten" dress.

When Warren was about 15 he wanted some high boots and breeches, which were all the style then. He begged and begged until my parents finally gave in. He was so proud of them, but he soon tired of lacing the boots up since they went way up to the knee.

My mother had a treadle sewing machine. I was anxious to learn to sew so I could make doll clothes. She let me start using the machine when I was about 10, although my dad was a little worried that I would put the needle through my finger or something. I got along fine and took sewing in 4-H when I was about 14. I made a lot of my own clothes after that.

My dad cut our hair. He cut mine and Vickie's just below the ear. I never liked short hair. When I was in seventh grade they let me grow it long. Home permanents came out and I started giving myself perms when I was in high school. My mother had long hair that she wore in a bun but when it got to be the fashion to have "bobbed" hair she had Daddy cut it. He didn't really like it but wanted her to be in style and knew it would be much easier to take care of. While my mother's hair was long she curled the sides when she was going somewhere. She used what they called a crimper. She lit one of the kerosene lamps and stuck it down in the chimney to get hot, handles up. That worked quite well.

My mother cut my dad's hair. The clippers were not electric so it wasn't easy and my dad was fussy about it. He would sit on the stool with a dish towel over his shoulders and a mirror in his hand giving her instructions.

Our mailbox was about half a mile from us. It was at a crossroads and the mailboxes were on a wagon wheel so the mailman could turn it to put the mail in the half a dozen or so boxes there. Our mailman was Hermas LePage from Mentor. He had a machine called a snowmobile. It was actually a Model A Ford with extra wheels, skis under the front wheels and a caterpillar track. He could get through any road with that! Hermas was related to the Tom Hauge family.

Linda and Lester with Vickie and June
wearing their fashionable "tams"

Neighbors

Our closest neighbors were Ingbret Akre, Bennie Kittleson, Harlow Jorgenson, Jacob Ganzhorn, Jens Rude, Tom Hauge, Ted Austinson, Helmer Kittleson, Selmer Johnson, Floyd Foreman, Elmer Trandem and Tom Haug. They were all Norwegian except Ganzhorn who was German and his wife was Swedish. The Broskes were Bohemian but weren't in our district, even though they were actually closer to our school than Hillside. They were allowed to come to our school one year. Norman was a little disruptive in class so they weren't allowed to come back.

Lester and Selmer Johnson

One time the kids asked Warren what nationality he was and he said he didn't know. They said "Well, you're just nothing then." That remark prompted him to find out where the Colebanks came from. It was England. My mother was pure Swedish, but I guess Warren didn't think of that.

The Norwegians were very reserved. They watched you for a while before they made friends. Once they decided you were okay they were very friendly. If you visited them, they always gave you coffee and a dessert. The farmers had breakfast, lunch, dinner, lunch and supper. When we first moved there they would talk in Norwegian right in front of us. They didn't know my mother could understand them. She was amused by it. They didn't do it any more after they knew she could understand them.

Lester, Linda, Warren and June about 1930

Illnesses

We had the usual childhood diseases. I had 3 kinds of measles, whooping cough, and small pox. My brother had the mumps but Vickie and I didn't get them.

There was a smallpox epidemic one year and they came to the school and vaccinated all of us. It was too late for Vickie and me, however. We had been already exposed and came down with the pox two weeks later. I wasn't so sick but Vickie was very sick. She had them in her eyes and mouth and everywhere. My mother called Dr. Sturmans out from Erskine to look at us. She wanted to be sure it was smallpox rather than chicken pox. Dr. Sturmans pronounced it smallpox. He said he had seen enough of it in the Army to know.

At that time there was a lot of tuberculosis around. Someone was sent out to give us the Mantoux test to see if any of us had TB. Warren and I both reacted to the Mantoux test but nothing showed up on the x-ray. The Strand family lost several members to tuberculosis. They lost a baby, a 10-year-old girl, and an older girl who was married. I believe the father died of it too. The ten-year-old, Marian, was in Warren's class. We went to her funeral. It was so sad.

Another funeral I remember was for Ottman Ganzhorn, who drowned in a reservoir. He was 18 or 19 years old. The Ganzhorns had the funeral at their house. I remember two of the young neighbor girls singing for it. They started crying and couldn't finish the song.

There were a number of sanitariums around. One sanitarium was in Crookston and another in Walker. One winter Warren coughed real hard all winter. My mother did everything she could think of for it. When he went into the Marines they told him he had scars on his lungs from TB so that must have been when he had it.

One time a couple of the kids brought seven-year itch (scabies) to school. Vickie and I got it. My mother was quite upset about it. We had to change clothes every day, hang up our bedding outside every day and use some sulfa salve. It was really hard to get rid of. Now days they have medicine to kill it right away.

Once I got impetigo on my legs. The doctor said I probably got it from playing in the dirt.

When I was 11 years old my dad had what they called a "nervous breakdown." Mrs. Wrist from North Dakota had bought the Jake Ganzhorn farm next to us. She was getting a divorce from her husband and wanted her two teenage boys to live on a farm. She had two girls younger than them. After a year on the farm she went back to her husband and wanted to rent out the farm. She begged my dad to farm it and he finally agreed. We moved into that house, which was very nice, but it meant my dad had to farm two farms and it got to be too much for him.

The breakdown came on slowly until one day he wanted to know where his gun was. He wanted to shoot our neighbor, Ingbret Akre, who was actually his best friend. My mother told Warren to get the gun and hide it – which he did. My mother then called Dad's brother John to come over. They realized he needed to go to a hospital. They got him in the car and headed to Fergus Falls. On the way they stopped for gas and he got out of the car, jumped over the hood and took off. He stayed overnight at some farm and in the morning turned himself in. He was in the hospital six months and they gave him therapy and shock treatments.

That was a very hard time for my mother. Warren was 15 and wanted to quit school to help but Mama wouldn't hear of that. She asked one of John's boys, Maynard, to come and help. He was older than Warren. Then she got Grandma Roof to come and help her because we all got the flu and were all in bed at one time. We had it quite hard – I was even delirious. Mama got a terrible sinus infection and Warren's tonsils got so bad he couldn't hear. She took him to the doctor and had them taken out but he bled a lot afterwards. The doctor asked, "Why didn't you tell me he was a bleeder?!" After that he got his hearing back. That was a bad winter for my mother.

Fergus Falls State Hospital

My dad got out of the hospital in May. Before he came back home my mother moved back to our log house. Right away we took a trip down to Madelia to visit relatives. He enjoyed the trip and it was very good for him.

My dad had stomach ulcers and always had bad spells in spring and fall. There wasn't much they could do for them at that time. He went to the doctor but the doctor said he wouldn't treat him because he smoked. He heard about some pills that he could order through the mail. They were Pfunder's tablets. I think they were mostly antacid pills. They would help temporarily. He was in terrible pain at times. My mother seemed to be fairly healthy.

Once when Vickie was very small she had a fever and didn't feel good. Mama was giving her a sponge bath to take her temperature down and Vickie said, "Don't touch my sore foot." Mama looked at her foot and here she had a big boil on the bottom of her foot. She opened it up and it was full of pus. She soaked it and Vickie got better immediately.

When I was in the eighth grade I got Tularemia or rabbit fever, probably from a wood tick who had first been on a sick rabbit before biting me. I remember one had gotten stuck on the left side of my temple. I was so sick I just stayed in bed. I had sores on my face. My mother took me to the doctor, who did a blood test. I fainted. A while later the doctor sent word that it was tularemia. I was in bed for a month. I just barely got well enough to go to my eighth grade graduation in Crookston.

Linda, Lester, Vickie and June in 1940

Food

We fared quite well during the Depression because we raised a big garden and had our own eggs, meat and milk. My dad butchered a calf and a hog, usually in the fall when it was cool. My mother canned most of the beef. The pork was cut into pieces, salted down, then wrapped in paper and put down in the oats in the oat bin. It kept very well there.

In our garden we raised peas, carrots, corn, tomatoes, turnips, squash, pumpkin, cucumbers, lettuce, parsnips, radishes, cabbage, rutabagas, and Swiss chard. We also had a big raspberry patch. Mama canned several hundred jars of food and put in the cellar. Foods like squash, pumpkin, parsnips, and rutabagas would keep in the cellar without cooking. She also always made a big crock of sauerkraut in the cellar.

Every summer my Dad bought a crate of peaches and one of pears, which my mother made into sauce. Dad also bought one box of apples and one of oranges. We were allowed one a day, either an apple or an orange. My dad usually ate an apple before he went to bed. In summer he ate corn flakes.

A typical meal would be meat, potatoes, a vegetable and a dessert (usually sauce.) We also had bread and pickles. My Dad insisted on having potatoes in some form at every meal. In cold weather my mother thought we should have a hot cereal. We had a lot of oatmeal and got tired of it. For breakfast we had cereal and then if we finished that we could have bacon and eggs and fried potatoes. For the lunches in between we had cake or cookies with a drink. If there was something on the table we thought we didn't like, Mama would make us eat at least a teaspoon of it every time. All three of us learned to like most foods – except oatmeal. My mother and dad drank coffee but we weren't allowed to have it until we were grown up. My mother thought it wasn't good for us.

Sometimes we had a kind of Kool-aid – it was a liquid in a bottle called nectar and you added it to water along with some sugar. We got that from the Raleigh man or the Watkins man who made periodic visits. My dad always got a salve for the cows from the Watkins man and my mother got vanilla and spices and nectar.

My mother was conscientious about having a balanced meal. We didn't have salad except in the summer when the lettuce was ready. She put a dressing of cream, vinegar and sugar on it and it was so good.

Sunday dinner was always special. Mama would get out her best tablecloth and dishes. She usually fixed fried chicken. Afterwards, my dad helped her with the dishes. That's the only time he did until us girls got big enough. He didn't believe in working on Sunday so we went visiting or relaxed at home. I remember my mother and dad going for walks in the pasture.

My mother had various kettles for cooking. She had an iron frying pan which was sometimes called a "spider." At first my mother did her canning in a big copper boiler that she also used for boiling the white clothes to get them white. My dad made a wooden rack to go in the bottom of it. Later she had a smaller pressure cooker for meals and a big one for canning. Once the big pressure cooker exploded and cracked right down the side. Food splattered everywhere. Fortunately, no one was near it at the time. One of the cats got some on her but not enough to injure her. My mother sent the pressure cooker back and got a new one in exchange. The old one evidently had a flaw in it.

My mother didn't have any good dishes until one year she got some for Christmas. My dad took me to Erskine to the hardware store there and had me pick out some dishes. I chose the Virginia Rose pattern made by Homer Laughlin. I was told not to tell Mama. I kept the secret and later my mother could hardly believe

I didn't spill the beans. I suppose I was around 8 years old at the time. She used the Homer Laughlin dishes on Sundays after that.

Homer Laughlin Armand (Virginia Rose)

When my mother taught school she had summers off except for two summers when she went to Mankato State and Winona State colleges. She usually worked out other times. One time she worked for a family named Yates in Madelia. They were apparently well-to-do and had a lot of famous people for visitors. Mrs. Yates was very fussy. She had a white tablecloth for every meal and it had to be set correctly. My mother said she learned a lot there and would often tell us things about "When I worked for Yates."

Christmas and Birthdays

Christmas 1943

We always had a small Christmas tree. We had candles on it. We didn't dare have them lit for very long because of the fire hazard. In school we made popcorn chains and colored paper chains for our trees. We had a few other ornaments including icicles, red and green ropes, etc. At first we opened our presents in the morning but my folks didn't like us getting them up so early. They decided we could do it the evening before. We were told to go upstairs and then we would hear the door open and feet stamping and loud ho-ho's. A while later we were told we could come down now because Santa had left. We knew it was our parents but we didn't care. It was exciting any way.

We didn't get a lot of presents except one year my mother had let me raise 16 chickens and I got to keep the money for them. If I got just toys for the money I had to wait until Christmas to get them. I couldn't wait so my mother sent for a big 26" doll named Dorothy, a small tin doll buggy and a miniature set of Blue Willow doll dishes. I had hours of fun with them.

One year my mother made big cloth rabbits for us. Warren called his Peter and I called mine Nellie. Warren had a smaller brown rabbit made for him by a friend of my mother's. That rabbit and Peter were the only two toys he kept by his bed. I still have the pattern for that rabbit. I made one for Warren after he was in the wheelchair but I'm not sure he was thrilled with it.

June with her dolls in August of 1938

My mother made three kinds of candy – fudge, divinity and penuche, a brown sugar fudge. My parents bought one sack of nuts and one of hard candy. We probably fared better than some of the other kids in the neighborhood. When we went back to school after vacation we had to tell what we got for Christmas. One family was Jehovah Witness and didn't give presents for Christmas. They gave their kids some presents on New Year's, however, so they wouldn't feel left out.

On our birthday we always got a birthday cake and some little gift. When I was eight or nine I decided I wanted to have a party, so we invited about half a dozen neighbor kids. I remember one little girl brought some homemade summer sausage. Nobody had much money to spend. One year my Aunt Clara sent Uncle John to town to get a birthday gift for my mother. He picked out very nice teapot. Aunt Clara really wanted that teapot but he wouldn't give in. My mother always served cocoa in it since we didn't drink tea.

June – Summer 1941

Religion

When my parents first moved up north they went to church, probably the one across the road from them. No one spoke to them or shook their hand, not even the minister, so they wouldn't go back and didn't go to church for some years. Aunt Clara didn't let that stop her — she went right in and introduced herself. Uncle Rob got converted to the Jehovah Witness sect and then it took him ten years to get Aunt Esther convinced. My mother hated that because that was all they wanted to talk about when they came over.

The neighbors thought we kids should be in Sunday School, so sometimes Selmer Johnson would pick us up and sometimes Akres did. I always loved to go to church. When I went with the Akres the sermon was all in Norwegian but I didn't care — I liked to go anyway. The Sunday School was in English.

My mother taught me the prayer "Now I Lay Me Down to Sleep" at an early age. My mother had a Bible with lots of illustrations in it. I would sit by the hour and look at the pictures. Finally my mother gave it to me. My brother said, "Why does she get that Bible?" She probably told him it was because I was so interested in it.

One year we had parochial school (like DVBS) in our school for a month after school was out. I dearly loved that. We had lots of handwork, memorized scriptures, heard stories and learned some songs. Our teacher was Miss Oin. I don't know where she was from. She had long hair which she wore in a bun. She had an autoharp, and that fascinated me, too. She taught us "Come to the Savior" and "Savior, Like a Shepherd Lead Us," among others.

Farming

The soil was very good on our farm. The only problem was the short growing season. My dad raised oats, wheat, barley and some corn for silage. He didn't have a silo so he dug a pit to put it in. He used most of the grains to grind up for feed for the chickens, cattle, horses and pigs. He had a feed grinder that was run by a gasoline motor.

Threshing time was a big deal. Selmer Johnson had a threshing machine and he pulled it over to whatever farm they were working on. There were six or seven men in the ring. They took turns being first. Selmer always got all black in his face from keeping the machine going. They brought their hayracks and horses and hauled the shocks to the machine and had to feed it into the machine. Someone stood on the other end holding the bushel sacks that were being filled with grain.

Each housewife was expected to provide lunch and a dinner. They always fixed a good meal including pie. The grain had to be hauled to the granary. My mother, Warren and I had to do chores as it would be too late when they quit threshing. Since they got so dirty working my mother set water, soap, towels and a basin on a bench outside so they could wash before they ate.

Cars

When my mother and dad got married they each had a car. They kept my mother's car and sold my dad's. Hers must have been the better of the two. She had a 1919 Model T Ford cloth-top touring car. Later my parents got another Model T that was enclosed and had glass windows. After that they had a Model B Ford.

When Warren was 15 or 16 he wanted a car. He found a used model T he could get for $15. As I remember he and his friend Aurel Hauge went in on it together. That didn't work out so well so I think he let Aurel have his half.

Linda Colebank and her Model T.

Drawbacks

Lest you think my childhood was all happiness I will tell about several not-so-good incidences that happened. We had little room in our cabin so when company came I had to share my double bed. One of my uncles came and stayed overnight. I was very young, probably about three or four. My mother put my uncle in bed with me thinking it was alright. Well, it wasn't – he fondled me. When I told my mother she was very angry and she said "My own brother! I would never have thought it." The same thing happened with a great uncle (which probably happened first) and I didn't tell my mother.

Another time an old couple moved into a house near us. My mother and my playmate's mother thought it would be nice for my friend and I to walk over and visit. So we went, not knowing we were walking into the house of a pedophile. When we got there he had us sit with him on the davenport and he immediately began fondling us. I didn't like it so I resisted. I remember his wife came and looked and saw what he was doing but said nothing about it. She went back out to the kitchen. I never could understand that. Then he wanted to take us outside. He took my friend -- who was only about four years old – with him into the barn but left me outside. On the way home I asked her what they were doing in the barn and she told me. He had raped that poor little girl. When I got home I told my mother what had happened. My brother was standing there and said, "She's making that up." But my mother believed me. She got in touch with my friend's parents and told them. The father was so angry they had to restrain him from going over there and beating the neighbor up. Too bad they didn't let him as he never got punished for any of his molesting. So, mothers take heed and don't trust any man with your daughters.

Another thing that I remember from my childhood when I was around five I suppose. I am embarrassed and kind of nauseated to think about it. Warren had some of his friends over and they were playing out in the yard and I wanted to join them but Warren said no. I was that pesky little sister who wanted to tag along. My mother said no, too. I was quite upset about it and went out in the woods. I happened to find a snakeskin that some snake had shed. I took it with me and went and stood by the boys chewing on one end of the snake skin. I'm sure Warren yelled for Mom and I was made to come in. I only got a scolding.

L to R: Colebank cousins Henry Jr., Warren, June and Maynard in 1929

High School

I was excited about going to high school since I would now have more than one teacher and more than one classroom. In the fall of 1940 I started high school in Mentor, Minnesota, which was about seven miles from us. It was a very small town. The school was two stories. The lower floor had the elementary classes and the gym and the second floor had the high school students. There were 18 or more students in my class. My cousin John was in my class and they thought we were twins at first.

In the fall of my freshman year we had two weeks potato-picking vacation. I went with my cousins to a farm near McIntosh. It was hard work but we were glad to make some money. I think the farmer's name was Widseth and he was single. He paid me extra money, so Cousin John said I must have rolled my eyes at him.

Mentor Public School

The school bus came right by our driveway which was very nice until the snow came and our road was not plowed. The bus couldn't get through, so I had to ski two miles out to the county road to catch the bus. We stuck our skis in the snow in the ditch and no one ever bothered them. Our bus driver was Serenius Swenson. He was always very nice to me. He always said good morning to me and not the others. I don't know why except I think our neighbor Mrs. Selmer Johnson was his sister.

One morning on my way to the bus I looked to my left and there was a buck coming out of the woods. It was coming right for me. I took off on my skis as fast as I could go, and when I got by Selmer Johnson's place I stopped and turned around to see if he was following. He had come as far as the road and standing still. Then he looked back and kind of nodded his head. Here came his small herd following him across the road.

The summer after my freshman year I got a letter asking me if I would like to come and stay with my grandparents in Madelia. My grandma (Martha Colebank) needed help with the housework. I was very thrilled at the prospect of going to a larger school and living in town. My parents said okay.

Uncle John's were going down to St. Paul for the State Fair so I could ride that far with them. We stayed overnight with my mother's cousin Alma and Ben Fredrickson in St. Paul. Then they put me on the train to Madelia. I arrived there in the middle of the night but was met at the train by the local cop, Leonard Larson. He took me to Grandpa and Grandma's. He was an old friend of my dad's.

Madelia was a lot different than Mentor. It was bigger and there were about 60 kids in my class. There was one big room where everyone went before class called the assembly.

I discovered that my cousin Viola Nasman was sitting right behind me. I met another girl who was staying with her aunt and uncle to go to school there. Her name was Donna Loosbrock. Viola, Donna, Irma Nelson, and Litana Ikier were my closest friends.

June's friend Donna Loosbrock

I was so thrilled to see they offered subjects that I couldn't get in Mentor that I enrolled in six subjects. Besides English, algebra, history and biology I also signed up for typing and home economics. It was a full load with no study periods. I loved typing

June attended the new Madelia High School on right

and eventually could type over 100 words a minute on a manual typewriter. Our teacher was a red-haired, freckled, heavy-set old maid by the name of Miss McKechnie. She was very strict and crabby. She seemed to favor the boys. One time I got up and pulled the shade down behind me because it was in my eyes. She told me that would be a zero for the day because I didn't ask permission first. She was always telling Viola she would get a zero for some little thing. It was during the war and teachers were hard to get so they had to take whatever there was.

I really liked home economics. My teacher was Miss Waite. We had cooking for half the year and sewing the other half. One time we were divided into groups and were given a dollar with which to make a meal. We had to get the ingredients ourselves. Our group decided on chicken. I went uptown, bought a live chicken and dressed it. I don't remember who killed it. I saved a lot of money by getting it live. Sewing was fun too. We got to make an apron first and then a dress. I made a dress for myself and also one for Vickie.

Once in a while I would go home with Viola for the weekend and sometimes with Donna to Wilmont, Minnesota, where she was from. That was the first time I went to a Catholic Church.

Martha Jane McIndoo Colebank and June

I had to work hard for Grandma but I didn't mind it. I had to do dishes, mop the floors, dust, and pump the water for washing. (She had a cistern in the kitchen that had soft water.) I had to empty the washing machine and rinse tubs and mow the lawn. I had to put on storm windows and take them off in the spring. I also had to go down in the basement and bring up corncobs and coal for the heater in the dining room and stove in the kitchen. There was a small room in the basement with no light where the coal was kept. There was a dim light in the basement, however. I was scared to go down there but I made myself do it. Grandpa L S always worried about the light bill. He didn't want it to go over a dollar a month and it usually didn't.

I went to church with Grandpa and Grandma on Sundays. They went to the Church of Christ. I really enjoyed it. Rowland Wilder was the preacher. I started going to their youth meetings on Sunday nights called Christian Endeavor. Maurine Hammond became a good friend. Her mother played the piano. After hearing their (the church) teachings for several months I decided it was the closest to the Bible that I had ever heard. When I was around 12 or 13 I realized I needed to be baptized but there was nowhere to do it, so I prayed that I would get a chance to be baptized when I was 16. That came to pass – I was baptized on Easter Sunday in 1942.

Donna and I were chosen to carry the flower-covered arch for the Junior-Senior Banquet that year. We had to hold it while the students passed through. It was considered an honor.

I think I went home on the train. I was anxious to get home because I got a little homesick. By fall, however, I was ready to go back to Madelia. Again I took six subjects including bookkeeping and shorthand.

Irma Nelson, Donna Loosbrok and June before the
Madelia Junior-Senior Banquet

This year I started going out on some dates. Several mothers at church would have liked me to go with their sons but I didn't feel any vibes.

That summer when I returned home my cousin Ann asked me to come with her to Walker, Minnesota where she was 4-H leader for Cass County. She had a room over Rode's Cafe and she was pretty sure I could get a job at the cafe. Walker was a pretty place right on Leech Lake. It was a resort town. Lots of rich people had summer homes around the lake. I did get a job at Rode's. I was still quite shy and wouldn't tell anyone my name. The local patrons had a bet over who could find out my name first. I finally told the barber, so I suppose he won the bet. I worked behind the fountain. Lots of boys would hang around there and finally Mr. Rode told them to leave if they weren't buying.

Mrs. Rode wanted me to meet her boys. One was my age and one a little older. She invited me to come up and hear them play the violin. No interest there either.

I did go out with one of the football boys a couple of times. I heard later that he (Charles Teenus Carlson) got on the Gophers team at the University of Minnesota. One of the girls that worked in the cafe was Betty Countryman. She was my age and very nice. I went home with her a few times. Very nice family.

Ann had to put on a 4-H program at the Cass County Fair and she asked me to play the piano for their singing. It was so cold the night of the program I could hardly move my fingers to play.

The post office there had a regular boat run around the lake to deliver mail. For a small price you could go along for the ride. I was all set to go once but we didn't get very far. We had to turn around and go back because of the strong wind. So I never got to make that trip.

Soon it was time to go back home for my senior year. I wanted to be there in Mentor so my folks could attend my graduation. By this time I had 16 credits which was all you needed to graduate. The superintendent asked me why I hadn't graduated yet. Of course I still had three required subjects to do. I enjoyed my senior year because I didn't have much studying to do. I graduated with a B average. My brother also had a B average and my sister Vickie was valedictorian of her class.

June and cousin John

That summer I got a job as waitress in the Felix Cafe in McIntosh. I went out a few times with Chester Castleman, who was a farmer with 400 acres of land, his own airplane and a real nice car. I thought he was too old for me. He was probably in his 30's. He was a very nice man.

Belvin Aaseng came into the cafe and asked me for a date and I declined. Then he brought his friend Emery Stordahl and Emery asked me for a date and I decided to try him. They were very nice boys who had been in 4-H. Belvin asked me if I knew anyone he could go with. I suggested Viola. They both came down to see us later in Madelia and Belvin and Viola got serious. Emery and I broke up for religious reasons.

June in front of the Felix Café in McIntosh

I didn't work there long because the owner kept trying to get me alone. He probably was a bit senile – his wife ran the cafe. So I went home again and sent in an application for an office job. I must have taken a test because it was a civil service job. I soon got offered a job in St. Paul. At the same time Grandma wanted me to come back so I had to choose one or the other. My parents heaved a sigh of relief when I decided to go back to Grandma. They didn't like the idea of me going to the cities alone.

So I started looking for work in Madelia. The first one I found was at the turkey plant plucking turkeys. It was a messy job and you had to wear overshoes because of the water on the floor all the time. Viola worked there too. I started watching for another job and got one at Larson's Gas Station that had groceries and a little cafe room. I worked in the cafe part. Then I heard about the insurance office needing a typist. Maurine Hammond was working there. I got that job right away. The boss had gone with Aunt Jennie and had a soft spot in his heart for her.

A while after that I saw in the paper that there was an opening in the post office. You had to take a test for that. When I took the test there were about 6 others who took it. I got the highest grade. The postmaster could take his choice of anyone who passed the test. He chose his nephew, but the nephew was called into the army and he had to choose another one. He came to the insurance office and talked to my boss, and later I got offered the job. He was a little skeptical about it because there were no other women working there. It was the highest paying job I could get at that time. It paid $1.00 per hour.

About this time Maurine and I decided to go roller skating in Mankato. I think we took a bus to get there. We were both skating along when here came this guy who started skating in front of me backwards. He could do fancy steps too. He finally asked me if I would skate with him.

One of the first questions I asked him was what church he belonged to. When he said the Christian Church I thought he might be an answer to my prayers. (Bob laughed about that later.)

Bob and his friend had seen us skating and they flipped a coin to see who would get who. He got me. He asked me to come and watch him play ball at a church game so I did. He got so nervous seeing me there that he couldn't hit the ball. We started dating after that. He had a car and came over to Madelia quite often. My grandma thought he was okay because he belonged to the church where Aunt Jennie went.

Bob soon got tired of driving back and forth so he looked for work in Madelia. He drove over one time in a blizzard and his dad told him he was crazy. He got a job in the shoe shop run by Howard Bristol, a member of the church. He also helped in a threshing run that some of the church men were in. He always said he really enjoyed that work. He stayed with the Lloyd Davis family.

Bob didn't really like to go to church but he went because of me. Sometimes he went out for a cigarette. He told Viola, "June thinks she has to go to church every Sunday – that will change if we get married." Well, he didn't have to sit under preaching very long until the spirit began to move him. So when I decided to go to Bible college he decided to go with me.

I broke up with him for a while and went with Harlan Johnson. Harlan was a neighbor on the farm up north. A very nice and talented man. Our parents would have been very pleased if I had married him. But I kept thinking about Bob and decided to go back to him.

Bible College

We had a preacher in Madelia who had gone to Nebraska Christian College in Norfolk, Nebraska. I could have gone to the one in Minnesota but thought I wanted a smaller school and chose that one.

Bob smoked his last cigarette just before they picked us up to go to the college. I had told him I wouldn't marry anyone who smoked and he was having a hard time quitting. He smoked a pack or more a day.

Guy B. Dunning was president of the school. He was a well-known preacher up and down the valley and had started a number of churches. Mr. Schnelle was the dean, and Lila Brauer was secretary. They all taught classes. I really enjoyed the classes.

I stayed in the girl's dormitory run by Mrs. Carr. I took chalk art taught by Mrs. Radcliffe. Bob took it for a short while too. We had come there in the middle of the semester in January.

When school was out my roommate Doris Keeney and I taught DVBS in Wayne, Nebraska. I remember the preacher was Alvin Geise and he had a two-year old son that they let come to DVBS. Every time Doris or I would ask, "Should we do this or that?" he would yell out "No!" Later that boy became a preacher.

There was a snowstorm while we were there – on the 28th of May, I believe. The snow killed the garden plants. We went from there to Madelia where we held another DVBS. Larry Davis was in our classes.

My grandma had saved up for a trip to Oregon to visit her daughters and other relatives out there. I don't think she had ever been there. She said she would pay my way if I would go with her. I was delighted to. We traveled on the train and even had a sleeper. I took my camera and took all kinds of pictures and later put them in an album for her.

I had a wonderful time out there. They had a picnic and reunion of the relatives and over 100 were there. Grandma's sister Ida came from California, Anna from Nebraska, and Ella from Oregon. It was the first time they had been together for 40 years. My mother's twin sister, Esther, and her family came too. They lived in Tigard, Oregon. My dad's older sisters Lizzie and Clara lived out there too. They both had large families and most of the children were married with families too. We got there just in time for the funeral of one of George McIndoo's sons. George was Grandma's (Martha McIndoo Colebank) brother.

1947 Colebank family reunion in Oregon

After we got back, Bob and I planned to get married before we went back to college. Money was scarce so we weren't planning on having a big wedding. When the church people heard about our plans they said "You have to have a church wedding and we will help."

So on August 20, 1947 we got married in the Church of Christ in Madelia. My sister Vickie was bridesmaid and Bob's brother Jim was best man. We stood up with our friends Doris Keeney and Dale Scheffler about a week before so we asked Dale to be an usher along with Bob's brother Harvey.

We asked Doris to sing and Maurine Hammond to play the piano. Maurine's mother offered to make the cake. Our flowers were from the funeral of one of my Sunday School girls who had died

Bob and June's wedding picture

a few days prior to the wedding. They were very nice, mostly gladiolas as I remember.

Bob's brother Jim thought he would play a trick on us and put a heat bulb right above us on the stage. It was quite hot standing under that bulb. The trick backfired on Jim because he had to stand under it too. I wore a light blue suit, carried a white Bible and had a bouquet of white roses. Bob had a tan pin-stripe suit. Money was scarce in those days so I decided not to have a long wedding dress. I thought a suit would be useable afterward — which it was. I think Nancy has that suit.

After the ceremony we went to Mankato to have our pictures

Just married!

taken at the Snow studio. Vickie and Jim went along. Then Bob and I took off on our honeymoon. We only got as far as St. Peter and stayed in the Nicollet Hotel there. We stayed at a lake resort somewhere on the way and then went on to Osakis to visit Viola and Belvin and little Donna. Then we left for Norfolk.

The Nicollet Hotel

Our first apartment was in the basement of Glen Williamson's house. It was only one room. We had an ice box, table and two chairs, desk, and a rollaway bed. I got pregnant in October and it would have been born in July about the same time as Doris and Dale's son Stephen, but I had a miscarriage. We called the doctor to come to our apartment. He had to go around behind the furnace to find our room. He said "If you're planning to have a baby you better find a better place to live."

Glen Williamson house in Norfolk, Nebraska

For a short while we lived in the girl's dorm basement which was lighter but we still needed more room. Vickie had come down to go to college and was staying with us.

The Army had fixed up a bunch of Army barracks to be rented out and we got one of them.

By this time I was pregnant again. Barbara was born December 21, 1948. It was a very traumatic birth. I went to the hospital the evening of the 20th. Towards morning I was having one steady

The old Army barracks where Bob and June
lived when Barbara was born

pain. The nurses kept asking me when I was having a pain I said all the time, but I don't think they believed me. I didn't know much about having a baby so I thought it was all part of the process. A student and friend from the college wanted to be there for the birth and was there until she was born. Her name was Beth Killough.

When the doctor arrived around 7:00 a.m. he got very angry and said, "I should have been called hours ago." He realized the baby was stuck, due to a hook on the end of my spine. He worked real fast and tried to get her out but to no avail. Then he called in an old, experienced doctor to come and help. Between the two of them – one pulling and the other pushing – and the use of instruments, they got her out.

Barbara had died just before they got her. Immediately they started working on her and got her to breathe. She was a gray color and her head was somewhat misshapen from the manhandling. They kept her in the hospital for three weeks. She had trouble keeping any milk down. I attribute her recovery to

Beth Killough's care. She was an RN and worked there. Every chance she got she would rock Barbara and coax her to eat. After we took Barbara home, Dr. Surber had me bring her back in a couple of weeks. He picked her up, took her over by the window in the light and looked in her eyes. Then he heaved a sigh of relief and said, "Oh, she's all right." I think he thought she might have some brain damage.

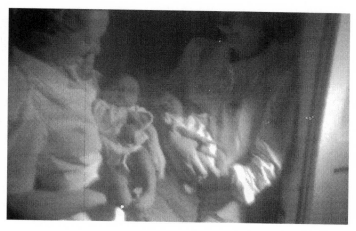

June and infant Barbara on right

After she was born Bob went back to school. I didn't come out of the anesthetic until noon, and I had hemorrhaged and was very weak. When Dr. Surber noticed that Bob was gone he called up the school and talked to him. He scolded him and told him to get right back down there so he would be there when I came to. Bob didn't realize what all had happened.

That winter was a bad one. It seemed like there was a blizzard every weekend. Bob was preaching in Oakdale, Nebraska and I usually went along. I shudder now to think of me taking that baby out in that weather.

Barbara started noticing her clothes when she was three months old. When I laid her down after putting a dress on her she would grab her skirt and pull it up where she could see it and grin. I sewed a lot of dresses for her.

When Barbara was about five months old she got a bad cough. The doctor thought it was whooping cough, but I wonder if it wasn't bronchitis. I held her all night. Bob couldn't stay awake to watch her.

That summer we stayed with Alvin and Ruth Petersen on the farm and Bob worked with Alvin. Barbara learned to walk there.

Bob didn't want to go back to Norfolk because he disagreed with them on some things. So we went back to Madelia until Dale was born in the hospital there on December 26, 1949. Dr. Surber had told me that when I got pregnant again I should send him the name of the doctor, so I did, and I suppose he told him about Barbara's birth. I didn't have that trouble with Dale though. I didn't even have an anesthetic. The doctor was upset that he had been called away from his Christmas dinner so he didn't give me an anesthetic. I got along okay though.

We heard about a church that was looking for a preacher in Montieth, Iowa. They accepted us and we moved into a little house out in the country by there. While we were there I had Dale in the buggy and pushed it out onto the enclosed porch. The

Dale at five months old

porch slanted a little and the buggy took off and hit the outer door. It flew open and down the cement steps and on to the sidewalk it went. Dale rolled out. I had him wrapped good, however, and he didn't seem to be hurt at all. It gave me quite a scare though.

While we were at Montieth twelve men quit smoking.

Bob wanted to go to college at the Midwestern School of Evangelism in Ottumwa, Iowa, so we went there and found an apartment on Green Street. Our apartment was right over the furnace and the floor got very hot.

I was expecting Rebecca by this time. On the night of January 1, 1951, she decided to be born. There had been an ice storm and the streets and sidewalks were so icy you could hardly walk. We left Dale and Barbara with the Loren Daley's and somehow made it to the hospital. Rebecca was born three hours later on January 2nd. The doctor hurried her along because there was another lady ready to deliver outside the door. I wanted to go home in three days but the doctor really didn't want me to. He said I had had a retained placenta and could hemorrhage at any time. He finally let me go but said not to tell anyone that he had let me go. Bob's parents came for a few days after she was born. Grandma Blanshan was amazed when Barbara, who had just turned two, went to the bathroom all by herself with no help. Dale had just turned one.

While we were living here Dale swallowed a bunch of unused staples. He had climbed up on bob's desk and found them. When we noticed he had a mouthful of staples I took them out of his mouth and called the doctor. He said to feed him some bread and they would pass through. They did.

A student from California, Max Bakke, had bought a place on the edge of Ottumwa that had a little house on it. He offered it to us. It was mainly one big room and a full basement. One day I went down in the basement to get something and there was a big sewer rat sitting by the drain. He got up on his hind legs and bared his teeth like he would attack me so I retreated to upstairs. Later I put a quart jar in the drain so he couldn't get in again. I heard him rattle the jar later. We could hear mice and rats running up in the attic so we got some d-Con and all was quiet after that.

Rebecca was a little over a year old and was learning to talk. One day a high soprano opera singer was on the radio. She listened a bit and then said, "Oooh chickie!!"

The next house we lived in was on Taft Avenue, I believe. Beryl Blair Anderson stayed with us that summer. She was a student at MSE.

There was a peach tree in the back yard with a lot of peaches on it, and I was waiting for them to ripen. One day we got home and they were all gone. A neighbor boy about 15 years old came and told me his mother did it. "They weren't ripe anyway," he claimed.

Barbara and Dale at the house on Taft Avenue

We heard they needed a preacher in Centerville, Iowa, so Bob applied there. We moved there to a house near the old ice plant.

It was here that Dale lost the sight of his eye. Rebecca had a habit of taking off whenever she got a chance, so Bob made a wire pen in the back yard to keep her in. The neighbor lady, Mrs. Ball, and I were walking in the back yard one day and she noticed a stiff wire on the pen. She thought one of the kids might get hurt on that so she tucked it under some wire. Dale saw her do that and went to pull at it. It snapped back and hit him in the eye.

We rushed him to Iowa City and he was admitted to the hospital. In those days they wouldn't let parents stay with the children so we had to leave listening to him cry, "Let me up and I'll be good!"

They had him tied down so he wouldn't touch his eye. I felt so bad that I had to leave him. They operated on his eye the next day. They sewed it up but didn't know how much sight he would have in it. They said it was best to leave the eye in there because his head was still growing.

Aunt Sandy, Bob holding Dale just out of hospital, Rebecca

Bob was getting burned out by this time what with working full time, preaching on Sundays and going to school. He had finished school except for a paper he had to write. The school mislaid it somehow and said he couldn't graduate without it. So we moved to Tilden, Nebraska, to a house on a farm not far from Alvin and Ruth. It belonged to Alvin's brother Walter's son.

Dale was a cute little boy and had dimples. One of the ladies at the church called him "Dimples." He talked early and I remember him standing in the back seat of the car singing "Standing on the Promise City God." (We sang a song about "Standing on the Promises" and there was a town called Promise City nearby so he just put them together.)

We took Dale to some sort of doings in Tilden, Nebraska and they were showing little pedal tractors for kids. We put Dale on one of them. He got the giggles and didn't know how to pedal.

Dale and Rebecca in 1951

While we lived at that house Barbara and Dale went to a country school nearby. That left Rebecca and me home alone. Rebecca talked and talked to me. It must have been the first time she had a good chance to be heard.

I was pregnant with Nancy by now and she was born November 3, 1954. When I brought her home the other three kids were coughing, and it turned out to be whooping cough. Nancy came down with it when she was only two weeks old. I was very worried so I took her to the doctor. He gave me some little gray pills that I was to grind up, add a little water, and feed her. They seemed to thin the mucous so she could handle it. I ran out once and she started turning blue right away so I got more as soon as possible.

Barbara got thin with blue circles under her eyes from the coughing and vomiting. Dale did okay. All the kids in the church came down with it so we met at the Petersen home and had Sunday School for them. The mothers stayed there too, of course. We kept a five-gallon bucket handy in case anyone had to vomit.

Bob's mother, sister Donna, and her son Harold came to visit us. Harold wanted to hold the baby so bad but we told him he couldn't. I put Nancy in the bedroom for a nap. A little later here came Harold carrying her out and holding her up by one arm and saying "See, I can too hold the baby."

When Nancy was born I thought I wanted a boy. When I came out of the anesthetic and was still not all there, I noticed the lady in the next bed with her baby. I asked her what she got and she said "A boy." I said "How would you like to trade?" As soon as I saw her I wouldn't trade her for anything. She had a cute little pug nose like I did when I was born.

Bob and baby Nancy

Bob was working at Alvin's and I was home alone with the kids when a storm came up. The sky was a greenish color which I had never seen before, so I took the kids and went into the storm cellar. Bob came rushing home and found us there. We could hear roaring outside and the windows breaking. The hail was the size of baseballs. Bob had to see what was going on and held a chair over his head while he looked.

One night we sent the kids to bed upstairs and they kept making a lot of noise, so Bob hollered up the stairway, "I want silence and plenty of it." It went very quiet, then Barbara piped up, "Daddy, what are silents?" I guess she thought if he wanted plenty of it she better find out what it was.

Some bees got in the upstairs and one night when I went to put on my nightgown it was full of bees. I did quite a dance for a while. Bob thought it funny.

A little later we moved to another house a little further away that was owned by some people by the name of Downs. Nancy learned to walk and talk there. She liked going on picnics and one day she said, "Let's go on a parknic."

Downs House near Tilden – 1955

We lived in the Downs house during the winter. One night about midnight a loud pounding came on the door. Bob got up to see about it and it was a drunk guy who got stuck by our driveway. Bob put his clothes on and went to help him. He got him out and on the road again. He was so drunk Bob had to put him in the car. He took off and Bob came home hoping he made it to wherever he was going.

Barbara in dress made by June

Meadow Grove, Nebraska

Our next move was to Meadow Grove, Nebraska, not far from Tilden. Bob didn't have a job and things were scarce. We were down to a few jars of canned goods when a letter came from Dan and Betty Escritt with a check for $25.00. God was really looking out for us.

We had a scare one night when we were asleep. The click of a door woke me up. I got up and went and looked and found the door to the outside was open. When I looked out, there was Dale running down the street in his pajamas, crying all the way. He was headed right for the highway which wasn't very far from us. I had to run out in my pajamas to get him – he was walking in his sleep.

Another time Barbara was going to the bathroom or something in the night. We were asleep when suddenly a loud scream woke us. It sounded like someone was hurt. Bob leaped out of bed right over the end of it and got to Barbara in a hurry. She thought she had seen someone. All we could figure out was that the shadow of a tree branch was coming through the window. It was moving so it looked scary.

June and baby Nancy in front of Meadow Grove house

We were crossing a one-way bridge one day and we saw another car coming. The other car didn't stop even though we were already on the bridge. Bob tried to put on the brakes but they failed, even though he had had them fixed a few days before. We hit the other car head on. I had my hand on the door handle and the impact bent my hand back and broke my right wrist in seven places. I was expecting Suzanne and I was worried about her. The doctor set my wrist and put a cast on it from my elbow almost to the tips of my fingers. I had the cast on for eight weeks. It was very hard to change Nancy's diaper with one hand.

Suzanne was born on May 2, 1956, when we lived in Meadow Grove. Bob's folks had come down to be there when she was born and she was five days overdue. I took a dose of castor oil and it started things almost immediately. I went to the hospital in Tilden. After I was there for a time the doctor said it looked like it would be a while, so Bob went home. He barely got in the door when the hospital called for him to come right back.

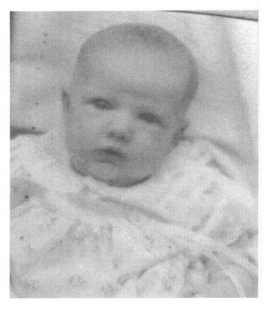

Baby Suzanne

I picked out Suzanne's name. A gal from California came to visit her aunt in our neighborhood when I was in grade school. I thought she was so pretty and I loved the name.

We moved back to Oakdale and lived next door to Elsie and Carl who were crazy about Nancy. Suzanne got bronchitis that winter and coughed until spring.

While we were here Rebecca, who was about six years old, got eczema quite bad on her legs and arms. She was scratching it like mad. We decided to take her to Omaha to an allergy clinic. They injected her all down her arms and back with different substances to see what she was allergic to. The doctors were amazed at how she sat still for the tests and made no fuss at all. It turned out she was allergic to dairy products, dust, cats, smoke and other things. I realized why she had gagged when she tried to eat cottage cheese. We had to give her a shot every week for about a year. The shots desensitized her for some of her allergies.

Once when she was younger we were at Bob's parents and they were serving fish. Rebecca began gagging and we thought she had a fishbone stuck in her throat. We called the doctor who said it was an allergy and we were to give her Benadryl. Later we found out she was very allergic to fresh water fish.

Meanwhile Bob was looking all over for work. He found they wanted a juvenile probation officer in Lincoln, Nebraska. He applied for the position and got it. There wasn't a church there and he thought maybe he could start one.

The first house we found was located in Denton, a small town outside of Lincoln. We rented from a family next door by the name of Rosecrans. They also liked Nancy. (She was pretty cute.)

While we lived in Denton Nancy got in my purse and swallowed a bunch of aspirin. Barbara saw her chewing something and checked it out. I grabbed her and took her to the bathroom and put my finger down her throat until she vomited. A little while later she acted like she might faint so we rushed her to the hospital where they pumped her stomach. They said they didn't get anything. I must have got it all.

Bob in his office in the courthouse in Lincoln

A woman in Lincoln had shot her husband while he was sleeping and was on trial. She had a two-year-old son who probably saw it all happen. Bob's office was placed in charge of the boy, Dennis. They put him in foster homes but he wouldn't eat. They had him in the office and Bob picked him up. He really liked Bob, who looked a little like his Dad. So they told Bob to take him home and see if we could do anything. It was breakfast time and I had made pancakes. We put him in the high chair and he ate seven pancakes right down.

Dennis was used to getting his way by throwing himself on the floor and having a fit. He tried that at our house and discovered the floor was very hard (it was cement) and it kind of hurt. So the next time he tried it, he laid himself down carefully and then had his fit. He didn't do it anymore after that. His mother went to prison for a few years. People testified they had seen her husband abuse her so she got off easier. Dennis was given to a relative out west.

One night I heard some heavy footsteps going around our house. I got up and investigated and it was a cow who got loose. Bob didn't like it that I didn't call him instead of checking on it myself in case it was a man.

Rebecca and Barbara in Lincoln

House on 36th Street in Lincoln

We finally found a place in town at 810 S. 36th St. It was close to an elementary school called Randolph School.

House at 810 South 36th Street in Lincoln

Barbara had a friend whose dog had puppies. They found homes for all but one. She told Barbara that they would have to kill it if they didn't find a home for it. Barbara felt bad and had her friend bring the puppy for us to see. We couldn't resist keeping the little black and white rat terrier puppy and named her "Penny." She was a nice addition to the family and was with us 14 years.

Our neighbors were Mr. and Mrs. Herman and they were from Russia. Mrs. Herman didn't want kids playing in her yard and was known to be crabby. I got to know her and she really wasn't crabby. On Halloween I didn't let the kids go to her house because I didn't know if she would like it or not. She came over the next day and asked why the kids didn't come – she was waiting for them.

There was a pair of twins next door, Jean and Jane, who were Barbara's age. Across the street was an older lady who worked in the courthouse. Behind us across the alley were the Picards who had a little boy, then James and Eileen Davis with 3 children – Melody, who was Nancy's age, and a younger girl and boy.

Twins Jean and Jane

On the other side of the Hermans were the Suddeths. They had a 14-year-old girl named Patty. I had her babysit once and the kids locked her in the basement. After that, I decided Barbara was old enough to babysit them. Patty had a water spaniel dog. When she filled the tub to take a bath she had to shut the door because her dog would jump in it whenever it had a chance.

Bob took part in a manhunt for a man named Charles Starkweather who murdered 11 people. First, Charlie and his girlfriend Caril Fugate killed Caril's mother, father and little sister. Then Charles shot an old man who was his friend.

The police didn't know where he was so they were going house to house looking in garages, etc. He was already out of town, however, and they caught him out west a short time later. The movies "Natural Born Killers" and "Badlands" were based on Charlie Starkweather.

Caril Fugate and Charlie Starkweather at the courthouse

We had a full basement and plenty of room for the kids to play. We saved up milk cartons which were square and made nice building blocks. I got my first automatic washing machine and dryer when we lived there.

Nancy started kindergarten in Lincoln. She somehow hurt her ear on the gate between the house and driveway and we had to take her to the doctor to have stitches put in. One day she came home from school and said she had a terrible headache. I gave her aspirin and put her to bed and rubbed her back. I think that was a migraine headache because she got more of them when she was older.

We took a trip up to see our parents and my grandmother who was in the nursing home. My grandma had saved a ring to give to me for Nancy because she was named Jane after her. I don't know how she ever kept track of that ring because her mind wasn't good. Nancy later gave it to her daughter Mandy because the ring had the initials MJC on it. Grandma died after that but I didn't go to the funeral because we had just been there and couldn't afford another trip.

A young man from the church in Cozad, Nebraska wanted to come and stay with us and go to school. He wanted to become a doctor. His name was Glen Conway. He was there a few months when he made the mistake of looking at cars and bought a Renaud. With payments on the car, he couldn't afford to go to school so he went home. While Glen was living with us Dale had to have the hallway for his bedroom. He was very fond of reading and read the World Book Encyclopedias all the way through. We had just gotten the set.

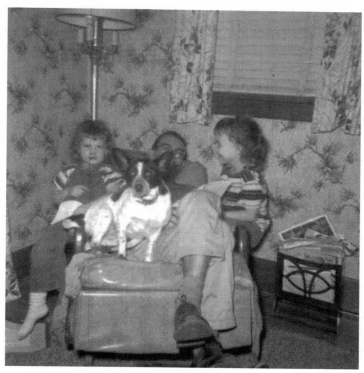

Suzanne and Nancy and Glen Conway with Penny in front

Bob got a small congregation started and they met in Penzer Park Youth Center. One time we forgot Nancy there and had to turn around and go back. She was sitting on the steps crying. I was glad she stayed there.

The school PTA asked me to be secretary. I didn't really want to because I was pregnant by now and didn't want to get up in front. But I did it. They asked Barbara to play a violin solo. I made over a dress for her. It had a black velvet top and full pink organdy skirt. She looked so cute up there and I was very proud of her. None of the other school kids were asked to perform.

I became pregnant with Davie and he came two weeks early. Bob was out in western Nebraska giving a speech on juvenile delinquency. I called him and told him to go to the hospital because I thought I would be there by the time he got there. When he got to Lincoln he went straight to the hospital. He couldn't find me so he went home. I was still home as the pains had let up, but they started up again so I did go to the hospital then.

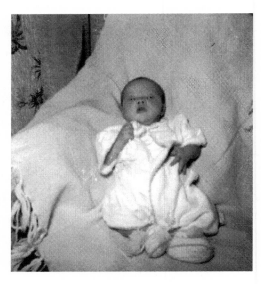

Davie - April, 1960

When Davie was born on April 17th I didn't notice anything wrong with him but Bob did. After I got Davie home I could tell he wasn't just right. We took him to the doctor who said he had Down Syndrome. That was a shock to me because I hadn't had much experience with that type of thing. They said he was educable though.

They noted Davie didn't have any muscle tone in his legs. So we took him home and I rubbed his legs whenever I gave him a bath. He walked at 18 months which was good for him. We had a walker in which he learned to get around really well. I think it strengthened his legs. Once Davie got real sick and could hardly breathe. He made a whistling sound with every breath. We rushed him to the hospital and they put him in a tent with cold air blowing on him.

I told them Davie had been exposed to measles and it might be that. They didn't put him in isolation, however, until he broke out. There was no rail on his bed and he started to fall out, but the nurse caught him. When she tried to give him a shot it wouldn't go in so she pounded on the needle to get it in. Bob was upset about that. Davie recovered nicely though.

A library up town was closing and they said anyone could come and take what they wanted. So we got quite a few nice books for the children.

When we got ready to move to Walton, Bob asked a man to come and help him load our upright piano. He waited and waited and the man didn't come so Bob pushed it out on the porch. The man still didn't come so Bob dragged it down the steps. Still he didn't come so Bob put one end of it up on the pickup and then got hold of the other end and lifted it up on there. He was strong in his arms from all the digging he did while working for his dad.

Walton

Our next move was to Walton, Nebraska, a little town a few miles east of Lincoln. We found a big farmhouse near Walton. We thought it would be nice to be out in the country and have a bigger house. The house was big – 5 bedrooms, and large kitchen, dining and living rooms. The ceilings were very high. The house had electricity but only one faucet for water and no drains. There was an old-fashioned wood-burning stove in the kitchen and a propane gas space heater in the dining room.

The house in Walton

I remember one night it was very cold and the wind was blowing, so we took our blankets and laid on the floor in front of the space heater to keep warm. During the night the wind changed and started blowing under the door in the dining room right on us so we had to move to the kitchen by the wood stove. The 3 older children got to have their own bedrooms and Nancy and Suzanne were in one together. We really enjoyed the room and the children enjoyed playing outside. There was a barn and shed too.

A cat had been left there at the house and she was pregnant. She had six kittens, one for each child. They were all different colors – black, white, dark tiger, yellow, calico, and tan. The kids had fun naming them and playing with them. One of the kittens was very cross right from the beginning. He fought with the other kittens for the least little thing.

Suzanne and Nancy in Walton

Suzanne was playing on the big propane tank in the yard and fell off and broke her arm. I think that was the first broken bone in the family.

Davie learned to walk in Walton. I put him in a walker and he learned to use his legs. They got strong enough for him to walk at 18 months, which was very good for a Down Syndrome child.

Davie learning to walk

I was pregnant with Amy and thought she would come on my birthday, January 29th. I went to the hospital on my birthday, but she wasn't born until after midnight so she had her own birthday – January 30, 1962.   When Amy was born they didn't show her to me right away. They said she was in the incubator. Several days went by and they didn't bring her to me. I was just sure there must be something wrong so I didn't dare ask. I was crying when Bob came in and found out why. So he called a nurse and told them to bring that baby to me right away. They did and I could finally see she was okay. They said she had been lethargic after she was born – probably from the anesthetic they gave me. In addition, she had white skin like I did when I was born.

We didn't know what to call her. I had picked out Laurie Jean but Bob decided he didn't like that. He went home and wrote down all the names he might like and I wrote one up in the hospital. When we compared them we both had written Amy Jo on the list. So Amy Jo it was. We had never discussed that name before so I don't know where that came from. She was my biggest baby, weighing in at over nine pounds.

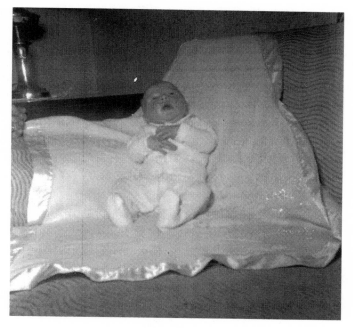

Baby Amy Jo

Both Davie and Amy learned to walk while we were in this house. One day I was doing something out in the yard and had them both with me. All of a sudden I heard Amy crying. They were both in the outhouse. Davie was looking down in the hole at Amy standing in the muck. Luckily she didn't fall down. She was only dirty up to her knees. I took her and dipped her in a tub of water about 3 times before using soap.

Walton was fighting to keep their school so they wanted Bob to help. I think he was president of the PTA. We did what we could but eventually they closed it down as they did all the country schools.

Suzanne started kindergarten in Walton. One little girl was fascinated by her name and went around singing "SUZANNE BLANSHAN, SUZANNE BLANSHAN!" Suzanne was chosen attendant to the homecoming queen.

One morning the kids started out for the bus as usual when Barbara decided to come back and get a scarf. When she got up to her bedroom and went into her closet, she looked up through the trap door to the attic and saw the roof was on fire. A brick had fallen out of the chimney right where it joined the roof, and sparks much have caught the roof on fire. Barbara came running down to tell us. I called Bob and the fire department. Meanwhile Dale climbed up in the attic and yelled for us to bring water. We brought him water and he got it out before the fire department got there. They had had an argument about whose district we were in and who should go. If Barbara hadn't come back for her scarf I'm sure it would have burned down since it was very old and dry. I'm certain God had a hand in that. It was quick thinking on Dale's part too.

Our landlords were an old bachelor and his sister, Bill and Dorothea. They had a big dog who was very cross. He was very protective of their pickup. Bob put his hand on it and he jumped up and bit him.

Another time the dog started to attack Rebecca and Dale jumped in between her and the dog. He got his jacket all torn up. Bob happened to have a cow's tongue in his hand and beat the dog off with that.

There was a pack of coyotes that ran across the field nearby. Our dog Penny got really excited but we couldn't let her go out there. They sounded like a bunch of kids with their yipping.

Blanshan family in Walton circa 1962

Bill and Dorothea

Bob had an attack while he was at work. The doctors thought it was his heart and put him in the hospital. One of his bosses had called and said "If you need anything call me." I didn't have a way to get in to see Bob so I called her and asked her if she could give me a ride. She said "Why did you call me? I haven't got time for that!" I was taken aback and had to find another way – one of Bob's clients. The doctor told Bob he was under too much stress (he was in charge of more than 100 boys on probation) and should quit that job.

Suzanne with broken arm in Walton

Lake Crystal, Minnesota

We decided to go back to Minnesota and Bob found a job as policeman in Lake Crystal. We also found a big house to rent there. A banker had built it and it was very nice except it was old. Elmer Peterson was our landlord. He was very happy to rent it to Christians. The house had 5 bedrooms, plus a large kitchen, dining room, and living rooms. Amy was about 16 months old when we moved there. We had just put everything in the house and hadn't arranged it yet. When she came in she said "Where's the po-port (davenport)?"

House in Lake Crystal

The house was about a block from the lake. Dale spent many happy hours going down there and diving for things. He found fishing poles, anchors, etc.

The house was heated by hot water radiators which worked very well. The rooms downstairs were arranged so that you could go around in a circle from room to room. I had gotten Davie a tricycle and Bob asked, "Why did you get that? He can't ride it anyway." Davie was a determined little boy, however, and kept trying until he could ride it. Dale brought home a horn from school and Davie wanted so badly to get hold of it. One day it was left unattended and he quickly picked it up and tried to blow it. When we tried to take it away from him he said, "No, mine!" That was some of the first words he said.

I came down with a bad cough and I thought I was allergic to our cat, until one morning I woke up and found I was bleeding in my mouth. I thought I must have tuberculosis. The doctor lived across the street and Bob went right over and got him. He had me come to his office for an x-ray. The bottom half of both my lungs were raw and bleeding. He told me to go to bed and stay there. He thought it was viral pneumonia. I was in bed 3 weeks. If I tried to get up I would hemorrhage again. It was a hard 3 weeks. I kept one of the three oldest home each day to watch Amy and Davie. No one came to help except one of the church ladies who came for a day and did my ironing. That was Anita Bristol and it was a big help.

We were attending church in Madelia and Bernie Bliss was the minister. He was going to be leaving and told Bob he should apply for the job. So Bob did and they hired him.

Bob on the job in Lake Crystal

Madelia, Minnesota

We moved into the parsonage which was just behind the church building. I was very happy to be in the church where I was baptized and married. Aunt Manie always put candy in her coat pocket for Davie. She got a kick out of how he made a beeline for her right after church. Davie always sat quietly through church but when he heard us sing the doxology he heaved a big sigh of relief because that was our closing song.

Amy and Davie in front of Madelia Church of Christ

Davie attended the day care center run by Harold Kerner that was held in the Presbyterian Church. He loved to go there and was learning to write letters of the alphabet. He was the youngest one there and the others fought over who got to help him take off his coat, etc.

Barbara was in her senior year of high school and she graduated from Madelia. She had been working at the hospital.

Barbara 1966

We went out to visit a church family (Omar Baade) one day and they gave us dinner. We had brought Amy and Davie along with us and they played outside for a while. The Baades warned us that the dog might bite as he had bitten their own little boy when he ran over the dog's tail with his wagon. He had to have stitches in his head. Things seemed to be going okay, however.

After dinner we were getting ready to leave and I put Davie's coat on and sent him out the door to the car. Unbeknownst to me, Mrs. Baade had put the leftovers in a dish for the dog and set it on the steps. When Davie went out he evidently stepped in it and the dog attacked him. Mr. Baade heard the dog growling and ran out to check. The dog had Davie down on the ground. Davie was wearing a parka hood jacket so the dog went for his face. He was so shocked he didn't make a sound.

We rushed him to the Madelia Hospital and they said they would have to wait a while before they could administer the anesthetic because he had just eaten. His nose was partly torn off and an eyelid and he had other cuts. After a short wait they decided to go ahead with the surgery and Bob sent me home with Amy while he stayed there. When Davie was put on the anesthetic he aspirated his stomach contents into his lungs and at the same time his heart stopped. Bob had to come home and tell me Davie was gone. I went into shock and they had the doctor come and give me a shot. When the Baades heard it Omar went out and shot the dog.

This was the worst experience of my life. The funeral was well attended with about 19 preachers there along with many other people. Dale Williamson did the sermon. He ended it with something about the way Davie used to say "Bye, see ya!" Ruth and Alvin Petersen sang "God's Way is the Best Way."

Amy was four years old at the time and Davie was her playmate. She always decided what to play and he would follow. After he was gone she wandered around the house and didn't play. I was getting worried about her.

After Barbara graduated we decided to move. The church at West Concord had contacted Bob and wanted him to come there.

June and Amy leaving Davie's grave in Minneopa Cemetery

West Concord, Minnesota

We moved into the parsonage in West Concord. It took me several years to get over losing Davie. What brought me out of it was getting pregnant with Brenda. Amy had been begging for a baby sister.

The parsonage after a blizzard

A physical fitness class was being offered for women and I decided to go. Maxine Avery from church also went. We got really fit, I guess, since about four of us got pregnant, including the Methodist minister's wife who hadn't had a baby for 14 years.

The doctor wanted me to doctor in Rochester because of my age (almost 42) and because it appeared Brenda was breach. I also had RH negative blood. Bob thought he was RH positive since that is what they told him in the service, but Mayo Clinic would not take his word for it. They tested him anyway and he turned out to be AB negative. Since we were both negative there wasn't any problem that way.

I had been told to come to the hospital as soon as I started having pains, so I did. They said nothing was happening, however, and told me I should go home. All that night and the next day I could feel the baby kicking a lot. When I did go to the hospital again they said she had turned herself around and was coming out the right way. The nurse kept telling me I wasn't ready but I knew by the strength of the pains that it wouldn't be long. We called the nurse back and she took a look and said "Oh, the head is crowning!"

They rushed me into the delivery room and Brenda came right away – didn't even get my doctor there or get an anesthetic. They held her up to the light right after she was born and she opened her eyes and stared at it. I asked them if she had Down Syndrome and one of the nurses asked, "Now why did she ask that?" One of the others answered, "Because she already had one." Brenda was born January 11, 1968.

We had gotten acquainted with the Dwight Hill family who lived across the street from us in Madelia. After we moved, the creamery where he worked had laid Dwight off. He got a job in the creamery in Claremont, which was not very far from us in West Concord, so we continued our friendship. We were glad to hear they were that close.

Dwight and Marilyn Hill

They had been somewhere the day Brenda was born and came to the hospital as soon as they knew she was born. The hospital wasn't going to let them in because it was after visiting hours. The Hills told them they came from out of town and the hospital let them in. Brenda was lying there with her eyes open and looking all around while the others were sleeping or crying.

I had an amaryllis lily that was getting ready to bloom in January, which was very unusual. It opened up the night Brenda was born.

While we were living in West Concord Nancy and Suzanne were invited to a birthday party at a neighbor's house. Suzanne was 11 and Nancy 12 ½ . The parents weren't home. They had built a fire in the yard to roast wieners and marshmallows. The fire died down and the older sister of the birthday girl squirted lighter fluid on the fire to make it a little bigger. The flame followed the stream back up to the bottle and although Suzanne was behind her, she was close enough for the flame to catch her hair on fire. She started to run but the older sister grabbed a towel off the clothesline and gave it to Nancy, who put out the fire on Suzanne's head.

We took Suzanne to the local doctor but he said to take her to Rochester because she had third degree burns. By the time we got to Rochester her whole face was so swollen she couldn't open her eyes. The hospital put her in isolation and used saline packs on her burns.

When they let her come home we had to continue with the saline packs. She was in the hospital a month. Her burn wasn't quite healed and initially they thought they were going to have to graft, but it finally made a bridge of skin across the sore and healed. She lost part of the rim of that ear and still has a scar on that side of her face.

The hospital hadn't washed her hair for three weeks and it was so singed you couldn't comb it. I got the idea to lay her on the kitchen counter with her head over the sink and she let me carefully comb it under running water.

Suzanne recovering from her burn

Dale graduated from high school in 1967. He graduated with honors and could have gotten a scholarship to quite a few colleges. He planned to go to Bible college in Ottumwa. Iowa at Midwestern School of Evangelism. The superintendent called Bob in and wanted him to try to get Dale to go to a different college. MSE was not accredited. Dale had his mind made up to go there, however. He couldn't play in sports because of his blind eye, but he was manager of the sports teams through high school. He got to go to the games that way even though it was a lot of work.

Dale was away in college when Brenda was born and when we called him and told him about her birth he wasn't very excited

The Blanshan Family in 1968

about another girl. When he came home for the summer he had a lot of fun playing with her, though. He even got her walking when she was only seven months old.

Barbara and Paul planned to get married on October 26, 1968. Barbara's wedding was a beautiful wedding. I made dresses for the ones in the wedding and also a little one for 9-month-old Brenda. They were a light blue taffeta.

We had been asked to come to the Bemidji, Minnesota church and decided to accept. We stayed in West Concord long enough for the wedding and then went up to Bemidji at the end of October, 1969.

Amy, Rebecca, Barbara, Amy, Paul, Paul's brother George, and
Nancy at Barbara's wedding in Eagle Lake in 1968

Bemidji, Minnesota

There was a family named Koster in the church and Mrs. Koster told me her boys were very happy to hear we had girls. We had five girls with us at this time.

The Bemidji church found a house for us to rent out in the country. It had a long driveway. While we were here we were gone a few days and someone had been in the house and left te door open. The furnace was going like mad when we got back and the bird was very unhappy.

The kids took a bus to school. When it got cold they had to stand and wait for the bus. The girls weren't allowed to wear pants to school yet and Rebecca's legs once froze so badly they were purple.

Church of Christ in Bemidji 1969

We decided it would be better if we were in town. We found a house on Bixby Avenue near Bemidji State Teacher's College. It was a large house with a finished off third floor. Rebecca claimed that for her room. She was the oldest one at home at this time. Then the landlord wanted to move back into it so we had to move.

Warren and Joyce were visiting us and we were driving around looking at houses when Joyce saw one. "How about that one?" she asked. It was a perfect location on America Avenue one block from the elementary school and one block from the middle school. The high school was right beside the middle school and it was only two more blocks to the college. The house wasn't fancy but would suit us. The church helped us put down a down payment and then we started making payments. Later on we added two bedrooms to it.

The house at 1517 America Avenue with addition

I decided to go to work to help out with expenses. I applied at the college. It was a civil service job so I had to pass a test. That afternoon I got a call from the library director who asked me if I would like to have a job in the library as clerk. I went right to work. They put me in the purchasing department and I loved working there. One of the workers was from Mentor and I had known her before. Her name was Marty Evenson. We became good friends.

Working in the BSU Library

Brenda was a year old and the lady next door (Mrs. Kirkpatrick) did babysitting, so it worked out perfectly. The girls could go and get her when they got home from school. She liked going there and called her "Packerch."

Brenda and her babysitter Mrs. Kirkpatrick

I had chances to work my way up and had to take a test each time. I advanced from clerk to clerk I and then to clerk II. Next came clerk III and finally library technician. This job was in the basement of the library in the curriculum department. I had my own office with girls working under me.

We had a steep stairway in this house and one day Brenda fell all the way down. Fortunately she didn't get hurt much. She was only four or five years old.

Around this time we received word that we had our first grandchild, which was born to Barbara and Paul. Barbara gave birth to Duane in June, 1969 and a year later to Bonnie. We were quite excited about having a grandchild.

Rebecca joined the Navy in October of 1969. Bob took her down to the Markham Hotel to catch the Greyhound for boot camp in Bainbridge, Maryland. As he saw her off on the bus, his eyes teared up. It was only the second time in her life Rebecca had seen him cry. The first was when Davie died.

Rebecca was a member of the Hospital Corps and was stationed at the US Naval Hospital in Bethesda, Maryland and at the Brooklyn Navy Yard. She spent one enlisted term in the Navy.

Rebecca catching the Greyhound for Navy boot camp

Our 25th anniversary came on August 20, 1972. I wanted to have a celebration but decided to have it in Madelia because that was where most of our relatives were. I sent for some pretty material from the J.C. Penney catalog and I made dresses for all the girls and me. I thought that way everyone could tell who was part of our family. We took Jon Larson along with us and traveled to Madelia. Jon and Suzanne played background music (violins).

Bob's sister Donna made a beautiful cake. As she was going down the stairs to the basement of the church she dropped it. There was panic for a while but she was able to repair it so that you could hardly tell it had been dropped. It turned out very nice.

The Official 25th Anniversary Photo

Bob's mother and sisters went together and bought us a set of silverware in a chest. Bob got me a silver service and Warren and Joyce gave us a nice set of stainless steel silverware.

I decided I needed to learn to drive. I took lessons from Mr. Raake who was teaching driver's training in school. It cost $30. I passed the driver's test with a score of 94. I bought a car too. It was a white Impala. Mr. Raake lived about a block from us and had a little girl in Amy's class whom she played marbles with. Amy had a little sack of marbles and the girl won all of them away from her. Amy was determined to keep trying.

Some time while we were living in Bemidji I had a little accident. Bob was driving ahead of me – probably in the truck. The roads were very slushy so I was not driving very fast. Bob turned around and came back and told me I would have to drive faster as that was too slow. So I sped up and hit a slushy spot which spun me around and backed me down a steep ditch. As we were sliding down, Nancy – who was in the back seat – yelled "Put on the brakes, Mom, there's a lake down there!" So I did and came within a few feet of plunging into it. I'm glad Nancy looked back. God was looking out for us again. Bob never said a word about it to me.

My sister Vickie was a missionary in Jamaica. My mother wanted to go and visit her and would pay my way if I went with her. I decided to go. I wanted Bob to take me to the cities to meet her there and fly out but he said I would have plenty of time if I took the bus.

When I was about half-way there the bus had a flat tire. The bus driver stood up and asked if anyone on the bus knew how to change a tire. They hunted up the nearest garage and even they had a little trouble figuring it out. We were finally on our way. The other passengers told me I would never get there in time. The bus driver drove as fast as he dared and made up time. I barely made it. My mother was frantically pacing in the airport wondering where I was. She was having me paged. We just barely made it on to the plane.

We arrived safely in Kingston and Vickie was there to meet us. We had a wonderful time meeting the people and seeing all the sights.

June and her mother Linda in Jamaica in 1971

Vickie had been in Jamaica 17 years when she got terminal cancer and had to return to the states. Bob and I decided we would like to go and work where she had been in Mandeville. We had to raise our own support from churches. We went to Lakeland, Florida to wait for our papers. We waited several months and nothing was happening, so Bob went to Miami and checked on it. They had lost our papers so we had to go through all that again.

While we were waiting for our papers we enrolled Brenda and Amy in schools in Lakeland.

Brenda in front of Lakeland house

I think it was March of 1975 that we finally left for Jamaica. We had about six barrels of belongings that had to go through customs. That could take a long time. The guy who was looking through our barrels came across a stethoscope. He got so excited about listening to his heart that he went around listening to everybody's hearts. He had so much fun with it that he didn't even go through our barrels but let us go on which saved us a lot of time.

We got some of my sister Vickie's furniture which was in Kingston and hired a truck to drive to Mandeville, which was about 60 miles west of Kingston. The Banton family, a church family, helped us a lot. They found a nice house near them for us to rent. It was fairly large. It had four bedrooms but the kitchen was tiny with no cupboards. Mandeville is up in the mountains – although they are not high mountains. Our house was uphill from downtown. We had to walk four miles to church and four miles back. Going home was the hardest. We were without a car for a long time. We walked most of the time but took a transport if we had something to carry.

It took some adjusting to get used to their ways. We had trouble understanding them at first. The girls caught on right away and began talking like them. They spoke sort of a broken English called Patois.

Brenda and Amy were seven and fourteen. The Jamaicans loved white children and really spoiled them. They were a big help with the young people.

Brenda with young Jamaicans

Bob took his work very seriously. We went out almost every day holding street meetings. We had a puppet stand which went over really well. I played the accordion and some of the Jamaicans played guitar. We would pick a spot and then begin playing music. People listened but when we brought the puppets out they gathered all around. After our singing Bob would preach.

It was amazing how the Jamaicans would stand for a long time. The meetings were quite successful and we got a number of converts that way. We had services at the church Sunday morning and night and prayer meeting Wednesday nights.

There were only one or two cars in the church. Sometimes we got a ride home with Brother Harris. He had been in England and worked quite a few years and came home with a car. He would give us a ride home. The only trouble was he was going blind and gave us a number of scares. His wife sat beside him and told him what to do. He was such a nice old fellow.

Jamaica 1978

We found out the church had a van but it wasn't running. Eventually we got parts for it. One time we used it to go to a rally in another town. The van was real full. It was on a Sunday and the gas stations weren't open. Bob forgot about filling it up on Sat. He was afraid we wouldn't make it home. The Jamaicans started singing a chorus called "I'm Going On Right On That's What I Know." They kept singing and miraculously we got within a block of our house before it ran out of gas.

The Bantons had a girl named Joy who was a little older than Brenda. Janice was Amy's age. We enrolled Brenda in the public school. Joy went with her. They put Brenda a grade or two ahead of her class since the U.S. schools were more advanced. Amy went with Janice to a Catholic school called St. Elizabeth's. Later we sent her to Beaconsfield which was more like a U.S. school. Brenda's school had about 1200 students when they were all there.

The girls missed a lot of school. Friday was market day and quite often they stayed home for that. They had to wear uniforms. Some couldn't afford them or they didn't have shoes so they didn't go to school.

Brenda was the only white girl in the whole school. They teased her some and called her "white pork." They didn't bother her so much when Joy was with her.

Most Jamaicans were very friendly. There was one problem though. If they worked for you they thought it was their privilege to steal from you. I had to have a maid to do my washing because I didn't have time for it. I didn't go over there to spend all day washing clothes, so we hired a lady to do it. It was all done by hand. You could expect to find little things come up missing all the time. You didn't dare leave anything out in the yard as it would disappear. Once at a later time when we had a car I heard a noise in the night. I got up and stood looking out the window for a while but I couldn't see anything. In the morning we discovered they were in the process of removing the wheels from our car. Evidently they saw me and took off, leaving their tools behind. God was watching again.

After we had been in Jamaica a couple of months I got word that Vickie wanted to see my mother and I since she didn't have much time left to live. I decided to go back to the States.

I took a bus to Kingston. That was scary as I was the only white woman on the bus. I know how it feels now to be in the minority. When we got to Kingston I had to take a taxi to the Christian school where Dale was staying. He had spent five summers working with the camps in Kingston. I gave the driver the address and he asked where that was. I wasn't familiar with Kingston. He drove and drove and I was watching the meter. When he finally found it I had just enough cash to pay for it.

Dale was not home and I had no way to get in touch with him. I went to the people across the street and asked where he was and they thought he had gone out of town. Luckily they had a phone and let me call another missionary there. I told him my predicament. Dale finally came home and I stayed overnight there. He took me to the airport in the morning in some kind of jeep belonging to someone else. I took a plane from there to Joplin, Missouri where Vickie was. Barbara brought my mother down.

June and her mother saying goodbye to Vickie

Vickie was very thin. She was so glad to see us. That was the hardest thing in my life to say goodbye to her knowing I wouldn't see her again.

The Jamaicans never worried about time. They were usually an hour late for church, which bothered Bob to no end. We sang choruses until most of them were there and then had the regular church service. They were wonderful singers and put lots of action into their songs. They used tambourines and guitars too. They also clapped to the music on the off beat which was a little hard to get used to.

I tried to learn how to do the tambourine. If I wasn't getting it right they would take it away from me and play it. I eventually got good enough so they didn't take it away from me.

I got a note from Brenda's school saying there would be PTA on a certain day at 4:00 o'clock. I got there at four and no one was around. I found a teacher and she said "Oh, they'll probably start at five." And sure enough, they did. I suppose they said four so everyone would be there by five.

I taught a ladies class out in the Cedar Grove district. I had to go out there the day before and tell them I was coming or they wouldn't be there. I usually took a lunch of some kind.

There was an old pump organ in the Mandeville church that I played for church. It leaked air so I had to pump hard and fast. I played the accordion for street meetings, etc. One time a little boy said to me, "I know how you play that thing. You just squeezy and pullee."

The Jamaicans always wore their best to church. The ladies wore hats, so I did too. The ladies didn't wear slacks to church at that time.

Once Brenda's friends decided to braid her hair in little braids all over her head, which would have been okay except they had put lots of vaseline in it.

Street Musicians

Amy got along well with the young folks and was a big help.

Out in Cedar Grove, I made each little girl a doll on her birthday. They were cloth dolls and I cut up wigs for their hair so they could comb it. I made them a tan color as that was mostly the color of theirs. One little girl came to me just before her birthday and said "Sister Blanshan, is it pure brown dollies you have?" I asked her how she wanted hers and she said she wanted a white one, so I made her a white one. I saw it a couple of weeks later and it was the color of the clay dirt around there. She must have played with it a lot. I probably made a hundred of those dolls while I was there.

Gabrielle and friend with the dolls June made them

Bob decided he wanted to raise some chickens. He made a pen and then bought some baby chicks. When they got bigger we had fried chicken quite often. We also got eggs so it proved to be a wise investment.

We met a young man out in the Cedar Grove district who had no job and nowhere to live, so we let him move into our maid's quarters under the house. He was later baptized. He was a big help in carrying equipment when we held street meetings. Later he got married and built them a house in Knockpatrick District. They had three boys and one girl, I think. Primrose died not too long ago and he is remarried.

Our water supply was a big cement open tank behind the house which caught the rainwater from the roof. Wells were extremely hard to dig because of the rock everywhere, so the city sold truckloads of water in case one ran out. We usually ran out in the winter months. Most of the Jamaicans could not afford to buy water so we let them come and get some out of our tank. They had to carry it by hand.

My sister Vickie had owned a cat named Angelique. One of the Jamaican families had the granddaughters of Angelique and brought them to us. One was calico and the other a dark stripe. Cats didn't fare well because the dogs were not leashed and ran everywhere. We could often hear dog fights going on at night. Bantons gave us a very nice dog. It was golden Lab or something on that order. We named him Burpee. One day he started bleeding and I took him to the vet. The vet said it was a venereal disease which he probably got from a female dog, so he had to be put to sleep.

It rained a lot in Jamaica. Sometimes there was thunder and lightning. One time when Bob was gone we had a bad storm. We saw a ball of fire in the kitchen. I turned off the electricity but the switches kept on clicking even though it was off. We stayed in the hall until it was over. We found out later that it had hit the transformer which was just outside our yard.

There was a Nazarene missionary in Mandeville who had quite a spread. He had a special building to broadcast from. He had a nice big house with two apartments In the basement plus two houses for caretakers. He also had a small orchard in which he had oranges, grapefruit, tangerines, etc. and an avocado tree. He had been there a long time but had to go back to the states for some reason. He tried to sell his place but didn't get any takers, so he came out to see us and asked us if we would like to rent his place. We said we couldn't afford a place like that. He asked us how much rent we were paying and said we could have his place for the same price. We would have to collect the rent from the renters. We decided to take him up on it and moved there. He had built the house American style with a big kitchen and lots of cupboards. The Lord really put us in a nice place. It had a big living room so Bob could have his training classes there. It was on high ground and had a deck in back where we could see the town down below. Mr. Pontius didn't want to rent it to Jamaicans as he said they would trash it. He had to leave his white dog there. Burpee asserted himself as the head dog and the white one didn't object. Leon moved into one of the little houses. The other one was rented out.

I had been invited to join a group of ladies who met once a month at their individual homes. It was composed mostly of white ladies whose husbands had jobs there. They were from England, Australia, Sri Lanka, and other countries. It was very interesting. We exchanged information about where we could buy certain things, etc. We also had lunch. I had them over once since we had a much nicer house now. One lady was a Nazarene missionary and she told of an experience her husband had in the U.S. There was a convention of preachers and a young preacher was asked to speak. He had a very good sermon about sin being like an octopus and getting into our lives a little at a time. It was a good sermon except he said "testicles" instead of tentacles. It wouldn't have been so bad if he said it only once, but he said it over and over again in his illustrations. The preachers had to try very hard not to laugh out loud. The young preacher must have been very embarrassed when he found out.

Amy had to walk alone now to school. I was very apprehensive about that and thought Bob should take her. He thought she would be okay, however. One day a young man grabbed her as she was coming home from school. She kept walking toward home and talking all the while. He went along with it and she got home okay. She told him he could come back some other time and see her. Bob went right down to the police station and told them about it. He asked them if he could take care of it and they said yes, and when you get done with him bring him down there and they would take care of him. When he came back Bob was waiting for him and sat him down and talked to him. He apologized and said he wouldn't do it again. We found out later he had some mental problems.

School was not compulsory there at that time. Many of the young men could not read because they had quit school. I offered to teach them and had a class at night for them. We were very proud when one of them stood up and read from the Bible in church.

Bob and the girls and I took a trip to the U.S. for two weeks one time and on our way back we decided to stop in Montego Bay instead of Kingston because we could get a train there that went close to Mandeville. We got on the train just fine with our luggage. We had brought as much as we could of things for the Jamaicans. After being on the train a short while we realized they only stopped a couple minutes at each stop, so we were wondering how in the world we would get all our stuff off the train before it took off again.

One of the Jamaicans on the train said, "You throw them out the window!" When the train stopped at our stop the Jamaicans on the train helped toss our luggage out, so we made it. It was about 6:30 in the evening when we got there and we still had to find a way to get to Mandeville. There were no taxies or transports in sight, so Bob started walking around in this very small village and found a man who was going to work in Mandeville. The only problem was he had a very small car and we had a lot of luggage. He was willing to take us, however, so the girls and I got in the back seat and then they piled as much stuff on top of us as there was room for. They put some in the trunk and Bob sat in front with some. We were very glad to get home!

Castro and his Communists were trying to turn Jamaica Communist. They even put up some road signs in Spanish and built a school for them. The Jamaicans weren't so thrilled with that. They said, "We know how to build our own schools." The Jamaican prime minister was a friend of Castro's. His government started trying to get some of the white people out of there, and they wouldn't renew our visa. We even had a white man come to our door and tell us if we needed to get out fast there was a ship at a certain place we could board. I don't know who he was. So, after two years in Jamaica we had to go back to the States.

We moved back to Lakeland and enrolled the kids in school there. Brenda didn't want to go to school. When I asked her why, she said "I don't want to go to school with all those white kids." So I told her I would go with her. When we got there her teacher was black and she was very happy then.

We moved back to West Concord, and this time we rented a house out in the country.

While we were in West Concord Bob was asked by Fred Miller to come and speak to the Jamaicans in London. We raised enough money so we could both go. It was in February and the temperature in London was in the 50's. I really enjoyed the trip since I have always been interested in things British, maybe because of my English ancestors. We got to see the Tower of London; walked across London Bridge; went to the British Museum and a maritime museum; went to a jumble sale and an auction sale; saw the changing of the guard, and visited St. Paul's Cathedral. We also got to see the play "The King and I" with the original Broadway cast including Yul Brynner. All this thanks to Fred and Charlotte Miller for taking us about.

Fred and Charlotte Miller family

At this time I was starting to collect teapots. I was able to bring several home with me from England. We arrived home with a lot more stuff than we went with I enjoyed that trip so much.

We had quite a few activities going. We had a Joy Club of around 70 children and a Bus Ministry. It was a lot of work preparing for those.

Brenda had various friends over to stay overnight – Heidi Avery, Vickie Brekke and others. Amy was going with Kevin Ellingson.

The school put on a play and Amy got a minor part. I thought she should have had the main one because she could sing right out and had a good voice. Later she got a superior rating in music contest, so they asked her to sing at her graduation. She sang

"The Holy City." The sound went off but she went ahead and sang anyway and her voice was strong enough to be heard. She got a standing ovation.

We decided to move back to Bemidji when Brenda was in the 7th grade. She joined the orchestra and played violin. The director wanted her to play the cello. She practiced about 3 weeks and then he put her in first chair. The girl who had been there had years of lessons but he wanted Brenda to be there.

The school held parent-teacher conferences and Brenda asked the teachers if it would be ok if she brought her grandparents to the conference. She thought it would be a good trick. When we got there we realized they thought we were her grandparents so we set them straight.

We were anxious to go back to Jamaica. We heard that they voted in a prime minister who did not want to be communist. We spent the summer of 1980 in Madelia before leaving for Lakeland in August. Brenda went to school in Lake Gibson Middle School. She played in the orchestra. She challenged the boy who was in first chair and she won. The boy cried and said "My dad will kill me!" She felt sorry for him and let him stay in first chair.

Back to Jamaica

We went back to Jamaica in June of 1981. We found a house on Ward Avenue. It was up on kind of a hill.

We kept hearing a rat in the kitchen at night so Bob decided to set a trap. He did so, but the rat took the cheese and didn't get caught. Bob tied the cheese on and had a length of pipe nearby ready to kill him with. When we heard the rat again the next night, Bob went out there, swung at him with the pipe and missed. Bob's feet slipped out from under him and he went down on his rear. The rat ran right over his stomach and got away. The next night the rat tried to get the cheese and got caught in the trap, so that was the end of him. We caught his mate the next night. We threw them down the hill and Jamaica's garbage group (turkey vultures) took care of it.

Nancy had just fixed my engagement and wedding rings. They were a little big so I left them at home in the dresser drawer so I wouldn't lose them. While we were at church we were burglarized. The burglars found the rings and took them along with other electronic things. I had lined the drawers with newspapers and Bob had put several hundred dollars under the paper. We were glad they missed that. I really hated to lose the rings I had had for 36 years.

We found a better place to live, but we were burglarized there also. They lifted up part of the zinc roof and climbed down into the house. I had some spaghetti on the stove for our meal when we got home from church. The burglar sat down and ate what he wanted and fed some to the puppy to keep him quiet.

We were pretty sure we knew who it was — one of our former maid's boys. We heard he had to appear in court over another charge, so Bob went to listen. He recognized he had on Wesley

Answer's shoes. Wesley Answer was a man who was staying with us. The judge called Mikie by name because he had been there before. Mikie was sent back to jail.

One day when I was in a store I saw a white lady. That didn't happen very often so I went over and introduced myself. Her name was Sandra Black and she and her husband were missionaries to the Nazarene Church. We had so much in common that we decided to visit each other. I think we visited at least once a week and I would make an American dish and she a Scottish dish. The Blacks had three children – two girls and a boy. They had a lot of stuff stolen from them because they lived in a more conspicuous place. They had lost a 100-pound tank of propane gas.

One night when David was gone Sandra heard some noise but thought it was the wind since it was blowing hard. She checked anyhow and someone was breaking into their locked garage to get their car.

After the Blacks were sent back to Scotland and Brenda was on her job in Scotland, I told her to look Sandra up. Here she was only a couple blocks away! The church where they attended was just across the street. What a coincidence!

There was a man named Mr. Heale who had a furniture store up town in Mandeville. We got acquainted with him, and he and his wife were very nice. He was part Chinese. He had a nice home on the ocean as well as the one in Mandeville.

One day he invited us to go with him to his seashore home for lunch. It was a really nice property. He was trying to sell it. His mother was living in one of his houses all alone. He was concerned about her being alone and asked us if we would like to live with her. We would have the living room, two bedrooms and kitchen. His mother was called Nana. She would have a bedroom and use of the kitchen. She preferred to use the little lean-to off the kitchen. It was all smoked up and black out there because she cooked with fire. I remember she bought a frozen chicken up town and put it up on the roof in the hot sun all day. I'm not sure what that was supposed to do for it.

I wasn't sure Mr. Heale had given her any choice in having us come and stay with her so I went and talked to her. I asked her if she was ok with it and she said "Yes, I like Americans." She had worked in Cuba for some Americans for some years. She was a very nice lady and we got along just fine. I always gave her some of the food I cooked and she seemed to enjoy that.

Street program in Christiana with Bonnie and Steve Williams

One Saturday night there was some really loud music up town and it was keeping everyone awake. I suppose they were dancing. Nobody thought to complain. The next weekend it started up again and Bob finally went down there only to discover it was the police putting it on. They agreed to turn it down some. About 4:00 in the morning they would start playing hymns.

Bob came down with Dengue fever or Breakbone fever as the Jamaicans called it. It was carried by mosquitoes. He was very sick with it. It featured a lot of pain and flu-like symptoms. It also affected the nerves. He would be sick a few weeks and then think he was getting well and it would come back again. I was glad no one else got it.

After we had been in Jamaica for another two years it was time for us to go back to the states again. We went back to Lakeland and then back to Bemidji for Brenda's 10th grade.

Orlando

Harrell Road Church of Christ in Orlando, Florida wanted us to come there so Bob decided that we would. By this time we had an old Airstream camper and a small boat. We filled up the truck with belongings and also put a lot of our belongings in the Airstream. Bob drove the truck pulling the camper and I drove the car pulling the boat which had bicycles in it. It was a scary trip for me because I wasn't used to driving much. I didn't know how to back up the boat so I had to always park where I didn't have to back up.

We made it there okay. I was worried about the truck making it up the mountains with the heavy load. It barely made it to the highest point before I had to stop and let it cool off. I was really glad when we got there.

We rented a house on Buttercup Lane that didn't have air conditioning and it really got hot in there. We wanted to get in the Winter Park School District since that was where the church was. I decided to go to the school and ask if she could start there since we planned to move into the district. At first they said no, but when they found out her grades and that she was in orchestra they said okay.

I really enjoyed working with the Harrell Road Church people, especially the ladies. Our group of ladies sang special numbers which I thought were quite good.

We found a house on 8204 Baja Boulevard which was closer to the church and in the Winter Park School District. Things went along fine until a Jamaican lady called and wanted to know if she could stay with us until she found a job and a place to live. She had two teenage boys with her. We said sure, she could come.

Later when the landlord found out about it he asked us to leave. I guess he didn't like black people.

A lady who lived near the church wanted to have us house sit while she was gone a few months.

We said "What will we do with our furniture?"

She said, "Oh, put it in the garage." So that's what we did.

Amy and Boyd and their two girls came to stay while they found a place to live. After this we were able to get an apartment about half a block from the church. It had two bedrooms and was in an ideal place for us.

I wanted to get a job but I knew my age was against me. I put an ad in the paper saying a mature woman was looking for work. I got three answers. One was from an elderly accountant across town who needed someone to type tax returns. He liked me because I reminded him of his mother-in-law who was Swedish. I didn't like the idea of having to drive across town because there was a lot of traffic, but I did it. Later I saw they were looking for a worker in a yardage shop not far from our house. I have always enjoyed working with materials so I applied and was hired. The store had material for curtains and upholstery. The hardest part was figuring how much material they would need.

Barbara, Paul, Suzanne and Curt came to visit us. They drove over to Cape Canaveral to watch the Challenger take off. Bob went but I had to work. I think it was quite a shock to watch the space shuttle explode.

It was while we lived here that Barbara sent me four place settings of (Royal Doulton) Royal Albert Country Roses pattern. I was really surprised when I got them. Not much later she sent four more settings. After that she and Nancy and Brenda sent other pieces. I still think they are the prettiest dishes I ever saw.

Brenda with her perennial popcorn birthday cake

One day a little girl about 12 came to the door and asked if she and her mother could stay with us because her mother's boyfriend had kicked them out. I had the little girl in Sunday School. The mother had some speech defect and didn't like to talk so the girl did the talking. I said they could but the only room I had was on the davenport. That was okay with them. They came bringing their belongings which included a cat and five or six kittens. They were there several weeks before they found a place to go.

Brenda graduated while we lived in Orlando. There were about 600 students in her class. Bob didn't like to think of watching that many kids cross the stage to get their diplomas. He wanted to leave as soon as Brenda got hers, but I said that wouldn't look good. They had the first ten kids with the best grades sit up on the stage. Brenda was one of them.

Brenda rode the bus for a while but she didn't like that. She wanted to drive there herself. She wanted to drive our pickup as that was kind of a status symbol. She was a very good driver to we didn't mind that.

Bob had a lot of health problems which were causing him a lot of pain. He tried to get in the VA Clinic in Tampa but they said they couldn't take him as they had too many already. He had a hernia which was giving him a lot of trouble, had just had a mastectomy and had kidney stones. He finally had Dale call to some of the VA hospitals up there and see if they would take him. Dale did and said that St. Cloud would take him. The pain was getting bad enough that he went right up there and they took him in.

Brenda had a temporary job at FMC. When we decided to go back to Minnesota she was torn between staying in Orlando and going with us. She told FMC that she needed to have a raise so she could get an apartment and a more permanent job. They created a job for her so she could stay on and has been there many years since.

Bob did not feel like coming back down so I had to do all the closing of things. Nancy and Linda came down and helped me. We had the truck and a U-Haul. We made the trip okay. I don't remember if we went to Brainerd or Bemidji. Shortly after that we decided to move to Williams, a very small town in extreme northern Minnesota. There was a small group of Christians there. We found a house to rent.

The church in Williams

Taking Care of Mother

While we were there we got word that my mother had fallen and broke her hip. I drove down to Madelia and went to see her in the hospital every day. She didn't remember that at all. When the hospital got ready to release her I got all her clothes and put her in the car to head for Williams.

I got up early to get a head start because they were predicting icy road conditions. I thought I could get ahead of it but I was wrong. We hit icy roads not far out of Madelia. It was glare ice. We slid off the road several times. The first time I was able to drive back on the road but the second time I had to have help. There were guys standing along the road ready to help. We made it to Brainerd where Bob was waiting for me. The roads were fine from Brainerd on. It was a scary trip for both me and my mother.

We had a little dachshund named Lady at that time. She was quite concerned about my mother. I put a bell by my mother's bedside so she could call me whenever she needed me. Lady would always run to see whenever she rang the bell. One day my mother had a terrible nose bleed. I was just ready to take her to the emergency room when it finally quit.

The hospital in Madelia had given me exercises to have my mother do and we followed it faithfully. She finally got so she could walk well and wanted to go home. She had been with us six months. I took her home and stayed a few days to make sure she could be by herself.

She did okay for about a year and then I got a phone call from her neighbor saying I better come and see my mother because she didn't look well. I drove right down and found her sitting in her chair looking kind of dazed. She thought she had the flu. She hadn't even gotten her mail so I knew she was sick. I took her right to the doctor the next day and he said she had overdosed on her pills. He kept her in the hospital a few days and then said she couldn't be alone any more.

We were talking about finding a place to live and my mother said, "You might as well move in with me." I was surprised when she said that, but that's what we did. We put a lot of our stuff in the basement and some upstairs. We got along fine and she seemed to like the idea of me staying there.

Amy was pregnant with her fourth child and she asked me to be there at the birth. Sterling Joseph Eser was born March 28, 1989. It was the first and only time I got to experience a baby being born. It was a wonderful feeling, especially when they put him in my arms first. I remember his little lip was quivering – I will never forget that.

After a while in Madelia Bob wanted to be where he could do some preaching and teaching. He always loved the people in the Bemidji church so he went back up there and got an apartment in Evergreen Acres and I stayed with my mother. He left the car for me. That worked for a while and then he wanted me to come up to Bemidji. He found a house to rent on 15th Street right next to the Alvin Hymes family who were members of the church. We locked up my mother's house and moved up there. It worked for a while but then we realized that Mom would do better in her own home.

While we were in Bemidji my mother fell and got a hairline fracture in her hip. We put her in a nursing home to recuperate. One day I was pushing her down the hall in her wheelchair and we passed by a lady sitting in the doorway of her room yelling "Help, get me out of here!" Mom looked at her and said "Oh, you look alright,'" to which the lady said "Well, who asked you!"

My mother's mind was getting worse. She didn't think Madelia was her home. She was reverting back to some former home – probably the farm because one night she was sure she hadn't put the chickens in. That was a worry on the farm because wild animals could get them if they weren't inside. She got quite upset about it so I told her I would do it. I went outside and went around the house and came back inside. She was satisfied then.

I wanted my mother to see my brother Warren before she got any worse. He lived in Bremerton, Washington. We set out in the camper and we hadn't gone very far before my mother wanted to go back home. We kept going, however. Before she broke her hip she had been going out to visit him every year so I thought she would be fine with him. Bob and I wanted to visit some preacher friends who lived some miles away. Warren told us to go ahead and take our time visiting and they would be fine.

We hadn't gone very far before we got a call from Warren desperately wanting us to come back because mom was quite upset about us being gone. Warren asked her what she was upset about and she said "I don't like to be dumped. I think they have gone off to be married." In one way it was funny but in another way it was very sad. At least my brother got to see what her state of mind was like.

Linda, Joyce and Warren

She got steadily worse so I got a monitor to put by her bed so I could hear her at night. She hardly slept at all but laid there and called "Help, help!" When we asked her what she wanted she would say "I don't know." She didn't even take a nap – only slept about five minutes at a time. My wrists were getting sore and I needed a carpal tunnel operation.

Barbara stayed with my mother while I had the carpal tunnel operation done and when I was recuperating. I had both wrists done at once. That took a lot out of me and I realized I was quite run down. I was no longer able to take care of my mother so we had to put her in the nursing home here in Madelia. She started having seizures and ended up having grand mal seizures. The nursing home staff gave her medicine that kept her in a state like she was asleep all the time.

My mother had always put great store in birthday celebrations, so when her 100th birthday came in June we put on a program for her. We placed her in a wheelchair up in front. She appeared to be out of it but Amy saw her open her eyes and look a few times,

so I think she was listening and maybe comprehending some of
it.

Linda in the Luther Memorial Home in Madelia

I was not able to visit with my mother because she didn't
respond. Bob had been wanting to move out to Loveland,
Colorado. They had been asking us to come for some time, so we
decided to go. We stayed a year and then got word that my
mother was very bad and not expected to live.

We went right back to Madelia. When I went in to see my mom
her blood pressure was very low. When she saw me, however,
she perked right up back to normal. She must have been very
glad to see me.

While we were in Colorado we had some interesting experiences.
We were living in the church basement because there were
several rooms down there that they were not using. Sometimes
we would hear someone come in the door upstairs and hear the
footsteps walk up to the front. We thought it might be Richard
Snell having come up to study in his study up there, but when we

went up to see, no one was there. We also had a window peeper. He ran away when Bob came out.

We went to the Colorado State Fair also. They had a lot of mules which we hadn't seen at a fair before.

There was a lot of beautiful scenery around Loveland too. We visited several of their parks. There were statues all around town. One was a life-size little girl sitting in front of the library. It was so real that I brushed the snow off the book she was reading when it had snowed outside. I think they had conventions for sculptors there too.

I was working on my family history at the time and had written to a historical society in Illinois asking for information on my great great grandfather William Cunningham. I got a letter back saying it was funny I wrote because she had just gotten a letter from a lady in Loveland asking about the same person. She gave the name and I immediately got in touch with her. She turned out to be about a fifth cousin. She gave me a lot of material on her side of the family. Her name was Kathleen Allen. She was a very nice person.

 One of my cousins died and her obituary was in the Madelia paper. I noticed she had been living in Loveland, Colorado and had a son there, so I looked him up too. He was an air traffic controller at the airport in Loveland. They were also very nice people. Two weeks after they met us they called and asked us if we would stay in their house while they went on a vacation in the mountains, so we did. They had a very nice new house with a hot tub. We didn't try it out however. We thought they were quite trusting to trust us that soon.

I had seen a beautiful china closet in a second-hand store that I really liked but it was $400.00, which was a little more than I wanted to spend. I kept checking it out until one day a sign was on the door "Under new management."

I went in to see if the china closet was still there and it was. It was marked down to $200.00, so I bought it. My husband wasn't so thrilled and said "How are you gonna get that thing home?" When it came time to go home I took the six sections of rounded glass — which were removable — and wrapped each section in blankets. I then put them up on the upper bed in the camper along with the glass shelves. The other part we were able to get on the floor in the middle of the camper. It arrived home without a scratch!

The china cabinet with June's Royal Albert china

The summer of 1994 was a busy time. My high school class had a 50-year reunion and it was also an all-school reunion. We had a good time and saw a lot of people we hadn't seen for years.

I also got word that my cousin Henry in Michigan was dying of lung cancer and emphysema. I hadn't seen him for years either so I was glad to get the opportunity. We also got to visit with his sister Doris and her husband.

Back to Madelia

Barbara and Paul had bought our house in Madelia and decided to make it larger. They hired two guys, Clem Kunz and Reynold Knickeram, to do the work. I did a lot of work picking up broken plaster. It was very dusty and was hard on my asthma. Bob tried to help and fell off the ladder and got quite a bump on his head. Another time a hammer fell and hit him on the head also. He seemed to be accident prone.

He was asked to preach in Davenport, Iowa, and on his way back he began to feel very sick like he would pass out. He also noticed a terrible smell. He quickly drove into a gas station and opened the car door. He got out and looked in the trunk and saw that a can of gas he had put in there had tipped over and was running on the carpet, causing a chemical reaction that was very toxic. He didn't feel good for hours after that.

It was a very busy summer. Bob was very good at calling on his relatives and mine, so we did a lot of that because we had a lot of relatives in the area. We also called on some church members. Bob preached off and on at the nursing home for their chapel service.

We both did a lot of programs for seniors. I had a hat program. I played my auto harp and sang and wore a hat for each song. I also performed at the meeting of the Senior Federation which covered our district which met once a month. One program I had used antiques. I would sing a song like "'When it's Lamp Lighting Time in the Valley" and I would display a kerosene lamp, etc. There was a young fellow there who was there in some sort of leadership capacity. He was very bored with my program. I'm sure he thought we should have some rock and roll music instead, but the seniors were enjoying it. One man said "Oh, I could just listen to this all day."

I was also working on my family history book. I called it "William Cunningham." William was my great-great grandfather. I was writing about his ancestors and descendants. We didn't have all the programs on the computer to help us at that time. I had to send out a lot of inquiries to historical societies to find out information. I also wrote to relatives. I found a descendant of my grandmother's brother, George, in Green Bay, Wisconsin – Carol Buckley. I invited her and her husband John over and she, John and sister Marie came and spent the day.

I was also still collecting teapots. I was asked to put some of them in their display case at the library. I put one from each country that I had.

I had learned how to reupholster furniture while we were in West Concord. I had been reupholstering chairs and davenports ever since, and at this time I reupholstered our davenport and love seat.

My mother died on August 13th, 1994. She had reached 100 years old. The funeral was in the Baptist Church in Madelia. My sister-in-law Joyce flew in from Washington; cousin John F. Colebank and wife from Kansas; Fred and Liddy Hintz and son Freddie from New York; Grace Anderson and Lowell Roof; Janie Robertson and son Mark from Missouri; Lois and Lee Haggerty; Aunt Bunn Oleson and daughter Candy, and many other relatives including our children came to the funeral. My mother was buried beside my father in Riverside Cemetery in Madelia. My mother was 100 years old at the time of her death. I think I would have lived that long too if I hadn't gotten cancer. My mother didn't have much wrong with her except high blood pressure. Her siblings all had high blood pressure and died of strokes in their old age. None of them lived to be 100 like my mother, though.

Shortly after that we went back to Colorado. We helped in the church there as much as we could. Bob preached, I played the piano, accordion, and auto harp and sang. We did a lot of calling. We met a lot of new people and enjoyed working with the Snells and the church people. In October Boyd Eser (Amy's husband) flew out and drove the camper pulling the truck back home for us

In November we made a trip up north and visited friends in Bemidji, Rebecca in the country by Shevlin and Dale and Linda in Warroad. Amy came with us and she and Bob went hunting. They didn't get anything but enjoyed being out in the woods. We had the camper so we parked in out in the woods and I stayed in it. I think they brought me along to cook. They hunted several days but no luck, so we went back to Madelia.

We had Thanksgiving at our house in Madelia. Most of the kids came, even Brenda from Florida, and Brian and Cathy Price from Iowa. Barbara and Paul were in Thailand.

Back to Florida

By this time it was getting cold and had snowed and we thought a lot about Florida. We took off on our journey December 24th and went as far as Boyd and Amy's in Forest City, Iowa. We had Christmas dinner there at Amy's. Nancy and Dennis and girls came from Mason City. Brian and Cathy were there too. We left the next day and made it to Brenda's. She had a nice four-bedroom house in Maitland, a suburb of Orlando. After visiting her and other friends we went on to Lakeland to visit Dale and Jerri Williamson.

Tom and Phyllis Richards let us live in one of their cottages. They ran a sort of assisted living place.

We had a busy winter helping with the church activities. Bob preached off and on and we both taught classes whenever asked to. I also did special numbers with my auto harp. No one could remember what it was called. One man asked me when I was going to play that thing again. We also did a lot of calling with Dale and Jerri.

We attended a Christian breakfast and got to meet the Speer family and Jimmy Roberts from the Lawrence Welk Show. We also helped with the chapel service for the Richards group. We very much enjoyed going to the many flea markets that Florida has. While visiting Brenda in Orlando we found out Judy and John Colebank were there. John is a double cousin to me and only a couple weeks younger. They stayed overnight at Brenda's and then we met them at the Olive Garden for lunch. Dale and Jerri and I enjoyed going out to eat off and on. I found out I really liked Cracker Barrel's catfish.

We went to Barefoot Beach and spent a day with my cousin Virginia Fredrickson Gustafson and her husband Roland and son

Greg. We got to see her brother Milton and his wife who were visiting them also. They were from Minneapolis or St, Paul. I hadn't seen any of them for years.

There was also a wedding of an older couple in Lakeland: Signa Jackson and Mr. Biggs. I was asked to play the organ for that.

We also had some visitors, the Ritesmans from Loveland, Colorado and the Maloneys from Madelia.

We took time to go and visit some friends of my brother's and mother's In New Port Richey. They were Conrad and Juanita Burgess. I remember she had very red hair and had decorated her house with orange and lime green. They were very nice people.

Another couple we went to see were Fred and Charlotte Miller who now lived in Claremont, Florida.

The James Blackwood Quartet came to the Civic Center in Lakeland and we got to hear them.

Bob enjoyed getting to go fishing once in a while, especially going with Don Spencer from Orlando and fishing in the ocean.

On March 16th, 1995, Bob, Boyd Eser and I went to Tampa and took the plane to Jamaica. Patrick and Roger were there to meet us with a small truck. We stayed at Patrick's house. We had such a good time visiting with all our Jamaican friends. They asked Bob to preach. I couldn't resist going to a restaurant and having some curried goat. It tasted so good but that night I got real sick. Guess my stomach wasn't used to it.

One Sunday while we were there they had what they call "Missionary" which was really a rally. They had several preachers speak including Bob and a preacher from Mocca Tree. Someone from each church represented got up and brought greetings from their congregation. There were a lot of items: Special numbers, ordination of two deacons and lots of good music. Jamaicans are naturally good singers and sing harmony well. There were guitars and tambourines and clapping. We thoroughly enjoyed it even though it lasted from 3:30 to 7:30.

Patrick took us around to see some of the sights, including Dunn's River Falls. The only thing that dampened our spirits was that both Bob and I caught cold. On April 3 we went back to the States.

We left Orlando on April 5th and headed for Virginia where we visited the Van Voorhis and Collins families. Then we went on to New Paltz, New York, where Bob's ancestors settled in the 1600s. They had helped found the town, which was very hilly. We saw some really old buildings, some of which were built by Bob's ancestors. We also went to see the Statue of Liberty and then on to Boston where we visited a Jamaican family who had moved there. We kind of got lost and we asked a guy for help. When we told him the address he said, "That's the black district." We said "We know and that's where we want to go." We had a real nice visit there.

Our next stop was in Syracuse, New York to visit my nephew Fred and wife, Liddy. Then we headed home, stopping in Mason City to see Nancy and Amy and families.

Paul's mother died and her funeral was in Mankato on April 20th. Barbara and Paul came back from Thailand for that. Barbara stayed a couple months but Paul returned to Thailand. Their children came to the funeral – Duane and Katie from Idaho, Bonnie from Ohio, and Chris from Mankato.

We decided to sell the camper. Bob always was looking for something better so we went through several campers. This time we got more than we paid for it.

We needed a new car so we got one from R and R in Madelia. It was a Ford F150XLT. The owner always gave us a good deal on a car.

Our dear friend Marilyn Hill Balfe was killed when she pulled out in front of a truck. We went to Owatonna for her funeral on May 30th.

June and Marilyn Hill Balfe in August of 1984

Kim, Jeri and Dale Williamson

On June 4th, 1995, we went to Oskaloosa, Iowa for Dale and Jerri Williamson's 50th wedding anniversary.

All through the summer I went to flea markets and had rummage sales. I had inherited all my mother's things and had too much of my own so I tried to sell some.

I was working all the time on my Cunningham book, and also did some work on the Blanshan's. I found out I was related to Dick Ellis in Ottumwa, Iowa. His great-great grandma was a sister to my great-great grandpa. I think there might have been one more great in there.

We had a small birthday club consisting mostly of relatives – Minnie, Velma and Jean who were stepsisters to Viola; Lorraine Joblinske (Viola's cousin); Margaret Stordahl whose daughter Lavonne married Minnie, Velma and Jean's nephew; Ezurina Meyer who had married their cousin; Viola (my cousin) and me. We met whenever someone had a birthday. We gave cards and gifts and went out to eat.

Back row, L to R: Velma Feder, June, Debbie Aaseng, Viola, Lorraine. Front row, L to R: Ruthie, Linda, LaVonne.

The guys were working on the house and building a two-car garage all summer.

Amy and Boyd lived in Iowa so we went there off and on to visit. We attended the Centerville Rally on August 15, 16, and 17th of that year.

We raised a garden so I was busy canning and freezing. We got corn from some farmer and froze a lot of corn.

June's brother Warren and his wife Joyce

My brother Warren passed away on October 16th, 1995. I was going to go out there by bus but Joyce called me and said she would pay for airfare so I got to fly out. The funeral was very nice. The children did the whole ceremony. Ann and Mel were there along with Geraldine Stahlnecker, son Dennis and wife Margie. Joyce showed me where Warren would be after he was cremated. I would like to have seen him one more time but I didn't get to.

Nadine Colebank Olson was in the hospital with ovarian cancer. I spent one night with her so she wouldn't be alone. She didn't want to take morphine because she said it made her act silly. I rubbed her feet and sang to her all night. She slept off and on. She died November 1st. She so wanted to reach her fiftieth birthday on December 7th but she didn't make it.

Nadine and children Marynda and Steve

Our davenport and love seat were such a faded color that I decided to reupholster it. It was hard work as it was so well made and hard to get apart. I used material I had gotten in Florida.

Blanshan Family 1995

We had a nice Thanksgiving at our house. All the kids were able to come and also Fred and Liddy and Jane and Jeff. Evelyn came with Brenda from Florida and Bonnie from Ohio. We had 44 people at the table which stretched from the dining room into the living room. We always have a good time when we get together and play a lot of music.

On December 17th we left Madelia and got as far as Roscoe, Illinois where we visited Leland and Merna Vandeveer. Then we traveled on to Alvin and Jean Petersen's in Mooresville, Indiana. We got to Brenda's in Florida on the 20th. We went to the Rally at the Harrel Road church in Orlando. John Van Voorhis and Bruce Runner were speakers.

Bob found a camper he liked in Sanford, FL. It was a 1984 Toyota Dolphin. It was just our size.

We went on to Lakeland to see the Williamsons. We enjoyed our usual winter of helping with church activities, going to flea markets, calling on people and enjoying meals with Dale and Jerri.

Brenda went with us to the state fair in Tampa. We saw a lot of music performances, some gospel and steel band, some Bolivian Indians who sang, jugglers, high divers and magicians.

Brenda had a surprise birthday party for me for my 70th birthday. She had it on the day before my birthday. I was really surprised. There were about 18 people there including Fred and Charlotte Miller from Claremont and Miriam Spencer and her sister Enola who was visiting Miriam from Iowa. The next day Bob took me out to eat at the Olive Garden.

On March 16th I was asked to speak at a Ladies Rally in Orlando. We had a good turnout. We had invited the ladies from the black church to come and they did. I spoke on being a servant. We had a delicious lunch of salads and dessert.

We were thinking about going home so on the 17th we left Lakeland. We decided to go by way of Texas and visit Bob's brother Jim in Donna, Texas. On the way we saw the battleship Alabama in Mobile, Alabama. We went through New Orleans and went through the French Quarter and reached Jim and Florence's on the 21st. We had a nice visit with them as well as with Minnie and Glen Sprague who also spent winters down there. I was not impressed with the scenery in this part of the country. I guess most of them come down here year after year to see all their friends. We made several trips into Mexico and bought a couple of blankets and miniature violins.

We left on the 27th. On our way back we stopped and saw the Alamo and in Waco to see the place where the Branch Davidian standoff took place. It was all plowed under and nothing remained. We stopped in Wellington, Kansas to look up some relatives of mine but they weren't there any longer. We also stopped in Mason City, Iowa to visit Nancy and Amy's families, arriving home April 1st.

Bonnie came April 25th and the truck arrived the next day with Barbara and Paul's furniture. We put some in the house and some in the garage.

Barbara and Paul came back May 12th. Barbara and I tried to arrange the furniture so as to get it all in.

We left our car with Barbara and Paul and took the camper up to Bemidji. We attended Jessica and Abby's graduation out at Steve and Bonnie's. Both had been home-schooled. They found a nice place among the trees and put up a stage. Steve and Dale both spoke. Quite a number of people had come. They had set up benches and places for them to sit. Refreshments followed. It was a beautiful ceremony.

We came home in time to go to Mandy's graduation reception. It was held in Nancy and Dennis' home in Mason City. Mandy was home-schooled also. The weather was good, the crowd good, and the lunch good.

Paul left for Singapore May 29th.

We went up to Bagley for Gillian's graduation from high school.

Amy and Boyd were now separated and Amy and four kids and two dogs arrived July 26th. She was able later to get an apartment in the apartments down by the river. We took the boxer, Sadie. She was a very nice dog and she adored Bob but was a bigger dog than we wanted. We found a good home for her with a car dealer on the edge of town. They had a little girl who really liked Sadie. Every time Bob would go there Sadie would be overjoyed to see him. One time he was in the truck and opened the window and Sadie immediately sailed right in on his lap. I don't know how she did that since she was such a big dog.

On July 27th a Blanshan reunion was held in the Garden City Fairgrounds. It was well attended. All our kids were there.

We traveled back to Bemidji on July 29th. We helped with their DVBS. Pam and her sister Charity Vanderveer were there to help also. While there we went with Bonnie and Steve to a Mountain Man Rendezvous in Deer River.

We were getting anxious to return to Madelia but went on a short trip instead. On August 19th we started out and went as far as Hill City and visited with Bob's cousins, Ira Lee Clark and Ardelle Manthey. From there we decided to go to Duluth since we hadn't been there. We went to Duluth and up to Two Harbors and Ely. Then we went to International Falls where we spent our 49th wedding anniversary.

Anna Williams and Travis Edwards wedding was August 31st of that year. They had asked Bob to lead the ceremony and Dale and Betsy sang. It was in the Presbyterian Church as ours was too small. The reception was in the basement of the church. It was a very nice wedding.

Before going home we attended the Jack Pine Retreat which is held near Williams, MN. We arrived home September 15th.

Paul came home from Singapore Sept. 26th. I think the first thing he did was fence in the backyard. That was so nice to have for the dogs.

Barbara and Paul left for Madison, Wisconsin on November 5th where Paul was working.

We picked up Bob's great nephew, Adam Schultz in New Ulm and took him along up north to go hunting with Bob. We stayed at Dale's in Warroad.

Barbara and Paul came home for Thanksgiving which we had at our place again. Nancy, Amy, Suzanne's families came and also Rebecca and Gillian.

Rod and Amy got married in Alaska on December 20th, 1996. She and the kids moved up there.

December 21st we went over to Sun Prairie, Wisconsin to visit Barbara and Paul. My cousin Rodney's daughter lived in the area so we invited them over to visit. She and her husband and three-year-old son came. Their names were Carolyn and Michael Hollenbeck and their son was Curtis. Michael was Canadian. While we were there we went to Roscoe, Illinois and visited Leland and Merna. It was just across the line from Wisconsin and only an hour drive from Barbara and Paul. We came back to Madelia on the 26th.

Highlights of 1997

It was a cold and stormy winter. We left for Ottumwa, Iowa on the 24th. Bob was to speak for chapel at the college that week. Wednesday night was so cold and stormy that we didn't go to church. We were staying with the Hunts. They called Raymond and Grace Lyon and Phillip who lived just down the road to come over and we had a Bible Study.

On January 17th we left for Florida. It was cold all the way even when we got to Florida. We stopped for the night in our camper and nearly froze. We arrived in Orlando on Sunday January 19th. We went to the Harrell Road church and they asked Bob to preach that night. I sang and played the auto harp as I usually did. On Wednesday we went on over to Lakeland. They asked Bob to preach on Sunday and I played and sang. We enjoyed visiting with Dale and Gerri Williamson. We went back to Orlando on the 27th where we celebrated our birthdays and helped Brenda clean up her yard. Bob went with her to buy a new car, a blue 96 Oldsmobile for 12,000. Then we drove back to Lakeland. We got word that Rebecca had fallen on the ice and broke her right leg just above the ankle.

The Orlando church had their annual ladies retreat on March 8. Gerri and I went to that. The speakers were Miriam Spencer, Charlotte Miller and me. We had a good turnout and the black ladies came again. Bob was asked to preach in Lakeland on the 9th and I sang again.

We had brought Brenda's old car to Lakeland to sell for her and we were able to sell it for $1200. Bob preached again on March 16th. We drove to Claremont that afternoon and visited Fred and Charlotte Miller, then went to church that night in Harrell Road.

Then we drove over to Brenda's where we painted her house yellow with white trim. It took us several days to do it. Brenda was going with Steve Turner and going to college and working full time.

On Tuesday the 25th we started out on a trip to see Barbara and Paul. We stopped in Mt. Airy, North Carolina and visited the James Gibbons family. We got to Barbara and Paul's the next day in Parkersburg, West Virginia. While there we visited the Fenton Glass Company and I found a dish just like I got at a rummage sale for 25 cents. It was the Hearts and Vine design in carnival glass and was listed as being worth $375.00. Bonnie came while we were there.

On the 29th we went over to Nelsonville, Ohio to visit our friends there. Again Bob was asked to preach on Sunday and I sang. We had a good visit with the Russes, Ronnie and Barbara Mash and Carolyn and David Axiom.

While there we got word that our first great grandson had been born on April 3 and named Grayden James Lyon. Barbara and Paul came to visit us while we were there.

We left for home on April 13th and got home the next day. Several bad things happened this month. On the 12th we found out Bob's older sister Donna had been diagnosed with acute leukemia and only had a couple weeks to live. This was a great shock for us all. Not long ago she had had both hips replaced and both knees fixed and also a foot and thought she would be pain free now. So sad that she didn't get to enjoy that time. She died May 23rd.

Larry Davis' mother had also died of cancer and their funerals were the same day. Enid Davis's funeral was at 10:30 in the forenoon at the Church of Christ in Madelia. Donna's was at the Eagle Lake Church of Christ later that day. Donna was cremated and she wanted her ashes to be scattered on her parents grave in Minneopa Cemetery near Mankato.

We attended several graduation doings that year. Emily graduated in Bagley, Renata in Edinburg, North Dakota and Betsy in Warroad. There was also a wedding in Pequot Lakes, Minnesota for Jessica Blanshan and James Lyon. It was an outdoor wedding and was very pretty.

James and Jessica Blanshan Lyon and Grayden

There was a lot of flooding on the Red River that spring. It was very bad in Grand Forks. The basement where Rebecca was staying to go to law school was flooded way up to the ceiling. Thankfully she had gone home before it happened.

The Blanshan reunion was held in the Garden City Fairgrounds again on July 26th.

On July 15th we had a surprise visit from Lance Hanson and his wife. I went to country school and high school with him. They lived in Kent, Washington and had just been to see her relatives in Cass Lake, Minnesota.

We decided to make a trip out east. We left July 28th, stopping in Eaton, Ohio at the Historical Society to look for information about William Cunningham. I found nothing on William Cunningham but I did find a picture of his wife's brother, Silas Dooley. Our next stop was in Zanesville, Ohio at the pottery place there. Then we traveled on to Toronto to visit the Mossors and stayed overnight there. We attended Bonnie and Blaine Randolph's wedding on August 1st in Richmond, Ohio and the reception in Weirton, West Virginia. We left after the wedding and went as far as Fremont, Ohio where we stopped at the Rutherford B. Hayes Library. I tried to find out William Cunninghams's connection to him but couldn't find anything. He said his mother was a first cousin to Hayes.

We arrived home on August 4th and left again on the 14th for Sharon Bluffs Camp where we held our BPW (Blanshan Petersen Williamson) reunion. The families took turns serving the meals. On the 15th we celebrated Dale Williamson's 76th birthday. The Centerville Rally was the next week so we stayed there for that. Our anniversary was on the 20th so we had a cake and lunch. I sang for their special numbers on Wednesday night with my auto harp.

We were back in Minnesota by the 23rd when they had a 50th anniversary celebration for us at the Church of Christ in Madelia. We had a good crowd (around 150). Our kids put on a good program. Rebecca wrote a nice song for us – "The Anniversary Song" – which the kids all sang. Out of town guests were Bernice, Bud and Bill Roof from up north; Doris and Peter Ratcliffe (Doris is my cousin) from Michigan; Mr. and Mrs. Dale Scheffler (Dale was an usher at our wedding) from Missouri and Bob's cousin Ardelle Manthey and her husband Francis from Hill City,

On Saturday the 16th we attended Tom and Maxine Avery's 50th anniversary in West Concord. All their kids were there and a lot of people.

September 10th we went up to Warroad for the Jack Pine Retreat. Bob helped get the campground ready. Bob preached Saturday night. Sunday we went to church in Bemidji and then left for home.

We sold our truck to someone in Mankato and bought another in New Ulm. On November 7th we went up to Warroad so Bob could go hunting. No luck.

We had Thanksgiving at our house again. Brenda came from Florida and I think the other kids were here except Amy who was in Alaska. Barbara and Paul came from Wisconsin. I fixed two turkeys. Paul went back to Janesville and Barbara stayed here.

December 5th we left Madelia, got as far as Wentzville, Missouri and stopped to see Dale Scheffler and his wife. We left the next day and went to Nelsonville, Ohio to visit the Russ family and others. Barbara came over from Bonnie's in Richmond to see us. She went back to Bonnie's and Bonnie had her baby on the 11th. It was a boy named Matthew Blaine, 8 lbs.7 oz.

The church there in Nelsonville had sold their building so Bob helped them move their things out. We left there on the 15th and arrived at Brenda's that night about 10 p.m. We looked around for a camper but didn't find one. We got to Orlando in time to go to their winter rally starting on the 20th. The speakers were Bruce Runner, Don Spencer, Dale Williamson, Don Renner, Fred Miller and Stuart Fitzgerald. We both helped with the services.

Brenda got the flu and a few days later I got it. I was very sick for a week and then coughed a lot for a long time. Bob had gone on ahead to Lakeland but I stayed in Orlando because I was still sick. Brenda and Steve Turner brought me to Lakeland later. We bought an old camper and put it in Dale's back yard.

1998

We went to Orlando on January 22th for Brenda's birthday. We worked on her flower beds and Bob mowed the lawn. Carrie and Crystal were there so Bob took them to Cape Kennedy and Playalinda Beach. We went back to Lakeland that evening.

On January 24th Bob was working under the camper with the jacks to try to get it more level and one of the jacks slipped. The camper fell on him. He was able to get out of the way a bit. Dale took him to the emergency room for an x-ray. One of his arms hurt for a few days but there were no broken bones. He seemed to be accident prone. He usually came out okay but his guardian angel must have been getting worn out.

January 29th was my birthday and Bob took me to Hardee's for breakfast. That was a treat because I really love their biscuits and gravy. Then he took me to Walmart at noon for taco salad. Dale and Jerri took us out to eat at Ryan's. It was buffet style which Bob liked. There were so many things he didn't like.

For Bob's birthday Dale, Jerri, Kim and I went and ate at the Historical Restaurant in Auburndale. I had catfish which was very good. We had the service at the residence earlier that day. Then we went to Orlando. We went to see Opal Barber in the hospital. She was diabetic and they were going to take her left foot off.

We stayed with Brenda a couple of days. About this time the Olympics opened in Japan. Steve Turner's parents were missionaries in Japan so he was interested in that. Then we traveled back to Lakeland again.

I was working on my family history and found out a descendant of William Cunningham's sister lived in Sarasota. I called to see if I could visit her and she said yes. We went over the next day. She went by the name Pattji (Patty Jay) Weber. She was really into genealogy. She had one room just for that. It had shelves all around with many notebooks on them. She gave me all the history of William's sister Martha which I was very glad to have. Pattji had multiple sclerosis at that time. I have lost track of her.

Dale and Jerri learned on the 13th that Jerri's brother Elden in Reno had had a massive stroke. We took them to the airport in Tampa to fly out on Delta. He died right after they got there.

We painted Williamson's house. Bob did the main part and I did the trim.

On the 21st Steve and Brenda and Bob and I went to Lake Wales and picked up Crystal at Warner Southern College where she was attending. We tried out Spook Hill and took them to Bok Tower.

Bad tornados had struck at Kissimee, Winter Garden, and Osceola County and 38 were known dead. Brenda called to say that the trailer court where Steve lived with his folks was hit. Their trailer was wiped out but they were safe. In Kissimmee the trailer court across from the Bible college was really wrecked. The Bible college, which was just across the road, was not damaged at all. The students took blankets from their beds and food and went over right away and did all they could to help. The newsmen were so impressed that they reported it on CNN. They got letters from all over sending them blankets, etc. What a testimony!

We left for Orlando on the 25th going by way of Claremont to visit Fred and Charlotte Miller.

We went to see Opal again. She had all of her toes taken off and part of her foot.

On March 20th we went to Epcot and Disneyworld. A friend of Brenda got tickets for us. We enjoyed it very much. I especially liked the president's show. They were life-size and moved off and on so they looked very real.

The Ladies Rally was on March 21 at the Harrell Road Church of Christ. Sharon Sutter, Miriam Spencer, and Helen Stoltz were the speakers. I sang "Little Flowers" and played my auto harp. They asked me to sing it again for church the next day.

On April 1st we left Orlando and drove as far as Abbeville, South Carolina. We went to the court house there to ask about William Cunningham's family but the dates that I was interested in had burned when the court house caught on fire, possibly set by Union troops in the Civil War.

We went on to Ashville, North Carolina. Bob was supposed to preach in a little church near there called Arden. They had a young preacher there trying out so they had Bob preach during Bible school and the young preacher for the main service. We were not trying out. Brother Hunt had given them our name. I sang "little Flowers" again. After church the whole congregation went to a cafe for supper. It was called Ryan's. We left after church and got as far as Indianapolis. We stayed at a motel and got up early (4:00 a.m.) We stopped at Nancy's in Mason City on April 6th but she wasn't home. She was in Madelia with her two dogs Benson and Brigita.

The first thing I did when I got to Madelia was go to the dentist, Dr. Fast. My tooth had been paining me quite a while. He pulled it and it was badly abcessed. He gave me an antibiotic for it.

Tornados had gone through Comfrey and St. Peter. We drove over to both places to see the damage.

Bob left for Warroad April 22nd.

May 2nd Barbara and I took part in the Tour of Tables at Trinity Lutheran Church. We chose the name "Everything is coming up Roses." We used my Royal Albert Country Roses pattern dishes. There were about 20 tables and all were different dishes. It was very interesting. They paid so much a plate and were served lunch at the tables.

On May 8th I went with Barbara and Paul to Grand Forks for Rebecca's graduation from law school. The speaker was Clarence

Thomas, Justice of the Supreme Court. We got to talk to him afterwards. Dale, Linda, Bobby, Bob and Nancy were there too. We stopped in Fertile on the way to Rebecca's to see Aunt Bernice. We went to Rebecca's reception in Shevlin and then on to Bemidji where they were having a special Mother's Day program. Bob preached and I sang "You are a Wonderful Mother."

We went home by way of Grand Rapids and then to Hill City to visit Bob's cousin Ardelle and her husband Francis Manthey. We made it home about 7:30.

On May 30th we went to Mason City to attend Mandy and Steve's wedding in the Evangelical Free church. It was a nice wedding and Mandy was a beautiful bride.

Winton Nasman, my cousin, had a stroke and recuperated in the nursing home. He had just driven home and was in the driveway when a strong wind blew him over. He hit his head very hard on the cement. He was taken to Mankato Hospital but never recovered. He died June 1st. The funeral was June 4th at the East Sveadahl Lutheran church in the country near St. James. Lawrence and Esther Colebank came from Bismarck, North Dakota. Three children of Aunt Mary's –La Donna from Faribault, Donald from Storden and Rodney and wife Thelma from Huron, South Dakota also came. We miss Winton very much. He always came to visit us often. He was the Nasman family historian.

Amy's husband Rod had a swelling in his neck. It turned out to be a bad kind of cancer – Non-Hodgkin's Lymphoma. We hated to get this news as we were very concerned.

We spent the 4th of July at Suzanne and Curt's near Mountain, North Dakota. Dale and family were there, also Rebecca, Nancy and Dennis, Barbara, Duane Katie and Bradley, Ann and Mel, Grace, Sherrie and Willie. In the forenoon we went to a parade in Park River. There were lots and lots of tractors of all kinds. A little boy who was standing by Bob said, "Boy does that bring back memories." He wasn't old enough to remember the old tractors. We had a nice lunch and then Curt had some fireworks. The Byrons came over that night for that.

Amy called and wanted us to come and stay with their 4 kids while she and Rod went to Houston, Texas to a cancer clinic there, so we went to Fairbanks, Alaska on July 7th. Amy and Rod left on the 10th. Mindy and Joci were both working. The church people had come over and laid their hands on and prayed for Rod before they left. Amy and Rod came back the 23rd. When they got back they took us to see the Rubber Duck Race on the river, which was interesting. Rod also took us up in a plane. He was going to show us the North Pole but Amy got sick so we had to go back. We got very close though.

While there we went to the University of Alaska museum. We also watched some Eskimo games. Rod bought a camper and we all went to Valdez. He parked near the dock and Bob and Rod went fishing. They caught some salmon.

On the 3rd of August we took a plane to Anchorage and visited there with my cousin Ann and her husband Mel Hagen. Ann had bought us all-day bus tickets. While we were on one of the buses the driver asked us where we were from. We said from a place you probably have never heard of. He still wanted to know what it was, so we told him. He said he knew that town because his sister lived there. What a coincidence! He was our grandson-in-law's uncle.

We went and toured a lot of places including Diamond Mall, the Federal Building, Eagle River, the Zoo, etc. Ann took us to their Senior Building for lunch, which was a nice big place. Then we went to a museum. We left Anchorage and flew back to Minnesota on August 7th.

When we got back to Madelia we looked at the Hartshorn Apartments and decided to rent one. This meant down-sizing for me, and it is always hard for me to part with things. Paul went to work in Mankato. We bought a camper in Lake Crystal.

We went to a flea market in Orinoco on the 15th. We saw Lawrence Colebank, and John and Judy Colebank (cousins) who had booths there. It was a real big place and would take you all day just to look at the booths. Lawrence was selling old telephones and John and Judy had a variety of dishes. I bought a few dishes.

On the 18th we took our camper and drove to Centerville, Iowa for the Centerville Rally. Jerry Weller, Earl Chambers and Tommy Johnson were speakers. We went back home two days later. It is always hot this time of year in southern Iowa so we were glad we had air conditioning.

We attended Bob's Aunt Alta Bares' 90th birthday celebration in Mankato on the 22nd. There were lots of relatives there, some of whom we saw very seldom.

I was having a lot of trouble coughing so I made an appointment with a lung specialist in Mankato on the 26th. I left his office with a nasal spray, Atrovent, an antihistamine, Gaviscon and a diet. I was supposed to come back on the September 21st .

Dale Williamson called to tell us that Opal Barber had died.

Ron Maloney also had a massive heart attack and died. Ron was a very nice guy and friend. He had a lot of experiences in WWII. He gave us a clock he had made out of a machine gear. His funeral was October 21st. I think Bob had the funeral or a part in it.

Bob went back to Bemidji on the 22nd and came back November 3rd.

Mary Russ had asked us to come to Ohio, so we left to go there on November 16th. We stopped in Cedar Falls, Iowa on the way to see Dwight and Vivian Hill. Then we stopped in Linn, Indiana where there was a surprise for us – Alvin and Jean Petersen had driven over from Mooresville to see us.

175

We arrived in Athens, Ohio on the 18th and stayed there nearly a week. Different ones invited us over to eat. Bob was asked to preach. Mary and Bob Russ were good friends we had gotten acquainted with in Orlando when they were there visiting.

On Monday the 23rd we drove all day to get to Brenda's that night. I remember we drove through a driving rain in Jacksonville, Florida and we could hardly see where we were going. We couldn't pull over because we couldn't see the shoulder, so we just had to follow the traffic and hope for the best. We were glad to get to Brenda's about 10:00 p.m.

Dale's family, and Crystal and Nancy were there in anticipation of being there for Thanksgiving. Fred and the boys, Lundgrens and Betsy and Winn also came. Thanksgiving was on the 26th and we celebrated it at Brenda's. They had borrowed tables and chairs from the church plus the piano, and two guys had just delivered it. There were 36 people there. Herbert Dawkins and wife, Jamaicans we had met in Jamaica, and son dropped by.

The night before we had ice cream and cake for Billy's 5th birthday. I remember how exuberant little Joshua Hintz was to see the cake and presents. I think he was more excited about it than Billy. We were happy to go back to Lakeland where our camper was parked.

Sunday the 29th Amy called to tell us that Rod had baptized Joci and Blaine. This was welcome news. Amy called again on December 3rd to say that Eliana Jo Davis was born around 7:00 p.m. the night before. The cord was wrapped around her neck but they got her out just in time. Now they have "his" and "hers" and "ours" children. We got another call from Amy to tell us their minister's wife had a baby girl a couple days after Eliana was born.

Eliana Davis at 3 weeks old

We were having a lot of problems with the car, so Bob got parts and fixed it. We also had trouble with the water system in the camper. Bob worked on that. Then Dale's van quit and had to go to the garage.

On December 16th, the U. S. began an attack on Iraq. I wondered how that would change things. It seems like there is war somewhere all the time.

December 25th came with no snow. It doesn't seem right to not have snow on Christmas. It made me a little homesick for Minnesota. We spent the holiday at Brenda's. She had Steve, Andrea and Nyume there. That night we went to services at the church on Harrell Road. That was the beginning of their annual Christmas Rally. Fred Miller, Bill Payne and Jim Book were speakers. They asked me to sing and play the organ.

Amy called that Rod was very sick with a temperature over 104 degrees. He was in the hospital and they had diagnosed pneumonia. We were very worried about him as his immune system was so low. He was much better by the 31st, but now Ellie was sick with a cold in her chest.

HAPPY NEW YEAR! - 1999

January found us still in Florida. We were busy making calls and doing church activities in the church on Combee Road where Dale preached. We also did chapel a lot at "The Residence." We had a lot of fun doing things with Dale and Jerri and having meals together. We also made another trip to Port Richey to see the Burgesses.

We were back and forth to Orlando to see Brenda. We spent our birthdays together. Bob got very sick with a high temperature and shaking, so he went to the Doctor in Orlando. She said he had a very bad UTI (urinary tract infection) and that if it got in his blood it could be fatal. An antibiotic took care of it.

I had a terrible nosebleed one night. It was so bad Bob took me to ER, but the waiting room was full. They put me in a room and we waited and waited but no one came. It finally quit and we left. We never got a bill. Bob did a lot of odd jobs for Dale Williamson and others.

Brenda had a workshop coming up in New York. We decided to take her up there and do some sight-seeing and visiting too. Brenda kept us entertained all the way by reciting States and their capitals and singing songs. We stopped in Washington D.C., then traveled on to Queens, New York where we stayed with some Jamaican friends. We saw the Statue of Liberty and declined to take all the steps up it – but Brenda did it. Then we left Brenda at her hotel and went on.

We stopped in Richmond, Ohio to see Bonnie and family and the next day we stopped in Illinois to see Leland and Merna Petersen Vandeveer. We got to Madelia on the 24th in time to attend Ernie Davis' (Larry's brother} funeral on the 26th.

On the 28th Bob went back to Bemidji. I went later. We took our camper to Grand Rapids and continued calling and looking for a place for our group to meet. We decided to move our things up to Bemidji and Ed and Arleigh Chandler volunteered to take their horse trailer and move them. We got it all in. It's surprising how much you can get in one of those. We moved into the Evergreen Acres Apartments in Nymore.

We got word that Crystal had been in a terrible car accident in Florida near her college. She had a broken pelvis, a head injury and a bad bruise on her hip. It took her a long while to recover from that.

May brought the graduations of Carrie in Warroad and Renata in Edinburg, North Dakota. We attended both.

In June we made a trip to Fairbanks, Alaska thanks to Rod and Amy. They took us to Denali Park, and the North Pole to watch a parade, then rented a camper and took us to Seward to an Army resort. Alaska has spectacular scenery. We got word while we were there that my cousin Laurence had died in Bismarck, N.D. He had a quadruple bypass and his kidneys shut down.

Rebecca had passed her bar exam and opened an office in Bagley, Minnesota.

The Blanshan reunion was July 17th at the Garden City Fairgrounds. We drove down for that.

On August 17th I had both feet operated on in Bemidji for bunions, spurs, etc. Dr. Espe said it was the worst case he had ever seen. I had to be in a wheelchair a while. I should have had it done sooner.

We took our camper to the Jack Pine Retreat near Williams in September, then we put the camper out to Ed Chandler's for the winter.

Aunt Bernice Roof (my dad's sister) of Fertile died October 28th and the family asked Bob to come and speak. The night before they had a little service where everyone who wanted to could talk about Bernice. It was so nice. She was 88 years old. She had always been such a quiet and gentle soul. She was always smiling.

On August 5th Bob's friend, Roger Deys, had a massive heart attack. He was operated on but only lived 11 days after that. They were living in Hawaii.

Bob and Amy went hunting that fall, but no luck.

Jessica and James had a 9-pound baby boy on November 5th. They named him Benjamin.

I made a lot of lefse during the year. I could sell all I could make. The people in the Evergreen Apartments really liked it.

A new grocery store opened in Bemidji and on their grand opening we purchased 10 cans of tomato soup, 20 pounds of chicken leg quarters, 20 pounds of flour, 6 dozen eggs and 1 pound of oleo – all for $12.45. That seems amazing now! The store was called Food 4 Less.

Our grandson Duane gave us a computer. Bob was worried that I would spend a lot of time on it. I didn't really get into it until we moved back to Madelia and I got on Facebook. I used it to type pages for my book too.

This year we had our Thanksgiving at Ma's Cupboard in Madelia. Our kids were there and also Jane, Jeff, Rhonda and Mark Robertson of Joplin, Missouri (my niece) and Bob's brother Al and Bonnie Blanshan.

Linda had a surprise party for Dale's 50th birthday. They were living in Warroad. We also attended that.

Bob had his left knee replaced December 20th in Bemidji. He got along fine and diligently exercised it.

On December 26th I got my first porcelain doll from Bonnie and Keren Williams. They had heard me say I would like a porcelain doll. That was the start of my doll collection. It had a lavender dress and was very pretty.

L to R: Amy, Dale, Paul, Rebecca, Wayne, Rod, Ellie having Thanksgiving at Ma's Cupboard in Madelia

2000

The year 2000 proved to be my worst year other than the year Davie died. We were still going back and forth to Grand Rapids. Bob built a fish house and put it out on Lake Bemidji and did a lot of fishing. I was working on my genealogy book. Bob's leg was healing but still gave him some pain. Things were going fine until Bob got another UTI infection and passed blood. Not long afterwards I passed some blood, so I thought I had a UTI too. I went to Dr. Benson and he said "No, you don't have a UTI. He sent me right over to the gynecologist who was in the same building. Dr. Kilgore examined me and after she had looked she said, "Oh, have we got problems here. You better get your things in order and tell your girls to have pap smears." I had lesions, my cervix was misshapen and there was a tumor. Then she said the dreaded word "cancer". She immediately made an appointment at the Fairview Hospital in Minneapolis with Dr. Cosin for March 7th. I had blood work, x-ray and an EKG. Dr. Cosin said they would do an exploratory operation and find out if it was contained. If it was contained they would do a hysterectomy and hopefully get it all. I was to come back on March 30th for that. I didn't like the wait but I suppose they were very busy.

We had our usual Winter Retreat at the church and Suzanne and Curt were there. Curt said "If I know June, she will rise above it."

Like it says to do in the Bible, I called for the elders and they laid their hands on me and prayed. I was not afraid. I had faith that I would get through it all right. I didn't panic.

We went down for the operation on the 30th. I think most of my family was there and also Al and Bonnie. They sat in the waiting room waiting for the verdict. A doctor came out and said it was contained so they could operate. Everyone was happy for a bit but a few minutes later they came out again and said they were mistaken – it had spread. That was not what we wanted to hear.

So began my six weeks of treatment. I had radiation five days per week. I also had several kinds of chemo. Twice I had Taxol, which took 8 hours, and twice I had the radioactive implant. That is where they inject radioactive stuff right into the tumor. They placed some kind of a contraption in me and I couldn't move much. There were high sides on the bed so the nurses wouldn't come in contact with it. I think that procedure took around 24 hours each time.

I had a lot of pain with it, a lot of severe cramps and diarrhea. This lasted for some time after I got home. They gave me opium in the hospital. I lost a lot of hair but not all of it. It came back in curly but that only lasted a month.

I had several interesting things happen while I was there. Several nurses said "You're a Christian aren't you?" I don't know how they could tell because I didn't have my Bible there. Another time a lady came in my room and apologized for coming in since she didn't know me. She said something kept telling her to go to me and pray for me. She asked if that was alright. Of course, I said yes and she prayed for me. I didn't see her again. The old hymns kept going through my mind. They were a great comfort to me.

Dr. Cosin was very encouraged by the results of the treatment. He said I now had only a 10% chance of the cancer coming back. It took me some months to get my energy back. I was in bed a lot at first but gradually got up a little at a time until I could be up and cook and do dishes.

I hadn't been home very long when I suddenly developed a fever. Suzanne was there and said I needed to go to the hospital. They took me to the hospital in Bemidji and I was immediately put in an ambulance and taken back to Fairview Hospital. They suspected an abdominal abscess. They gave me an antibiotic and two units of blood. I could feel improvement as soon as I had the transfusion. I was there five days and then went home.

The Blanshan Reunion was held on July 1st in Sibley Park in Mankato that year. I again put up my genealogy charts. We left for Bemidji that afternoon.

This was the year for the BPW (Blanshan/Petersen/ Williamson) Reunion too. It was held July 14th through 16th at Camp Delwater near Rebecca's up north. Quite a few were there, and Brenda made it too. I remember Bob marveling at how she went down the water slide yelling "Look at me, Daddy!" and then in a few hours she was on a conference call helping make big decisions for her company. I wasn't feeling good at all but went anyway. Bob and I had our own cabin.

Blanshan family at BPW Reunion 2000

All this time I was working on "William Cunningham," my great great grandfather on Grandma Colebank's side. Cousin Bernie (Solberg) from Gully was a big help. She even bought a copier and loaned it to me to use. She helped me put the pages together. She always brought apple pie from Hardy's with her.

On July 14th Rebecca and Emily found Wayne's mother Marie Hinrichs dead in her home. I can't imagine the shock that must have been for them. The funeral was the 18th in Bagley. It was a big funeral.

I was still having treatments on my side. Bemidji continued to do them. Finally, Dr. Dietz called from Minneapolis and asked if I still had that tube in. I said yes and he said that should have come out a long time ago. So they took it out and it didn't drain any more. I kept having pain there for a while, however.

On August 19th we got word that Norman and John Colebank (first cousins to me) had been killed in an auto accident in Orinoco. They both had booths at the flea market there and were leaving to go somewhere. Norman was driving and the sun was in his eyes. He didn't see the UPS truck coming and pulled out in front of it. They were both killed instantly. I miss them both as they were double cousins and I grew up with them. I especially miss John as he was so close to my age. Barbara and Paul had come to Orinoco that day and were looking for their booths but were told they had left. They drove by the accident and saw someone was on the ground but didn't know it was Norman and John. Bernie took me to Norman's funeral on the 25th in Valley City, North Dakota.

Bob got his first cell phone September 11th.

On September 28th we found another camper – a pull-type this time. We had looked all over, then found one a couple blocks from Barbara for $300. We had to buy a refrigerator and heater for it. We used it a lot in Grand Rapids. We finally found a good place to meet and that was in the meeting room in the new library.

I was working on a flower garden quilt. I had saved material with big flowers on it. I cut out the flowers and sewed them on a sheet. I think there was a lot of red in it. Nancy claimed it as soon as she saw it.

Thanksgiving came on November 23rd that year. We had it at Barbara's in Madelia. All the kids were there along with many grandchildren.

Bob was building a fish house which he did every year, then gave it away. He finished it on December 11th and put it out on Lake Bemidji. He had many hours of fun ice fishing.

Bob's Aunt Lila was in the nursing home in Big Fork, Minnesota. She died December 21st and they had the funeral in the Baptist Church in Hill City on December 26th. The family asked Bob to do the sermon. He was glad as she was one of his favorite aunts.

Bob's aunts Vera and Lila with Bob's sister Donna

2001

Dale and Linda moved to Oskaloosa, Iowa. They wanted us to go and get their stove, washer, dryer, refrigerator and dish washer from Warroad with our truck. We did that, loaded them up and started for Minneapolis so I could go to Dr. Doosenberry for a checkup. This was on January 8th. We stayed overnight at Emil and Linda Lorenz's and then went on to Madelia, stopping to see Albert and Bonnie in Belle Plaine on the way. We went as far as Mason City on the 10th and visited Nancy and Dennis. On January 11th we delivered the appliances to Dale and Linda who were fixing up a house.

We went to visit friends in Ottumwa on the 16th. While in Ottumwa the truck started making an awful noise and then quit. We called a friend, Greg Meyer, and he came and towed it to his garage. The belt on the tension pulley froze up and broke the belt. We were going to start out for Ohio and then Florida, so when we got back to Dale's we took Dale's car and left our truck with him. We only got as far as Mount Pleasant and it blew a head gasket. We called Dale and he came with his van and our truck. We put our stuff in the truck and started out again. We traveled to Mooresville, Indiana and stopped to see Alvin and Jean Petersen and stayed overnight.

On the 19th we made it to Nelsonville, Ohio to visit Bob and Mary Russ. We left there on the 22nd and arrived in Lakeland on the 23rd. We breathed a sigh of relief when the old truck made it all the way. Tom and Phyllis Richards loaned us a queen-sized bed and we put it in the shed behind Dale's house and that's where we stayed. It was his study.

On February 2nd we went over to Orlando to visit Brenda and Evelyn. On the 8th we went to Lake Wales to visit Crystal at Warner College. She was doing well there.

Bob painted Dale's neighbor's house.

On February 24th we left Lakeland and went as far as Atlanta, Georgia to visit Fred and Charlotte Miller. We left there on the 26th and traveled to Oskaloosa, Iowa to see Dale and Linda and family.

March 1st we stopped in Mason City and saw Nancy, then we went on to Madelia. We stayed there a few days and then went up to Bemidji on the 7th.

On May 8th Mandy had a baby boy which she and Steve named Josiah.

I joined TOPS on the 15th. It cost $20.00 to join. I soon had all that back by winning prizes for losing weight. It was a nice group to work with. We always had some kind of a contest going. We had entertainment too. One time they asked me to speak. I spoke on Jamaica.

We continued making our weekly trip to Grand Rapids. By May 1st we were able to take our camper there.

Drew graduated on the 20th and we went to Edinburg, North Dakota for that. He was valedictorian and also sang.

Barbara and Paul bought a house on East Main in Madelia to fix up and turn into an antique and tea shop they called Prairie Chic.

Roger and Carrie were married on May 26th and we went to their wedding in Iowa.

On July 7th we went to a Roof reunion on Island Lake near Lengby. Bob and I were sitting on one side of a picnic table and the person on the other side got up and over we went. No one got hurt and I guess it looked pretty funny.

We went to Mindy's graduation reception on July 20th in Madelia and stayed for the Blanshan reunion which was in Sibley Park in Mankato on the 21st.

Bonnie Lamm Randolph had a baby boy on August 25th. Barbara was there. She didn't think he looked just right. We found out later baby Corey had Down Syndrome.

The people in the apartments where we lived were very active and friendly. We had special meals together on holidays, pot luck on Sundays for whoever wanted to come, rummage sales, programs, pancake suppers and pie and ice cream nights. We also had card parties, bingo and other things. We did some of our own programs and they were very cooperative. They had a piano and an organ. I went down quite often and played the piano after supper. Sometimes Opal Guest would join me and play the organ. The people seemed to enjoy it and even gave me some money for doing it. Once a week a bus would come and take us to the grocery store free of charge. They let Bob have a little garden there. We got quite a bit of stuff out of it and I froze and canned at lot. We had a little trouble with a woodchuck.

On September 3rd we went with Ed and Arleigh Chandler to the Labor Day Rally in Fridley.

On September 11th we were sitting in our camper in Gene Taplin's yard when we heard about the attack on the Twin Towers. We were in shock. We wondered what would be next -- WWIII?

On October 5th we went to Tilden, Nebraska for Alvin Petersen's 80th birthday. He was in really good shape for his age. I believe he was Bob's closest friend.

On November 2nd we found a fifth-wheel camper for $1800. We gave our other small camper to Jason Corder. Seemed like Bob found something wrong with each camper and wanted to trade. My favorite was the LeSharo. It was small enough to park where a pickup could and yet had everything you needed. Bob said the parts were too expensive on that one, however.

I had a colonoscopy November 5th. They only found one polyp but said there were lots of adhesions.

Bob took the camper to Hill City and went hunting with Francis Manthey. He didn't have any luck.

Bob and I joined the senior chorus group called "The Third Street Singers". It was led by Mrs. Louma. It was fun to sing with them – Bob even had a solo part in one song. We sang at nursing homes, etc.

We went to Hill City on November and picked up the camper and went to Madelia. We stayed in the camper until it got too cold. (the heater didn't work). We stayed in Brenda's house then. Brenda had bought the house next door to Barbara and Paul.

Thanksgiving was on the 22nd. Rod and Amy hosted us all at their house. Forty-seven people attended. Everyone was there except Barbara's kids. Dale's wife Linda brought 17 pies. We had music and singing. Ellie was already trying to lead in things.

The Thanksgiving table at Amy's

On December 1st we went back to Bemidji and took the camper out to Ed's shed for the winter.

On December 2nd we got word that John Lorenz from Williams was found dead, probably due to a heart attack.

2002

Bob's cousin Lawrence Buck in Lake George told us about Florence Buck dying. We had met her once. She always wore the same black hat wherever she went. They placed it on top of her casket. I remember one of her grandsons got up and told how much he appreciated his Grandma and showed a quilt that she had made for him. Of course, that made an impression on me because he was an adopted Korean and thought so much of his grandma. The funeral was January 14th in Park Rapids and the reception was in the community center in Osage with burial in Osage as well.

Bob was getting in quite a bit of ice fishing. I made lots and lots of lefse. With so many Norwegians around I could sell all I could make. I think I was charging 4 for $1.00 which was cheaper than anyone else. They were dinner plate size.

We continued going to Grand Rapids for the weekend and coming back to Bemidji in time for the evening service at church. We always left early enough to have breakfast at Hardy's before church. I loved their biscuits and gravy. At that time they allowed seconds.

There was lots of excitement when the Bemidji Walmart store opened February 20th. The high school band played, there was a color guard, and Indian dances and introduction of the leading workers in the store. It was a 45-minute program. It proved to be a very popular store especially with the Natives. The parking lot always had cars in it. I will have to admit I loved their sewing department where they had a lot of fabrics at low prices.

The church in Bemidji was very welcoming to foreign students. We had a number of them over for meals. Two boys from India were favorites. One of them married a girl from the church and the other went back to India and got a bride and brought her back here and both found work and stayed here. A professor from China attended church too.

Both Bob and I enjoyed visiting with people so we had a number of people over for meals. Among them were people from the apartments, church people, students as well as others we met.

We had our annual Winter Retreat on March 2nd and 3rd at the church. Patrick Dougherty from Ottumwa, Iowa was the speaker.

March 7th we went to visit Dale and Linda and family who now lived in Knoxville, Iowa. Bobby had bought a 1929 Chevy which he planned to restore. Bob bought him a battery for it.

On the 12th we stopped at Nancy and Dennis's in Mason City, Iowa and stayed overnight. Nancy had gotten a new little dog, a little black poodle she called Bailey. It was so cute and loved to be held. We left for Madelia the next day. Cousin Jane Robertson was staying here with her daughter Rhonda. She was hoping to get some help for her. They had adopted her when they were in the Windward Islands (St. Lucia). They were staying downstairs in Brenda's house next door to Barbara, and Rebecca was upstairs.

When we got back we organized a rhythm band. We had picked up a number of instruments to use. There were at least a dozen or more who took part. I played the piano and Bob led. We performed at several nursing homes. They also played for our Easter supper at the apartments. Later on we found a drum for a man in the apartments that used to play in a band. He was a good addition to our band.

Gene Taplin, a preacher who was attending church in Grand Rapids, had to have a triple by-pass heart surgery. Arleigh Chandler in Bemidji had cancer that had spread to her liver. We went to see her in the hospital in Fargo. We stayed overnight at Beth Swanson's (a high school pal of Suzanne's).

Suzanne had a recital in the Presbyterian church in Grand Forks and about 60 people came. She did an exceptionally good job. Her teacher was there and was pleased too. This was April 13th. We were always proud of our kids whenever they accomplish things.

Bob's Aunt Lila died in the nursing home in Big Fork. The funeral was the 22nd of April. I think it was in the Baptist Church in Hill City. She was one of Bob's favorite aunts.

Arleigh Chandler died May 6th at her home. At the moment she died, their pet spaniel jumped up on the bed beside her. He had never been allowed on the bed. He seemed to know what was happening. Arleigh's funeral was the 9th and Bob, Jason Corder and Steve Williams performed the service.

May 9th Roger and Carrie had a little baby girl named Caitlyn. This was their first one.

June and Caitlyn – November 2002

Bob decided we should move back to Madelia in case my cancer came back. Ed Chandler loaded up our stuff in his horse trailer and took it to Madelia. Bob must have driven the truck. Larry Davis and the Martwick boys, Myron and Doug, were there to help us unload. We put the stuff in Brenda's garage. Her three-car garage was a great place to store things. We headed back for Bemidji and stopped at Grand Rapids on the way.

Ed helped us move the rest of our stuff to Madelia. We put everything in the garage again except the piano which we put at Rebecca's next door. Rebecca said we could move in with her. She said we could have the upstairs and she would have the basement and porch. I stayed with her and Bob went back to Bemidji again. He came back a week later.

We bought Larry and Norma's car when she bought a brand new one.

The Blanshan reunion was in Sibley Park again on July 20th.

On August 13th we took the camper and went to the Centerville Rally in Iowa. Speakers were Dan Smith, Jerri Weller, Patrick Dougherty, Ed McSpadden, and Jeff Dalrymple. We enjoyed visiting with old friends. There was a student reunion on the 16th which was held in the Country Kitchen. We camped at James and Jessica's in the country near Ottumwa. We stopped at Dale's on the way home. Betsy and Winn got married Aug. 24 in Bloomfield, Iowa. The next day was a graduation reception for Bobby so we stayed for that.

August 29th we went to the State Fair. Bob pushed me around in a wheel chair. We only stayed a few hours. We always tried to spend one day at the State Fair if we were in the area.

In September we had a nice visit from Dennis and Margery Stahlnecker and Dennis' mother Geraldine (Deenie) Stahlnecker. Deenie was my first cousin. They could only stay a few hours as they were on their way to Little Falls, Minnesota. They were from

Albany, Oregon. Geraldine was a daughter of Clara Strean, my Dad's sister.

All through these months I had a lot of pain in my hips, abdomen and back. Part of the time I was in the wheel chair. People brought in food and were very helpful. I finally got a shot of cortisone in my hip which helped a great deal.

Noticing that our health was beginning to fail we decided to take one more trip out west while we were still able. We left Madelia on October 1st, stopping in Huron, South Dakota to visit my cousin Rodney Cambronne, who was also our age. We went on to stay overnight in Billings, Montana at the Hampton Inn, thanks to Brenda. Our next stop was Proctor, Montana to see Dan and Betty Escritt. We stayed there several days.

We also got to see Dewey Obenchain and his wife Neela. They came over to see us and then we went over to their place to see their house they are building. It was really big.

We left there and drove through the mountains to Bremerton, Washington to visit my sister-in-law, who took us to see the crypt where my brother was buried. The next day we drove to Portland, Oregon to see Tom and Lois Zimmerman. We stayed overnight there. Then we went on to Molalla, Oregon to visit my cousin Kenneth Strean and wife Vivian and 90-year-old cousin Alice Strean.

We also drove over to Salem where we saw Harold Buckles, who was in an assisted living place. Bob had an Aunt Leora and Uncle Buck Gilson who were also in Salem. Then it was on to Albany, Oregon where we visited my cousins Dennis and Margery Stahlnecker.

Our next stop was Coos Bay, Oregon to see Ed and Sharon Werner. They took us to the coast to see a whole bunch of sea lions and also to a pretty waterfall which I don't remember the name of. We stayed overnight there and then went on to Culver, Oregon to see Joe and Bonnie Buckles. We drove on Highway 126 which took us through some beautiful scenery including a crater and lots of lava rocks and the Three Sisters Mountains.

We left there the next morning and headed for Meridian, Idaho where our grandson Duane Lamm and wife Katie lived. We got to see our great grandson Bradley.

We left there the next day and went as far as Provo, Utah. Brenda had reserved a room for us the Residence Inn which is a branch of the Marriot group. It was very nice. We weren't used to having it so nice.

The next day we drove 500 miles to Denver and stopped overnight with our good friend Don Heese and his wife Sandy. We left there and drove through Estes Park and Rocky Mountain National Park to Loveland, Colorado. We visited another good friend Richard Snell and his wife Thelma. We also went to see my cousin Eric Sorem and wife Nancy and Tom and Kathy Allen. Kathy was a fourth cousin, I think. We also visited with Dick German and wife who lived in Cozad, Nebraska. She fixed a real nice supper for us. They showed us their new beautiful motor home.

The next day we went as far as Tilden, Nebraska and saw Alvin and Jean Petersen. That night we went to a restaurant with them and Alvie and Zella Schwarting. Zella was Alvin Petersen's sister-in-law. How wonderful it was to be able to have fellowship with all these people on our trip! The next day it was back home again.

I was anxious to get things organized and made the mistake of carrying a twin-sized box spring from the garage to our basement. That set my back off and I had to stay in bed a couple days. I went to the doctor who x-rayed it. He said there was no cartilage between my lower back vertebrae, so I knew then I had to be very careful. He ordered about six weeks of therapy at the hospital.

Hunting time again! Bob made his usual trek up to Bemidji and Shevlin. I think what he enjoyed most was the anticipation of getting ready for it and visiting people. I always was glad he loved to meet people. He was always willing to stop and see my relatives as well as his own.

Thanksgiving came on the 28th that year and we held it at Amy and Rod's. Brenda had always done so much for our family that we decided to have a "Brenda Appreciation" service. Jon, Suzanne and Drew wrote a song for her and the sisters sang it. Bob wrote a poem. We presented her with a quilt with her name on it. Amy gave her a check for $100 (in payment owed her for all the times she had offered Brenda a quarter if she would rub her feet for her and never paid her.)

Kid's table at Amy's house

The next day Reid and Grace Hagen brought his parents, Ann and Mel Hagen, to see us. Grace was interested in antiques and wanted to see what Barbara had in her shop. Jon, Suzanne, Nancy and Drew were playing their instruments there. They were playing Christmas music and it sounded very good.

Bob built another fish house and put it on Lake Hanska. It seemed like he built one every year and then gave it away and made a new one.

We had Christmas with Barbara.

Barbara

2003

On January 10th I went to Dr. Cockerill in Mankato. He said one kidney was partially blocked and there was a possibility of a thyroid problem. He wanted to set me up for some tests in a month.

On the 18th we had a Blanshan cousin get together at Best Western in North Mankato. Twelve cousins were there.

On January 27th I went to the hospital in Mankato. Dr. Goldberg wanted to do a cysto-collagen injection in my bladder. They put me out for it.

I turned 77 on my birthday and we went to the Happy Chef in St. James. They gave me 77% off of my bill. I had golden-fried cod. The pie was free.

My hip was giving me a lot of trouble. On February 11th my back and hip were hurting so bad that Barbara and Bob took me to emergency in Madelia. They admitted me and gave me morphine. They kept me until February 2lst. After a CT scan and MRI they said my pelvis had cracked clear through on the right wing of my pelvis not far from the spine. The pain was unbearable. I never knew that cracks hurt worse than breaks on bones. They had me walking with crutches in the hospital and it hurt every time I tried to walk. After I got home my right leg started hurting, especially my ankle. An elastic brace helped that. They put a pain patch on me. Sometimes I still had to take Darvocet. I had to be in the wheel chair part of the time.

We got word that Bob's cousin's husband Francis Manthey had been shot in his bed. His wife Ardelle maintained that she didn't do it. The evidence all pointed to her and she is now spending life in prison. It is thought that she was addicted to gambling and trying to get Francis to give her money to gamble with. We felt very bad – we never thought she would do something like that. We went to his funeral in Eagle Lake on March 13th.

Prison photo of Ardelle Manthey

We got more bad news. Our good friend in Bemidji, Bunny Chandler (Howard's wife) had died. Bob went to her funeral but I wasn't able to.

Jane and Jeff came in March to do a week preaching for us. He was a very good speaker. They had their son Mark along too.

Bob's brother Garry came over off and on and went fishing with Bob. The ice went out on the lakes and Bob got out his boat. Fishing with him was usually an experience. The first thing that happened was that the boat got away from him while he was unloading it. I don't remember how he recaptured it. The next day he forgot to put the plug in and didn't notice it until he saw it filling with water. Another time he was out in the middle of the lake when the motor quit. He was standing up in the boat trying get it to go when it suddenly started and he fell out of the boat. As luck would have it he had turned the steering wheel and it went in a big circle and came right back to him and he was able to grab it. Another time when it quit he had to try to row with one oar to get back to shore. Yet another time he lost his rod but Garry snagged it three hours later.

Suzanne graduated from college and we went over to the University of North Dakota for it. There were 900 students graduating. Suzanne was one of only three music students to graduate.

June 1st Joci graduated from high school here in Madelia.

More bad news about this time. Our friend Dan Escritt died. Dan was a brother to Ruth Petersen. The funeral was in Oakdale, Nebraska in the Oakdale cemetery. Bob preached the sermon.

Life goes on and as one dies another is born. Nancy's Mandy had a baby girl on June 23rd that she named Grace Rene (Rowland).

July 3rd was the date for the BPW reunion. It was held at the same camp as the year before – Camp Delwater. We even had the same cabin.

There was another wedding in the family. Nancy's Crystal married Mark Egland and we went to their reception August 2nd in Mason City, Iowa.

The Blanshan reunion was in Highland Park in Mankato on July 19th.

On August 11th Dr. Goldberg tried some more surgery on my bladder. My hip and back were still bothering so I had a shot of cortisone in my hip again. On October 27th he tried another surgery but nothing much seemed to help.

Another close friend died August 7th in Lakeland, Florida. Bob went down for the funeral but I wasn't able to. I guess when you get our age you begin to lose your friends

Bob, Amy and Sterling went hunting up north again.

As the cold weather approached Bob started thinking "fish house" and he started building yet another one.

Just before Thanksgiving Rod developed chest pains and high blood pressure so Amy took him to emergency. They sent him to Rochester. One of his arteries was 100 per cent blocked so they put in a stent. Thanksgiving was held in the VFW building in Madelia. We had three turkeys. I was in my wheelchair and one of the little great grandsons stared at me for a while, then said "Are you my Grandma?"

This seemed to be a year for tragedies. My cousin Dorothy Sorenson was killed in a car accident as she was on her way to visit her son in Paynesville. The funeral was December 3rd. Amy sang for it. Our friend Shari Kilmer of Madelia had a heart attack and they put in 3 stents.

All this time I was finishing up my family history book. I ended up with 700 pages. I made about 75 copies on my copier and sold them for $30.00 plus postage. This did not cover the costs but I enjoyed doing it and thought I needed to write down what I knew while I still could. I also worked on quilts. I finished one with predominantly red colors.

We spent Christmas with Rod and Amy.

Marlene Davis, my home health aide was still coming at this time.

2004

On February 6th we started out to go to Texas and stopped at Dale's. Linda went with us from here on to help drive. We left on February 8th and went as far as Emporia, Kansas. We stopped again at Perry, Oklahoma for the night at Best Western. Paul had paid for two rooms for us. On the ninth we reached Brenda's in The Woodlands, Texas, near Houston. We brought Brenda's cat, Abu and Rebecca's cat, Fifi. They were pretty good travelers. We took Linda to the airport on the 14th. Brenda's friend from South Africa came. Her name was Leslie Booth.

We had a lot of fun exploring and going to the different stores. One store was Gallery Furniture, where they had one of Elvis Presley's cars on display. They also had a huge chair.

I worked on my crazy quilt that was in shades of blue.

One highlight for Bob was getting to go to George Foreman's church and hearing him speak. He also got to talk to him.

Bob bought a swing or glider for Brenda and put it out by her swimming pool. The water was too cold to go swimming, however.

We got word that Joel Rainer Howard was born March 24th to Carrie and Roger.

My hip started bothering me again so Bob got a wheelchair for me.

Jon and Suzanne came down on April 8th to drive us home. We left April 10th, stopping in Joplin, Missouri to visit Jane and Jeff. We arrived home April 11th.

My hip was bothering me and also my bladder. I went back to Dr. Cockerill on May 20th. He said "This has gone on long enough. I know one of the urologists in Rochester. I will call him and see if I can get an appointment." He got right on the phone while I was there and got an appointment for June 1st. I went to Rochester and they did several days of tests. The doctor told me I needed to have my uterus, bladder and colon removed and scheduled the operation for September 22nd. It would be done by Dr. Husmann and another specialist. One of my kidneys was blocked too. They were also looking for cancer but didn't find any. They said part of the bone on the front of my pelvis was gone (eaten away by the radiation.)

Jon and Suzanne were married on June 27th in the Covenant Church in Grand Forks. We were able to attend that.

I made a cat quilt for Brenda and began working on a crib quilt for Bonnie. I was also working on a lavender quilt made from curtains that I had when we were first married.

Another cousin's reunion was held at Best Western in Mankato again on July 10th and the Blanshan reunion was at Highland Park again on July 17th. A lot of people got sick after the Blanshan reunion. Bob got sick but I didn't. We couldn't figure out what caused it.

On July 18th we went to Springfield, Minnesota to attend the 50th wedding anniversary of Ernie (Bob's cousin) and Marlene Auringer. He was a square dance caller and gave us a little sample.

On August 8th we went down to Knoxville, Iowa to visit Dale and Linda. They took us to some sprint car races which we had never seen before. On the 10th we left for the Centerville Rally. Jason Corder, Dick Chambers and Jeff Dalrymple were speakers. We went home on the 13th.

Barbara, Nancy and I put on several rummage sales that summer. Nancy brought a lot of new stuff that sold well. In between times I did a lot of canning and freezing in spite of not feeling well.

We always loved to go to fairs. We went to the Garden City Fair and Jon and Suzanne took us to the State Fair. I took along my wheelchair. Another event we usually went to was Godahl Days. Godahl, Minnesota consisted of one little grocery store, but they have one fairly large building and room for shows outside. They always served a picnic meal at noon. In the afternoon there is a parade which is usually pretty good – lots of antique cars. Ellie got to be in the parade as she was chosen to be "Little Miss Madelia." I took my wheelchair again.

On September 15th I went to the Mayo Clinic for my pre-op examination. I was admitted in to St. Mary's Hospital on the 20th and the operation was scheduled for the 22nd. Before the operation I told them to leave my colon if they possible could.

The surgery took six hours. They had called in a colon specialist and he thought it would be ok to leave it in. When I awoke from the anesthetic I was alert and didn't talk silly or feel groggy. I don't know what they gave me. I asked the doctor why I didn't feel any pain down there and he said "Well, we kind of put it all to sleep." They were able to leave my colon in and I was glad I didn't have to have two bags. I got a lot of flowers and visitors and two dolls for my collection. I also got a lot of calls including one from Brother Ramsay in Jamaica. I went home October 3rd. A nurse came to see me the next day. I was in bed but she said "Well, look at you all bright and alert. I expected to see you with all four paws up in the air." We noticed a stent was coming out and the nurse called the doctor who said it was ok.

Bob had eye surgery at the VA hospital in Minneapolis on October 13th. On the 21st I had to go back for a check-up. Dr. Husmann took out the other stint. Everything was okay, but I had a little trouble getting used to the bag. A nurse came several times a week to help me.

I was busy making quilts during the year. I finished one for Dale and one for Rebecca. Also did some baby crib quilts.

November 13th was another cousin's get-together in North Mankato again.

Bob went up north hunting as usual and didn't get anything.

On Christmas we stayed home and had Barbara and Paul over.

I had Marlene Davis for most of the year for a home health aide. She was very nice and did a good job, but I think she was too old for the job. She had to quit because her back started hurting. After that I had Stephanie and then Wanda.

2005

2005 sounds a lot like 2004 except it was better for me health-wise. For most of the year my home health aide was Wanda Grenco. I had several different nurses who came once a week.

I was busy making a crib quilt for Mandy's Evan who was born January 17th.

Mindy started going with Neil Arkell of Madelia in January.

Bob did quite a bit of ice fishing. Garry came sometimes and sometimes he took others along.

In February Rebecca came back to Madelia from Texas. She brought Abu but Fifi had died. Her moving van came on February 14th. She wanted to have the basement and the porch. That was fine with us.

Paul did a lot of work on the house. Bob tore out a place upstairs for the washer and dryer and Paul finished it up. He put cupboards above the washer and dryer. Then they made the bathroom a lot bigger. The old one was real tiny. He put in a real nice shower and cupboards and a handicapped stool. He had to tear out some walls to do this. The old bathroom became our closet. New tile had to be put on the floor too. We really appreciated all the work he did.

We had a nice visit from Joci from Alaska in March.

We had several cousin get-togethers during the year, usually at the Best Western in North Mankato.

We enjoyed the company of Ellie when she came after school. She would always get some hot chocolate and ice cream. Bob always pretended he was mad because she was eating all his chocolate ice cream. We played a lot of games. She especially liked those where she could make up a story. She has a very good imagination.

I was playing organ or piano every Sunday for church here in Madelia. I also sang a lot of special numbers with my auto harp.

We played a lot of Uno, Racko and Aggravation (marbles) with Norma and Larry. We had many a good time visiting with them in the evening. When Norma was working, Larry would come over alone and we fed him many meals. In July Norma was diagnosed as having bone marrow cancer. This was a big blow to all of us. Larry came over whenever she was in the hospital.

We spent quite a few days entertaining at the Luther Memorial Nursing Home in Madelia. Bob was asked to have the chapel service in the forenoon quite often. I usually played the piano and sang with my auto harp. Sometimes I played the accordion. Whenever Jon and Suzanne or Dale came we had them play and sing. Amy did a lot of singing too. Ellie was only three when she stood on a chair and held the microphone and sang right out. Viola (my cousin) was in the nursing home and we went to see her quite often. We took sandwiches to her as she dearly loved a sandwich.

I was busy all year gathering information for my Buck History. Bob's Grandma Blanshan was a Buck. I found out they originally came from England.

We had a surprise visit from my cousin Dale Colebank and his wife Loita in May. Dale's mother Esther was a twin to my mother and our dads were cousins. Dale played the guitar and sang. Loita also sang. She gave us several CDs they had made. I took them out to the country to visit other cousins.

We watched our grandson Blaine (Boyd) graduate from high school here in Madelia on May 29th.

On June 1st we attended the funeral for Harvey's (Bob's brother) wife Mary. She was buried in Minneopa Cemetery.

We decided to go on a trip to Ohio. We left June 1st after the funeral and arrived on the 3rd. We had our motor home. We had a nice visit with Mary and Bob Russ and their daughters Barbara and Caroline and families. Our granddaughter Bonnie lived in Richmond, Ohio and she came over on the 18th with her three kids. It was fun to see them. We left on the 19th. We traveled by way of Mooresville, Indiana where we saw Alvin and Jean Petersen and stayed there overnight. We also stopped at Merna and Leland Vandeveer's. It was very hot going home and then our air conditioner quit working. I could hardly stand it until we got home. The nurse came the next day and my blood pressure was low. They took me to the hospital where they kept me long enough to hydrate me.

On Saturday, July 2nd we went to Renata and Greg's wedding at a Lutheran Church in Moorhead. It was a big wedding and very nice. I gave them a quilt.

Renata, June and Suzanne

On our way back to Bemidji we stopped in Lake George to visit with Bob's cousin Lawrence Buck and his wife Dixie. We went to Bemidji after that. From there Jon and Suzanne took us to visit Jon's parents at a cabin on Lake Burntside near Ely. The lake was beautiful. We had a very nice time. We drove back to Bemidji on the 8th and stayed overnight with Steve and Bonnie Williams. On our way home from there we visited Bob's brother Harvey in Baxter, Minnesota.

This was a very warm summer. We had six days in a row that were over 90 degrees.

Barbara had to close her shop "Prairie Chic" for health reasons.

The Blanshan reunion was in a different spot this year. It was at McGowan's Resort near Mankato on July 23rd. It was a nice place with plenty of things for the young folks to do. The Auringers also had a reunion on July 30th at Highland Park.

August is the time for the Centerville Rally. We left August 11th in order to visit Dale and Linda and family in Knoxville, Iowa on the way. The National Sprint Races were being held there, so we got to go there and see them. On the 15th we went on over to Centerville for the rally. The speakers were Patrick Dougherty, Jerri Weller, Dan Smith, Stewart Merrill and Jeff Dalrymple. We always had such a good time visiting with old friends and the local churches always served delicious meals. We got home on the 18th after running out of gas just four miles from Madelia.

We had a ladies tea at the Church of Christ on Saturday, August 20th. Amy and Ellie sang, Ettie Faye Palmer read a poem and I was the speaker. The theme was "Fill My Cup." We served a lunch afterward.

Neil Arkell. Mindy's boyfriend, was baptized on August 29th by Bob in the church in Madelia.

September 30th was the time for my annual checkup in Rochester. Everything was good. The doctor said "Whatever you're doing, keep doing it!"

We made our usual trip to the Minnesota State Fair but got very tired.

On September 3rd there was a get-together for Dawn (Al's daughter) and her husband Tom. It was nice to see them. They live in Texas so we hardly ever see them. The get-together was held somewhere near Al's in Belle Plaine.

Tom and Dawn

Our preacher friend, Ed Werner, came to Madelia on September 10th and 11th. He had a model of Noah's ark made to scale. Then he gave a very interesting talk about it. On September 13th we got the news that Jerri Williamson had a stroke.

Gillian's wedding was coming up so we headed for Bemidji. On the way we visited Al and Bonnie in Belle Plaine and the Mall of America in Bloomington. Then we picked up Brenda who had flown in to the airport. We stayed at Steve and Bonnie's in Bemidji.

The wedding was September 17th at the Hampton Inn in Bemidji. It was a beautiful wedding. I will always remember Ellie singing "Can I Have This Dance?" I think she was about seven. She did a wonderful job.

We went to church in Bemidji the next day. There were 18 of us Blanshans there. We left after lunch and stopped at Emily to see the Arkell cabins. They were very nice. The Arkell kids each have a cabin.

Naomi Olson, Emily Hinrichs, Gillian and Craig Beach

Ellie singing "Can I Have This Dance?"

My heart was beating erratically again so I went to the Doctor. He put me on Lasix and Metopropolol.

Another wedding came in October. Mindy and Neil were married in the church in Fairmont on October 29th. Garry and Mary Ann were there and followed us home and visited with us a while. I remember Garry saying "That was the prettiest wedding I ever saw." Brenda came for that too.

Amy, Mindy, Neil and Rod

Bob went up north for hunting on November 3rd and came back the 14th. No luck as usual.

Dale had a Youth Rally in Knoxville, Iowa. We went down on November 11th and the rally was the next day. Three generations of Blanshans preached – Bob, Dale and Bobby.

When we got back we took the camper out to Maloney's for the winter.

Thanksgiving came on the 24th that year. We held it in the church in Madelia as we had outgrown the homes. There were 50 there.

Amy played talk show host Jay Leno and interviewed the younger Blanshan cousins. Betsy's husband Winn emceed a game too. We always had funny skits, games and music at these get-togethers.

Winn Cradic emceeing the "Oldlywed Game" at
Thanksgiving 2005

The next day we got the sad news that Jerri Williamson had died.

Bob had surgery on his other knee on December 27th at the VA hospital. He had some trouble breathing when he came out of the anesthetic so they put an oxygen mask on him.

2006

Joci and Kyle were here visiting from Alaska.

Bob and I got cell phones thanks to Brenda.

Bob had not been feeling well for some time. He was having shots for blood clots, his foot was very painful and he had a high white count. Dr. Yvette gave him Amoxicillin.

February 4th was a big day this year because we had a celebration at the church for our 80th birthdays. Suzanne got me a pretty blue dress for the occasion. It was well attended. We were given $500.00 in all. Rod and Amy gave us tickets for an all-expense-paid trip to Hawaii.

Bob and June's 80th birthday celebration

Bob's cousin, Delorabelle, died in St. Peter, Minnesota. We attended the funeral on February 7th.

My left hip was painful again so I had a shot on February 28th.

Larry's wife Norma was very ill. Efforts to help her heal were to no avail and she died March 10th. The funeral was March 15th. Bob read the obituary, Barbara played, and Merrill Davis (preacher from Truman) gave the sermon. Norma was a close friend and we really missed her. She and Larry were at our house many times and we were at theirs. Larry was lost without her so we had him over every day for meals for a long time.

In March Bob had chest pains so he went to the hospital in St. James. His heart was fibrillating.

Alvin and Jean Petersen came for a visit April 6th but didn't stay overnight. They were on their way up to Bemidji to visit Bonnie and Steve. Dale's family came the same day around noon. They put on a special program at the nursing home.

I finished the crazy quilt I was making out of silk, satin and velvet pieces. Amy wanted it so I gave it to her.

It was time to use our tickets to Hawaii, and Amy and Rod went with us. Rod had spent some time in Hawaii when he was in the military. We stayed at the Hotel Hale Koa and Rod rented a car and drove us around. He showed us the resort which was especially for veteran's. I really enjoyed the Aloha Stadium Flea Market and found some bargains there. Rod had rented two electric chairs for us.

On the 29th we went up town where a couple blocks were roped off and a stage set up. They were celebrating Spam. It seems like the Hawaiians really like Spam. I guess they got introduced to it during World War II when so many soldiers were there. You could even order it in the cafes.

On the evening of May 1st we got to participate in a luau. It featured pulled pork and other Hawaiian foods. They also had a program which included hula dancers.

We left on May 3rd at 7:00 a.m. and got home at 5:30 p.m. What a wonderful time we had on that trip, thanks to Rod and Amy.

Barbara found us a nice davenport and tapestry-covered wing chair for $150.00. It was just the style I wanted. It fit nicely in our apartment when we moved there.

On May 11th we took the camper up to Bemidji to Bonnie and Steve's. Rebecca met us there and took us to her place for the night. The next day Rebecca and Wayne took us to Fargo to Jon and Suzanne's. On the 13th we all went to Grand Forks for Renata's graduation from the University of North Dakota School of Law. She passed the bar exam in September on her first try.

Renata had reserved a room at the Country Club for us all for lunch.

The next day eight of us went to church at the Valley Christian Church in Moorhead. We left after lunch and headed back to Bemidji, stopping at Lawrence and Dixie Buck's in Lake George.

Amy and Paul drove our car up so we would have a vehicle. We moved our camper out to Ula Hoffer's. She seemed so glad to have someone living in her yard as she was all alone. We left it there since we had to go back to Madelia.

On July 1st Barbara and Paul took Bob and I as far as Merna and Leland's and stopped for a while. Leland showed us how to get out to a campground. I think this was a BPW reunion. We had a room at the lodge that was air conditioned with a private bath and a double bed. Barbara and Paul were surprised when Bonnie, Blaine and family walked in. We had a really good time visiting with everyone. On Sunday we had a church service. Bob, Tom Williamson and Alvin Petersen preached. Alvin sang a song and I sang "What will you leave behind?" We came back on July 4th.

We went back to Bemidji again on the 8th. On July 9th we went over to Fertile to attend my (double) cousin Ann and Mel Hagen's 60th anniversary. I read the poem that had been read at my great great grandparent's 50th anniversary. Suzanne and Jon played their violins. Two of my classmates were there – Jean Rolland and Alice Janorschke Sebenaler.

Mel and Ann Colebank Hagen's 60th anniversary

We went back to Madelia on the 13th to go to Mary Ann's (Garry's wife) funeral. Barbara played. All of his children were there except Terry who was in the hospital with a kidney infection. Then it was back to Bemidji on the 15th.

We were in Bemidji a little over a week. I worked on a quilt for Brenda. We hooked up the camper and left Bemidji by way of

Minneapolis. We had Ula's great granddaughter along and took her home there. While we were there Bob went to the Vet's Hospital. When we got ready to leave the camper wouldn't start. We let it cool off a few hours and then it started. We left for Madelia and stopped at Al and Bonnie's in Belle Plaine.

Stephanie Carls is now my home health aide. She is engaged to cousin Nathan Fenske.

On the 28th we had to get a new refrigerator. We got it in St. James. It had an ice maker which we had never had.

The 5th Sunday Rally was in the New Ulm church this time on July 30th.

We made our annual trip to the Garden City Fair on August 4th. It was Senior Day and we got a free lunch.

Great grandsons Matthew and Bradley were here visiting Paul and Barbara. They borrowed our camper to entertain them.

August 12th we had our quilting party at the church in Madelia. The ladies brought quilts and displayed them on the backs of the pews. I gave a talk about "Patchwork Parables." I was using my walker by now and had picked up my lunch (pie) at the counter and took it over to the table to sit down. I forgot I had the pie on my walker and sat right down on it. It was good for a laugh anyway. We gave out prizes along with the lunch.

It was Centerville Rally time so we headed there on the 15th. Paul Barber was the speaker that night. I think we stayed in a room in the basement of the girl's dorm. Jeff Dalrymple, Jerri Weller and Smith were the other speakers. On Thursday night they asked me to sing for the service. I was honored because I had never been asked before. I had sung at their talent night but that was all. I sang "It Doesn't Matter."

On the 18th we went on to Ottumwa to visit Jessica and James, then went home the next day after stopping at Nancy's in Mason City on the way.

I didn't have a piano so I wanted to bring my mother's old upright over from Barbara's. Nancy and Paul rolled it over and put it on the porch. That piano had a lot of memories for me. My mother bought it before she was married and kept it all through the years. My sister and I learned to play on it. When we were going to have it tuned here the harp cracked so it didn't play well from high G and upwards. I could still enjoy playing it because the hymns didn't usually go that high. When we moved we put it on the rummage sale. I sure hated to see my mother's pride and joy ending up there. Bobby and Winn took some of the better boards off of it and some of the keys to make something out of. To my surprise someone bought it in that condition.

Although Madelia was losing some of its stores, a new Dollar General Store opened up near the highway. We soon discovered they had a lot of bargains, especially in paper products. They keep adding new items.

We went to the Minnesota State Fair on September 3rd. Bob pushed me around in a wheelchair for about three hours. Then we went over to the Fridley Church for their Labor Day Rally. Patrick Dougherty was the speaker and Jim Parks led the singing. We stayed overnight at the Emil and Linda Lorenz home. In the afternoon I was asked to sing so I sang "Leave Behind."

Mankato always puts on a Senior Expo once a year. This year it was on the 19th. There were many booths advertising things for seniors. We stopped at the hearing aid booth and signed up. A week or two later Bob got a notice that he had won the free hearing aids. At first we thought there must be some catch but there wasn't. He was fitted for two new hearing aids which he really needed.

Thursday, October 19th, I had been sick all night with a bad stomach ache. About noon I went to the doctor here and they gave me some pain pills and sent me home. Around 3 o'clock I started vomiting. I knew I was in trouble by the color of the vomit. I went immediately to ER and they put me in an ambulance to go to Rochester. David Smith was in the ambulance. He was the son of one of my friends. He had a nice bedside manner. My heart rate went up and my blood pressure too. Barbara had called Dale so he met the ambulance when it got to Rochester. They put me in St. Mary's Hospital right away. The first thing they did was put a big tube down to my stomach and pump it. Then they waited a while and gave me a lot to drink and a laxative. That remedy worked quite quickly. The blockage was gone and I didn't have to have an operation. They let me go home on the 21st, but I didn't feel good for several days after I got home.

A fifth Sunday came on October 29th. This time the Eagle Lake Church asked the other churches to come there. We talked Al, Bonnie and Garry into coming. Al sang a song, "Precious Lord, Take My Hand" and sounded real good. I sang "If We Never Meet Again." Barbara played the piano. They have a beautiful new building with plenty of room.

November 2nd was hunting time again and Bob, Amy and Sterling headed north. The Williams had fixed up a recliner out in the woods so Bob could hunt in comfort. I think he liked that but didn't get any deer.

Thanksgiving came on the 23rd this year. We held it at the church here in Madelia again. We had a special recognition for Rebecca. We gave her flowers , a corsage and a gift. Bob wrote a poem for her, Jon and Suzanne wrote and sang a song and Amy wrote a song. Dale played trivia with the crowd. He asked questions and whoever answered got to give Rebecca a hug. They also played charades and other games. Around 50 people attended. Jane, Jeff, Rhonda and Mark were there from Joplin, Missouri and Fred from Syracuse, New York.

Rod and Jon give Rebecca a hug!

We went to Rochester for my annual checkup on the 6th of December. I had all my tests (including a CT scan) on the 6th, then stayed overnight with Winn and Betsy in the country near Byron, Minnesota. On the 7th we saw Dr. Husmann and he told me everything looked good but I should have my heart checked. On our way home we stopped to see Tom and Maxine Avery in West Concord.

Bob had been having trouble with his heart and was doctoring at the Vet's Hospital in Minneapolis. December 12th he had his heart zapped and put into rhythm.

On Saturday the 16th we helped Amy and Rod celebrate their 10th anniversary at the VFW in Madelia. Barbara decorated and Linda catered. They had karaoke afterward. and Al sang among others. Quite a few of Rod's friends and relatives came.

Amy and Rod

Nancy, Dennis, Barbara, Paul and Brenda gave us a combination radio, record player, CD player and cassette player all in one on a stand.

On Sunday the 24th we left right after church and went to Dale and Linda's. We went to their candlelight service at their church that night. On Christmas day Linda fixed a delicious dinner. We opened gifts after dinner. We came home that afternoon.

Bob built another fish house and was anxious to use it.

2007

Bob liked to watch sports, especially those that his grand kids were in. This winter he got to watch Sterling play basketball quite a bit.

About this time I started getting books from the library. A volunteer would bring me new books every Tuesday and take back the ones I had read.

One of our old faithful Madelia church members died—Anita Bristol. Barbara played the piano and I played the organ at the same time for the funeral.

Going out to eat for Saturday breakfast had become a habit which we enjoyed at the Triangle Cafe.

In March we went to the Winter Retreat in Bemidji. We stopped in Kimball on the way and visited Mandy and Steve. We went to Rebecca's in Shevlin first and had supper. This year the Retreat was held at the Holiday Inn Express Motel. Van Palocek from Fridley was the speaker. He was a good speaker and the singing was wonderful. We went to Bonnie and Steve's for supper and out to Ed Chandler's to stay overnight. The next day was Sunday so we had the Retreat back in the church. Van spoke again.

After a fellowship dinner we went to Rebecca's and she fixed a nice supper for us. We stayed overnight with them and then met cousin Bernie Solberg in Foston at Bob's Cafe for a visit. Then we drove on to Moorhead to visit cousin Lois Haggerty and her husband, then on to Suzanne and Jon's in Fargo in time for supper.

The next day we met Renata and Curt at Culver's Restaurant. That night we went to a concert by Suzanne's 6th, 7th and 8th graders (strings). The next morning we went to Denny's for breakfast. When Bob went to pay the bill they said it had already been paid as an act of kindness. I never had that happen before. We met cousin Grace Anderson and her son-in-law Mark Vrem at a cafe for a visit, then back to Suzanne's for the night. We went home on Thursday the 22nd.

On March 28th Rebecca called to tell us that Natalie Rose Marcella Beach had made her entrance into the world. Gillian was the mother. This was also Sterling's birthday.

We made trips to Mankato off and on for groceries, etc. We always called Garry and Harvey to see if they were home and if they were we would stop by. We usually ate at Zanz Taco place.

I had a skin cancer spot on my ear which Dr. Jeff zapped.

Barbara and Nancy went to Texas for Brenda's graduation from Rice University with an MBA. We got to watch it all on the computer.

Brenda's friend Andrea, Brenda, Barbara, Nancy at Brenda's graduation from Rice University

On May 14^{th,} my sister-in-law Joyce and and husband Chet Simpson from Bremerton, Washington stopped by. They would

226

only stay about half an hour. I was disappointed about that. They were visiting all the places Joyce used to live.

Bob was able to go fishing quite often. Once he was fishing on Lake Hanska and the motor quit. He had to wade in water to bring it in.

Sterling graduated from Madelia High School. Amy had a reception for him at her house.

On June 21st we left with Barbara and Paul for Drew and Sam's wedding in Argyle, Minnesota. I gave them a quilt I had made. We stayed overnight at Drew's house since they were gone anyway. Back home on the 23rd.

Bob had been doctoring at the Vet's Hospital for some time now. He is having trouble with his heart fibrillating. He is on warfarin now.

June 29th we left for Ottumwa to attend the MSE student reunion. We visited James and Jessica and then stayed at the Fairfield Inn. The next day Lafe showed slides. Linda catered the supper and then we had a hymn sing led by Dale. There were special numbers in between including a duet by Lafe and Anita Culver and Dale's "Contenders" sang. The next day was Sunday so we went to the church where they had prayers, interviews and a talk by Lafe Culver with special music by the Gateways. We had lunch with the Spencers and Dale, Linda and Peggy. We left at 1:15 and were home by 6:45.

Bobby and Bob were planning a trip to Jamaica. In the excitement of getting ready Bob couldn't find his ticket or passport. We finally found them. On July 4th Amy took us to Al and Bonnie's in Belle Plaine. We left Bob there so Al could take him to the plane in the morning at 5:00 a.m. Bob called on the 13th. He had gotten sick in Jamaica and went to the doctor. It was another UTI.

On the 14th Joyce (Tresler) St. John from California was here visiting, so Ettie Faye (Hammond), Joyce and I went over to Larry Davis's where Doris was visiting him and had a get-together. I was their Sunday School teacher when they were in 6th grade and we hadn't been together since.

We heard that my sister Vickie's grandaughter Denise had moved to Lincoln, Nebraska from Scotland. Nancy and I went down to visit them. We went to the zoo and had a good time visiting. We stayed two nights and then headed home. We stopped in Sioux City to visit Carrie, Dale's daughter and her family. When we got home Bob was back from Jamaica.

Bob starting having bad dreams and acting them out. He thought he was fighting someone and grabbed hold of my hand and bent my fingers back. He woke up when I yelled. As I look back on this now I think this was the beginning of his Lewy Body dementia (similar to Parkinson's.) One of the symptoms was acting out hallucinations.

The Garden City Fair came around again and we went on August 4th. It poured down rain, however, so we didn't stay.

I had a sore on my left cheek near my mouth that wouldn't go away, so I went to Dr. Colmanares and he did a biopsy. When he removed the stitches he said it was basal cell cancer and I would have to go to a doctor in Mankato to have more cut out.

On August 11th I attended a baby shower for Mindy and I gave her the crib quilt I had made. That night we rode with Barbara and Paul to the Country Kitchen where they had a little celebration for our 60th anniversary. Quite a few of the family were there including Joci from Alaska. They read poems they had made up about us that were good. Rebecca gave us a $100 bill.

It was time for the Centerville Rally again so we headed down that way on August 14th. We decided to stay on the grounds and we got a room under the girl's dorm. It had not been cleaned and was full of dust, bugs, etc. Luckily I had brought along my hand vacuum cleaner. It was very hot (95 degrees). I had brought a fan thinking I might need it. There was no air conditioning in the building either but they had a huge fan on. I tried to sit near it as the heat bothered my asthma. Speakers were Jeff Dalrymple, Paul Julian, Jack Langford, Bill Payne and Jerri Weller. All were good speakers. The ladies of the surrounding area churches furnished the noon meal. It was always delicious with home-grown corn, tomatoes, etc. They also made some real good bread. We left at 2:00 p.m. on Thursday. We stopped at Nancy and Dennis's in Mason City, Iowa, who took us to Applebee's for supper. We got home at 9:30 p.m.

Dale called and said Jerri Weller had called him and told him they found Bob's car keys. He had lost them at the rally and we were using mine.

We went to Mankato on the 18th while Jon and Paul laid down tile in our kitchen.

August 20th was our actual anniversary. Jon and Suzanne took us out for breakfast and Bob took me to Olive Garden for dinner.

Paul and Barbara have two foreign exchange students – Mario from Chile and Cee from Thailand.

August 25th was Tom and Maxine Avery's 60th wedding anniversary. They held it at Hubbell House in Mantorville and Dale was emcee. All their kids were there and most of the grandkids. It was a very nice dinner. I had a sirloin steak and Bob had a hamburger. They had a nice program too.

On August 30th Neil came and worked putting new shingles on our roof. Neil is a hard worker. Dale and his boys came the next day and helped.

Barbara came and told us that Pam's husband Jim Burns was in the hospital in Rochester with cancer. We drove over to see him. While we were there the doctors had a conference and came and told Pam they couldn't do any more for him. Maybe they would want to put him in hospice in Mankato. Jim died the next day so they didn't need to send him to Mankato. We went to the graveside ceremony on the 12th.

On the 8th we went uptown during Younger Brother Days to hear Ellie sing. At noon we ate at the new cafe up town—Happy Days.

Stephanie quit so I had a new home health aide – Marnie Khorteum. She was taking nurse's training so I supposed she would quit after a while too.

Our good friend Shari Kilmer lost her mother. We went to the funeral at the Methodist Church on the 14th.

Amy and Rod were getting ready to move to Columbus, Ohio and put on a big rummage sale. We bought a bed, doll and small guitar.

On the 18th I went to Mankato to Dr. Donald Davis (dermatologist). He had to cut more out of the spot by the left side of my mouth because it was cancerous.

Larry Davis found out he had colon cancer and went to Rochester on Sept. 13th. Bob went over to be with him. It turned out it wasn't as bad as they thought it was going to be.

On September 26th the Vietnam Traveling Memorial came to Madelia. They had motorcycle escorts and everything. Bob went down to watch them set up. We went to see it the next day. I think it was in Watona Park.

On September 30th Mindy and Neil had a baby boy they named Nolan Dean Arkell.

Grandma Amy, Great-Grandma June holding Nolan, Mindy

June Taplin's funeral was October 1st at the Church of Christ in Fairmont. The family did the whole service.

I had always wanted a Maytag washing machine. Finally I got a chance to buy one for $100.00 It was owned by a bachelor who had it only a few months then had to go to the nursing home. It was just like new. The couple who were handling it for him were named Schaffer.

We called at the nursing home quite often to see my cousin Viola, Lorraine Joblinske, our neighbor McCabe and a classmate Betty Mitchell. Viola liked for us to bring her a sandwich — especially summer sausage which she called summer dog because that's what her mother called it.

On October 19th Neil helped me plant two trees out on the boulevard. They were some volunteers that came up in the back yard, probably some kind of maple.

Darlean Greeley and Marsha Pugh took me along to a ladies retreat in Albert Lea on October 27th. We went early and they served breakfast. They had a nice program. The speakers were Tay (Shields) Odor and Jean Karau. They had a four-lady worship team. They served a nice dinner. I saw quite a few ladies from other churches that I knew.

November 1st we left for Bemidji, stopping in Kimball at Mandy and Steve's cafe and had sandwiches and coffee.

When we got to Bemidji we went right to the hospital to see Emily and her new baby girl. She named her Joely Jane. Then we went on to see Bonnie and Steve Williams where we were staying.

Grandpa Wayne and Joely Jane Hinrichs Olson

The next day we visited Ula Hoffer and Ed Chandler and then went out to Rebecca's. Bob went hunting the next day in Steve's woods. That night we visited Darrell and Denise Magoon. Emily had us over for a nice dinner on the 8th. She lived on the edge of Bemidji on the airport road. Bob hunted every day but didn't have any luck. Jon and Suzanne took us out to eat at Perkins and we spent the rest of the day with them. We went to church in Bemidji on Sunday. They had a fellowship dinner and afterward had a dedication service out at the land they had just bought on which to build a new church. That night we went to the Bemidji Symphony Orchestra Concert which was held in the new high school. Suzanne and Jon both played in it. We left the next day for home, stopping at Steve and Mandy's cafe.

Thanksgiving came on the 22nd. It was held in the church in Madelia again. We fixed seven turkeys. Fred and family from New York, Jane and family from Missouri and Denise and Rene Docherty from Lincoln, Nebraska Came. Rene kept us in stitches all the time.

My cousin Viola's daughter Carolyn came and got Viola from the Madelia Nursing Home and took her to Oak Terrace Nursing home in Mankato. It is much handier for Viola's three daughters who live in Mankato to see her. Cheaper too.

We went to Rochester on December 3rd for my annual checkup. I had blood work, x-ray and a CT scan done. The doctor said everything was okay. We left as soon as we could because it was starting to get stormy. We decided to stay at Dale and Linda's and left for home the next day.

Our favorite store in Madelia – Duebers – was closing out and having sales.

We spent Christmas in Rochester again. We went with Dale and Linda to the candlelight service at the church. We opened gifts the next day. Dale read the account of Jesus birth and when he came to the place where it said "And they came with haste and found Mary and Joseph and the babe lying in a manger," Bob said "Wow, that must have been one big manger!" I got the giggles and had a hard time stopping.

Bob bought a portable fish house in St. James. Now he didn't have to ask for help getting the fish house on and off the lake.

2008

Amy and Rod left for Ohio. They stopped in Linn, Missouri to visit Joy (Banton) Arnett and her family. Joy was a playmate in Jamaica who married an American and came here. They had a good time reminiscing.

Brenda's birthday was on the 11th. I made her her usual popcorn cake with M&M's in it. Bob wrote a poem for her as he did for all the kids when they turned 40.

We had another Blanshan cousins get together at Best Western in North Mankato on the 12th. Only seven or eight attended.

On the 18th Molly Solheid started coming as our home health aide. We liked her from the start and had her for 6 ½ yrs. We are still good friends.

June and Molly Solheid in 2017

Bob wasn't entirely satisfied with his portable fish house as it was only big enough for one person and he couldn't stand up in it. So he had Paul and Mario (Barbara's foreign exchange student from Chile) help him put his big one on Lake Hanska.

We were both having a bad winter with coughing, etc. I finally went to the doctor and he gave me prednisone. Bob was doctoring in St. James with the veteran's doctor.

Dale told us he was singing and putting on programs at nursing homes and assisted living places. This is something he loves to do.

Brenda gave us a new Dell computer for our birthdays.

My cousin Rodney Cambronne in Huron, South Dakota died. He was one of my cousins that was close to my age. He was the son of my mother's sister Mary.

Bob was having a lot of trouble with his legs swelling and itching.

Bob's brother Jim was in St. Mary's hospital in Rochester, then he was put in a nursing home in Rochester to recuperate. We went to see him there. We stayed with Dale and Linda that night.

On April 3rd we flew to Columbus, Ohio. We got to see Rod and Amy's new house. It is very nice. Ellie wanted us to come to the Grandparent's Day at her school. On the 5th they took us to the Columbus Zoo. It was a huge one with lots of animals. I got very tired from all the walking.

Amy let us use her Lincoln and we drove over to Nelsonville to visit the Russes. We went to church there. Bob taught the Sunday School lesson and did the preaching. We went back to Amy's that afternoon. The next day Amy took us to Cambridge and Bonnie met us there and took us to her place near Richmond, Ohio. We stayed overnight there and she took us to Pittsburgh the next day to see the sights there. Then she took us back to Cambridge where Rod met us and drove us back to their place.

On the 12th we went to another town where Ellie competed in the District Christian School Bible Memorization Contest. She was in the 3rd grade group and got a superior rating. The next Sunday we went to Nelsonville again for church and Ellie went along and recited what she did at that contest. Amy took us to the airport on the 15th. We went by way of Milwaukee and Barbara and Paul picked us up in Minneapolis.

Brenda called April 28th to tell us she had a boyfriend named Richard now. I asked her what his last name was. She said she didn't know but she thought it started with a P.

Bobby had started dating Sarah. Romance was in the air.

On May 31st Barbara had a farewell for Mario and graduation reception for Cee, her foreign exchange students.

On June 14th we drove to Rochester for Polly's graduation reception at Dale and Linda's. On the way we stopped in Owatonna to see Florence and Jim. They were at Janda's rummage sale. Al and Bonnie came while we were there.

Polly at her graduation party

Then we stopped at Winn and Betsy's to see their place. They had an acreage on a farm near Byron, MN. Quite a few of the relatives were there. We went home the same day.

The next day was Father's Day. Barbara and Paul brought over a new big screen TV from Brenda. It was really for Bob but she gave orders that I could watch it too. It was great for Bob to watch his ball games on.

Our old car gave out. We bought a different one from Brad Kuebler, a 2003 Aztec Pontiac. It was a SUV. It was perfect for us because it was just the right height and we could see well.

Tom Avery of West Concord died and we went to his funeral on July 20th. Bob wrote and read a nice poem about Tom. He was cremated and I was impressed by the way they had a grandchild carry the remains and the rest followed behind him. We stayed at Dale and Linda's overnight and left the next day.

On August 6th my nephew Jim and Paulette Colebank from Washington came for the afternoon. We had a nice visit and Paul made a nice supper of grilled hamburgers and corn on the cob.

It was Centerville Rally time again. We left On August 11th. We stopped in Mankato to see Viola in the nursing home and in Mason City, IA to see Nancy and Dennis. We stayed overnight at Nancy's and went to Centerville the next day. We got a room at the end of the boy's dorm. Steve Heese preached that night. On Wednesday Dan Smith, George Conz and Steve Heese preached and the Gateway Singers sang. Thursday Jeff Dalrymple and Jerri Weller preached. They asked me to sing so I sang "What Can I Do for Jesus?" with the Omnichord. We left right after lunch, which was always real good. They always baked fresh rolls. We stopped in Mason City again and stayed overnight and went home the next day.

Our 61st wedding anniversary was on August 20th. We celebrated by having lunch at the Home Cafe in St. James.

We went to the Godahl Celebration on Sept 1st. They always had some good music, served a nice dinner and had a fun parade in the afternoon.

The Blanshan reunion was held at the McGowan farm again. The attendance was good. There were around 60 in attendance.

Bob's brother Jim and wife Florence with daughter Mickey and her husband Joe Merchant at the 2008 Reunion

We rode with Barbara and Paul to Mindy and Neil's in Lewisville for Nolan's first birthday. He was very interested in his gifts. Mindy fixed a picnic lunch for us. Quite a few relatives were there.

The Church of Christ in Madelia held a four-day meeting October 12th through the 15th. Mr. Zuck was the speaker. I was asked to sing Monday night, so I sang "Can He Depend on You?" They asked me to sing again on Wednesday night, so I sang "I Must Have the Savior with Me" with the Omnichord.

It was hunting time again. We went up to Bemidji on November 6th and stayed at Bonnie and Steve's again. We went out to see how their new church building was coming along. It was well along with the walls enclosed and dry wall up. While there, Bob had one of his nightmares where he thought he was fighting someone. He was pounding on me and I kept trying to get away until I fell out of bed. This was another sign of the beginning of Lewy Body Dementia.

239

Amy and Ellie came plus Amy's friend Mark from Hanska. On Sunday we went to church and enjoyed a fellowship dinner. Rebecca came and got Ellie and me on the 11th. Bob was hunting near them. Rebecca fixed a nice dinner and supper for us. Emily came and brought Joely, so we got to see them. Bob didn't have any luck so we went home on the 13th.

Renata had a baby boy on the 25th which they named Gunnar Gregory Selzer. He weighed only five pounds.

Grandma Suzanne and Gunnar

Richard, Evelyn and Brenda flew up on November 22. We got to meet the Richard that we had been hearing about. Bob talked to Richard about marriage, etc. and when he got done, Richard said, "We haven't really talked about that yet." So Bob felt kind of silly.

On the 25th Bob went to St. James and had an MRI done on his head. They didn't find anything wrong.

Thanksgiving was on the 27th. We had it at the church again. Sixty-one people attended and there was a nice program. One part consisted of interviewing Bob and I about our lives. The next day we held a baby shower for Crystal and Renata. Lois and Kathy Hill and their significant others came and spent the day.

Brenda, Richard and Evelyn flew back home on the 29th.

Bob had another nightmare and fell out of bed.

It was time for my annual checkup at the Mayo Clinic. We went to Dale and Linda's on the 9th of December. The next day I went to the clinic and had blood work, a CT scan and a chest x-ray, after which I saw Dr. Husmann. He said everything looked good. The lady that did my scan was Julia Clement. We knew her parents. We went home after that.

Bob had an appointment with Dr. Eatwell in St. James. He said Bob may have Parkinson's.

We spent Christmas with Dale and Linda. On Christmas Eve we went to the candlelight ceremony at their church. We opened gifts on the 25th and Dale gave his traditional recitation of part of Dicken's Christmas Carol and read the biblical account of the birth of Jesus. Linda fixed a delicious dinner as always.

I made lots and lots of batches of lefse and handed them out to friends and relatives. I enjoyed making it.

We saw the New Year in with Barbara and Paul. We went to Jake's Pizza in St. James and then watched a movie called "Where the Red Fern Grows."

2009

Bob picked up some kind of flu. He was sick on January 21st and passed out with his legs bent back under him. I got his legs out from under him and then called Barbara and she and Paul came and helped him get up. I got it the next day but Bob felt better. His back bothered him for quite a while after that. He had several weeks of therapy.

January 29th was my birthday . It was special because I shared it with Maddy Erickson, Winn Cradic and Greg Selzer. It was even better this year when little Eavan Grace Howard was born to Roger and Carrie.

Our good friend Minnie Sprague died on March 12th. She was in her nineties. She was my cousin Viola's step-sister. The funeral was March 20th.

On March 13th Barbara and Paul drove us up to Bemidji for their annual Winter Retreat. That night was especially for the young people so they took us out to Ed Chandler's where we stayed for the night. We went to church at 10:00 a.m. the next morning. Billy Wallace and Jason Corder did some team preaching. They served a nice lunch and the afternoon was spent in visiting with old friends. They had another service at 3:00 p.m. They had three kinds of soup for supper. We went back to Ed's for the night. Dale preached the next morning for church. They served another nice lunch. That afternoon we went out to Emily's along with some of Dale's family, Wayne and Rebecca and Barbara and Paul. She gave us supper and then it was back to Ed's. The next morning Ed fixed us a nice breakfast of bacon and eggs. Barbara and Paul picked us up late forenoon and we headed home.

Minnie's sister Velma had to have her foot amputated (she was diabetic) and we went to see her in the Pathstone nursing home in Mankato where she was recuperating.

Barbara and Paul took us to the Mall of America March 25th. It was a whole lot of walking so Bob pushed me around in a wheel chair. I enjoyed looking in the stores even though most everything was too expensive for me.

On April 1st Suzanne came down and brought her new $7,000 violin to show us. She actually got it for $5,000. It was a beautiful violin and had a nice sound and volume. It was made in Poland.

Every year the church in Truman puts on an Easter Cantata. People from Fairmont, Truman, Horicon and Madelia take part in the singing. Each year it is held in a different church. This year it was held in Fairmont on April 5th. Neil sang in the group and Mindy played the piano for it.

Bob had never been circumcised and now was having to have it done, so he went to the Vet's Hospital in Minneapolis on April 8th.

Lavon Avery, another good friend from the West Concord church died and we went to the viewing on April 12th in Owatonna. The family was all there so it was good to see them again. Lavon Avery was Lloyd's wife.

Barbara had both knees replaced on April 14th in Mankato.

On April 27th to May 3rd we had a visit from Merna Vandeveer and Lois Zimmerman. We enjoyed the visit and Barbara especially enjoyed it. They were close to her age and had known each other all their lives.

Mother's Day fell on May 10th this year. Brenda sent a lovely bouquet which I took to church for others to enjoy too. I also wore the corsage that Barbara gave me. Larry took us out to eat at the Triangle. I talked to the girls that afternoon on Skype. It's so nice to be able to see them and talk too.

Sunday, the 17th Barbara and Paul took us to Rochester for Peggy's graduation celebration. Lots of people were there. It was held at Dale and Linda's home.

Peggy Blanshan 2009

We traveled again on June 13th for Bobby and Sarah's wedding, which was held at Winn and Betsy's farm near Byron. It was an outdoor wedding and very nice. The reception was held in the barn which they had decorated and brought in tables and chairs. I presented them with the crazy quilt I had made for them out of silks, satins and velvets and put velvet on the back. Suzanne and Jon played string music for it and Peggy sang.

The reception line for Bob and Sarah's wedding

By this time my left hip was really giving me trouble. Dr. Kearny, a bone specialist from Mankato came once a month to Madelia. He gave me a shot of cortisone and that really helped for a long time. He thought it was bursitis.

Brenda came for the wedding and stayed a while. She took us to Mankato to look for recliners. We looked in three stores and finally found two nice ones on sale. They had heat and vibration. They were imitation leather. Really nice.

Father's Day was June 21st. I sang "My Heavenly Father Watches over Me" with the Omnichord at church. I fixed Bob his favorite dinner which was mashed potatoes, scalloped corn, peas and cheese salad, meat loaf and chocolate cake with chocolate frosting. The girls talked to him on Skype and Dale also called on the phone. Barbara and Paul gave him an alarm clock because he had trouble setting the electric one.

The girls had planned a sister's trip to Cape Hatteras, North Carolina. Barbara couldn't go because her knees were still giving her too much trouble after her surgery.

Bob's baby sister, Sandy, turned 70 on the 28th of June and they had a surprise party for her on the 27th at the VFW in Mankato. Lots of the relatives were there.

We decided that we could no longer afford two vehicles. It was time to turn our old faithful white Chevrolet truck in. It wasn't good for anything but scrap so we sold it to Brad Kuebler of St. James Auto Salvage on June 29th. It was like parting with an old friend. We had put many miles on it and hauled many a load in it. We had loaned it to friends to use, too.

This was the year for the BPW reunion which we held every three years. This time it was at the Rock River Christian Service Camp in Illinois. We rode with Barbara and Paul and Suzanne and Jon. Shari was taking care of our pets, Abu (cat), Molly(dog), and Chena, Amy's dog. We got there in the late afternoon on July 2nd. The meals were furnished and Bob and I had our own room and bathroom. Quite a few were there. It was so good to see everyone. Tim Petersen's two boys were there so we got acquainted with them. Saturday, the next day, it rained all day. In the afternoon we had an impromptu program of singing and speaking. Bob spoke and read three poems. I played the Omnichord and sang "Time has Made a Change". Each family contributed something. The next day was Sunday and we had our own service. Steve Rowland and Jimmy S. spoke. John Petersen sang some songs. Richard Homewood did the communion while Suzanne and Jon played their violins accompanied by Nancy. We went home Sunday night.

Brenda, June, Bob, Suzanne and Dale at BPW 2009

We found out that my cousin Viola Aaseng had died Friday night while we were gone. Her funeral was on July 8th at Trinity Lutheran Church here in Madelia. Belvin's 96-year-old sister Sylvia Jurgens was there from Fergus Falls. Viola was buried beside Belvin in Riverside Cemetery in Madelia.

That night Alathia, David and wee David arrived from Scotland. Alathia was my sister Vickie's daughter. Suzanne and Jon and Nancy came too. We had not seen Alathia for a long time. We

246

took her out to the cemetery to show her her mother's grave. We had a nice visit. On July 11th we had a surprise visit from Joyce Colebank Forde and husband from Savona, British Columbia, Canada. She is a distant cousin, one of the Canadian Colebanks. Joan Craig and daughter Paula from Thief River Falls, Minnesota also came for a day. Bobby and Sarah were one day visitors as well. These were all on different days.

The Blanshan reunion was again held at the McGowan Farm. The attendance was down some.

The church here in Madelia had Lowell Mason come and sing for one night. He will be remembered as a little person with a big voice. We had a good crowd.

We seemed to have a lot of visitors that summer. Richard and Thelma Snell came on July 24th and stayed overnight. We had such a good time of fellowship with them. They were on their way to Wisconsin to see their youngest son and family. I think Snells were living in Colorado at this time.

On July 30th Blaine (Boyd Jr.) went and enlisted in the Army. He will finish college before he goes in. We were disappointed that he wasn't interested in being an officer which he would qualify for but said he wanted to start at the bottom. He also enlisted in the infantry. He would not have it easy.

Of course we had to go to the Garden City fair on July 31st. We ate in the 4-H building. There were two ladies there who gave an interesting talk on raptors. They had brought along an owl, a falcon and one other.

On August 9th we had the Grace Harmony singers from Florida. They were a retired couple. They had written a number of songs which they sang. We experimented with having the service out in the parking lot. It was ok if it didn't rain, be windy or hot. Quite a few were there and we served ice cream afterward.

It was Centerville Rally time but we didn't go this year. We didn't feel up to it. We hated to miss it.

Our dear friend Opal Guest from the Bemidji church died, so on August 14th we left for Bemidji. Before we got to Lafayette we noticed we had a flat tire – something that we hadn't had for years. We stopped there and got it fixed. It had a big nail in it. We went to Opal's viewing that evening and then drove out to stay at Bonnie and Steve's. The funeral was the next day and it was a big one as she had lots of friends. Her age was up in the 90s. She was buried in the Aardahl cemetery out in the country. We went to church with the Williams the next day.

On Monday we went out to Rebecca and Wayne's. She took us out to eat in Shevlin and Emily and Joely came that night for supper. The next day Rebecca took us to Leonard to a big Western Saddlery shop. It was really big for tiny Leonard. We went with her to get some produce from a Mennonite family. I rode with Rebecca to Bemidji to get six guinea fowl

chicks. Emily came again at suppertime. We found out she worked a lot on people's feet at her nursing job so we asked her to do our toenails and she did – a job that was getting increasingly hard for us to do. We went home on the 19th.

Mary Russ called and told us that her husband Bob had died. We will miss him.

We always liked to go to Godahl for their Labor Day celebration. They had quite a parade. It lasted 45 minutes. There were lots of antique cars. We ate dinner there which was a picnic type of dinner. There was a good crowd and good music, usually country western.

On September 15th Paul took us to the Clay County Fair in Spencer, Iowa. We met Nancy there. Crystal, Mark and Oliver were there, plus Roger, Carrie and their kids. It was all very interesting but we got tired about 2:00 p.m. and Paul took us home.

Warner Martin Beach was born on October 6 to Craig and Gillian.

On October 14th Bob was really feeling washed out so he went to Urgent Care at the Vet's Hospital. They put him right in bed and said his heart was fibrillating. Four doctors saw him. After doing some tests they didn't come to any definite conclusion. They wanted him to go to neurology and cardiology soon. They took so long we held up the Watonwan County vet's van and we didn't get home until 7 o'clock.

Bob's nephew Harold Schultz died on November 7th. The funeral was on the 13th in New Ulm. They had asked Bob to do the sermon. Dale drove us there. Dale read the obituary and scriptures and sang two songs accompanying himself with the guitar. Bob was not in good shape but really wanted to talk for Harold's funeral. He started out good but then got kind of disoriented so Dale took over. Dale also did the talk at the graveside. Refreshments were served at the Bowling Alley following the service.

Brenda, Evelyn and Richard arrived on November 21st for Thanksgiving. It was on November 26th this year. We held it at the Madelia church building again. There were about 70 there. The kids had a kind of mock rehearsal of our funerals. Some people thought it weird but it was kind of funny. Bob's ashes were brought in in a minnow bucket

Renata, Peggy and Crystal on dish duty

Nancy's mother-in-law, Jean Erickson, died December 4th. Barbara and Paul took us to the funeral held in a Lutheran church in Mason City, Iowa on December 7th.

We had a life line installed on December 14th in case we fell or something while we were alone.

Dale and Linda had invited us to come for Christmas. The weather was a little stormy so Paul took us over in his 4-wheel drive pickup which made it with no trouble. We opened our gifts as usual on Christmas Day and Linda fixed a wonderful dinner. Bobby and Sarah were there from Louisiana. They had to leave on a plane that afternoon. On the 26th we helped Dale celebrate his 60th birthday.

It was time for my yearly checkup in Rochester. We were still at Dale and Linda's so Dale took me to the clinic for tests and I saw the doctor that afternoon. That night Linda had a surprise party for Dale's birthday. Nancy came and did the supper. Paul and Barbara brought Lu and Dee, their two foreign exchange students along. Lots of friends and church people were there. Rebecca took us home that night. We were tired out from our visit and didn't bother staying up for New Year's.

2010

Another little great granddaughter arrived January 18. She was named Bryleigh and joined the household of Mindy and Neil Arkell.

On January 28th we took the vets van to the Vet's Hospital in Minneapolis. Bob had appointments with the Physical and Neurology Departments. They told him he is in the early stages of dementia, probably Lewy Body Disease. Not good to hear. Can you imagine being told that was the sort of future you had to look forward to?

Amy and Barbara helped me celebrate my 84th birthday by taking me to New Ulm to the Chinese restaurant. I always enjoy eating out. I also got calls from most of my children and a couple of grandchildren. On Bob's birthday on February 4th Amy took him to the Bowling Alley at noon and Barbara and Paul had him over for a pizza supper. Ellie made him a chocolate cake. He also got quite a few calls and Dale came over from Rochester.

The Fairmont Church of Christ has an annual Love Banquet for Valentine's day. Amy took Larry and I to it on the 20th. They had a trio from the high school sing and another lady who sang and accompanied them.

Bob wanted to get his driver's license renewed so he went to St. James on the 24th. He didn't pass because they asked him questions about where things were on the car and he didn't know all of them because we hadn't had the car very long. A couple of days later he went to Mankato and tried again and he passed this time. Glad he could still drive me around.

Barbara and Paul, Lou and Dee took us to Bagley on February 27th for Rebecca and Wayne's wedding. It was 5:00 p.m. at the Legion. Jon played the piano, Jon and Dale sang, Amy and Eliana sang, Rebecca and her sisters sang and June Hinrichs read several things. Rebecca had 10 attendants and Wayne had six. Abby Cobb did the flowers. Nancy did the cooking. Sid Sletten did the music after that. It was well attended and was a really nice wedding. Everyone seemed to be relaxed and enjoying it.

Craig holding Warner, Gillian, Rebecca, Emily, Wayne, Aaron

Bob's brother Jim was in the nursing home with Parkinson's and Lewy Body Disease. It had been coming on a long time. Barbara took us over to see him on March 4th. Florence met us at a family restaurant for lunch. Bob and Jim had a good time reminiscing about old times and enjoyed Barbara's playing the piano.

I had been saving up money for some time to buy a headstone. Barbara took us to New Ulm on March 17th to Heritage Memorials. We ordered a stone with our name on both sides and also the names of our children. Having our name on both sides in big letters makes it so much easier to find. I thought it was rather expensive – even on discount it was $1,610.00. I was glad to get that done.

This year the Easter Cantata was held here in Madelia on March 28th. We had more than 100 people there. We served three or four kinds of soup. That seemed to go over very well. I think we had some sort of dessert too.

We realized it was time for us to move into an apartment. It was too much work for Bob to mow the lawn and shovel snow. On March 30th and 31st we moved into the Hartshorn Apartments. We got permission to move our piano into the community room. We soon got acquainted with the people there. They had coffee time forenoon and afternoon. The Senior Dining was also held there Monday through Friday. I took advantage of the meals but Bob didn't. We also brought our cat, Abu. Nancy took him to the vet on April 9th as he wasn't feeling good. The doctor gave him a shot.

On April 10th the Historical Society held a fund raiser at our church. Barbara planned it all and did a lot of it. Nancy did the cooking and Amy did the entertainment. We had about 80 ladies come. It turned out very well.

Homer Laughlin Eggshell dishes

June's Royal Albert Old Country Rose China

Shepherd Owen Cradic was born to Winn and Betsy on April 29th. This was also the day of Bob's cousin Marlene Auringer's funeral. It was at Our Savior's Lutheran Church in Mankato. There was no place to visit after the funeral except in the entry way. No luncheon afterward.

May 1st was a big day for Blaine (Boyd) Eser, our grandson. We went to Forest City, Iowa for his graduation from Waldorf College. A reception was held at the fire house afterward. They left me in Mason City, Iowa so I could go to Nancy's piano recital the next day. She had 38 students. She had it all organized so that it all went smoothly and was very good.

Ellie was in a play at school called Rip Van Winkle. We went to watch her on May 4th. She is very good at drama.

I had been having a lot of trouble with ingrown toenails. On May 10th I went to the podiatrist, Dr. Wactor, in New Ulm and had four toenails removed. I have never regretted having that done. No more pain.

On May 20th our good friend Velma Rogers and step-sister of Viola's died. The funeral was May 24th. Bob read a tribute to her.

Every year I tried to put flowers on the graves of relatives. On the 26th of May we went to Mankato to Minneopa Cemetery and put flowers on Bob's parent's grave, Garry's baby and Davie's. I put Easter lilies on Davie's because he was born on Easter Sunday. Then we came back to Madelia and put flowers on my grandparents, sister Vickie, my parent's, Nadine Colebank, and William and Mary Cunningham's in Riverside Cemetery.

Another graduation came up on the 29th. Barbara and Paul took us to Rochester for Jimmy Blanshan's graduation reception held at Dale and Linda's. All the kids and their families were there except Jeannie. Other relatives, friends and church people were there also.

Vivian and Dwight Hill paid us a visit on June 10th. We took them to Burger Night at the VFW for supper.

Rebecca had an operation in Fargo, North Dakota. On June 16th to have 3 overactive parathyroids removed.

John Petersen and son Dylan came on the 27th and John did a concert at our church. We served ice cream and sherbet afterward. John was the son of Alvin and Ruth Petersen, our very good friends.

Jim and Florence came to see us on July 3rd. Their daughter Mickey was camping at our local park and they came to help her celebrate her birthday. Jim was in a wheelchair.

July 10th was Younger Brother Days. We watched the parade with Amy, Mindy and Neil. Bob rode on the vets open wagon in the parade. Ellie was on some float too. Dale was narrator out at the site of their capture. This took place on the farm where my mother grew up.

On July 22nd Betsy came to visit and I gave her the quilt I had made for Shep.

On July 31st we went to the Garden City Fair. It wasn't as hot out this year.

Barbara and I took Abu, Brenda's cat that we took care of, to the vet. The vet thought he had lymphoma and probably had 6 or 8 weeks to live. He felt masses in his chest and stomach.

The Grace Harmony Singers came again and did a concert at the church on August 8th.

We wanted to go to the Centerville Rally in Centerville, Iowa once more time. Bob could not drive that far without getting tired so we had Bobby drive us down. Jessica and James brought their camper for us to use. It had air conditioning. It's usually pretty hot there this time of year. They asked me to sing for the service Wednesday morning. I sang "I Must Have the Savior with Me", with Omnichord. They asked me again for Thursday morning so I sang "He Restoreth my Soul." I don't remember who the speakers were. The rally was August 10th to August 12th.

The Blanshan reunion was on August 14th at the McGowan farm not far from Mankato. Not as good attendance as last year.

Our kids put on a little celebration for our 63rd wedding anniversary on August 20th. They held it in the community room at the apts. Quite a few people came including Bud and Dorothy Roof, Ann, Janice, Reid and Grace from Fertile, Minnesota; Grace Anderson and Jean Vrem from Fargo, North Dakota; Larry Colebank from Virginia and many others. The kids put on a nice musical program.

For weeks now we had been planning for a Colebank Reunion down at the park. Lots of arrangements had to be made. We told everyone it would probably be a one-time thing. We were surprised at the amount of people who came. My cousins Dennis and Margie Stahlnecker from Albany, Oregon came. Cousin Larry Colebank from Virginia Beach, Virginia, Bruce and Jim Colebank from Washington, Marty Colebank Smith from DeRidder, Louisiana, John and Joyce Colebank Forde from Savona, BC, Canada, nephew Bruce Colebank and his three girls and their families from Wisconsin, Eric and Nancy Sorem from Loveland,

Colorado, Ann and Janice Hagen from Anchorage, Alaska, all our kids and many others. Nancy catered the meals and brought a screened in tent. In the afternoon we had the different families come up to the front and tell who they were and where from. I did some of the talking because I knew who they were. That night we had a jam session as there were many musicians and singers. The next day was Sunday so we had a service there at the park. Jon had a session with the little kids and led singing. Bruce spoke and did a good job. We ate dinner out there. In the afternoon Johnny brought Clarence and Jeanette Nasman to visit Ann, Ruth (Marty) and Grace. A port-a-potty was even rented for the occasion so the older ones wouldn't have to walk so far. All in all we felt it was a big success.

June with Colebank cousins Ann Hagen and Martha Ruth Smith

Our dear friends Kathy Hill and Gene Jackel were married in Owatonna on August 28th. Barbara and Paul took us to the 11 o'clock wedding. It was held in Kathy's back yard. It was very nice. Suzanne and Jon played piano and violin. Nancy catered the lunch. It was nice to see all of Kathy's family.

Kathy Hill Jackel, center, with twin sisters Linda and Lois

We had a special meeting at the church August 29th through September 1st. The speaker was Lee Mason. I was asked to sing two of the nights. We also had Lee Mason and the Burnhams for dinner on Monday.

Labor Day came on September 6th. We went to the Godahl celebration. The parade was good as usual. The dinner was the usual picnic type. After dinner it started to sprinkle so we went home. Bob wanted to watch the Twins game anyway.

Selah Jeanette Egland arrived September 10th. Her parents were Crystal and Mark Egland. Another great grandchild for us.

We received the sad news that my cousin Johnny Nasman was killed in a mower accident. His brother Clarence said he was mowing down by the river in tall grass and didn't see a stump. When a wheel of the mower ran over it, it tipped the mower on top of him. It happened September 13th. The funeral was on the 17th in the East Sveadahl church. Lots of relatives were there. My mother was confirmed in this same church.

Joci came from Alaska for a visit on September 21st. On September 22nd we got six inches of rain during the night. That evening we were invited to Mindy and Neil's in Lewisville. Their yard was like a pond. Owatonna got seven inches. Many basements were flooded. Bob went over to the house we had been living in and the water had backed up in there too. A lot of the stuff that we had in the basement was damaged.

We went to Minneopa Cemetery to see our headstone that they had finally set up. It looked good and was very legible. We put the name Blanshan on both sides so it will be easier to read.

About 7:00 p.m. Monday night, October 18th, I started having pains in my stomach. They got worse so Barbara took me to the ER. They did x-rays etc. but didn't see anything. They kept me in the hospital until Wednesday. I wonder now if it wasn't a partial bowel obstruction.

On October 29th Bob took Abu to the vet to be put to sleep. He had quit eating and seemed to be in pain. It was hard to part with him. Bob held him while he was put to sleep.

On the 30th Lois Hill, Stu Main, Kathy Hill and Gene Jackel came and we all went over to Barbara's for lunch. Crystal and kids were still there also .

We enjoy going to the Triangle for breakfast on Saturdays. Sometimes Amy and Rod are there too.

At this time I was going over to the house next to Barbara's off and on to clean and get rid of things I didn't need.

We had a Thanksgiving supper at the church. Bob wrote a poem for the occasion. We took Ellie and Larry along. On Friday the 19th we had a Thanksgiving dinner at the apartments.

Paul and Barbara attended Ben Larson's funeral on the 20th. They picked up Evelyn in Minneapolis at the airport. Brenda and Richard came on Sunday the 21st,

Thanksgiving was on Thursday the 25th. We held it at the church in Madelia and 64 people came. We continued to celebrate the next day with a shower for Winn and Betsy's Shep. It was Billy's 17th birthday on the 25th, and Gunnar's 2nd on the 26th.

Bob, Brenda and Joely Hinrichs Olson playing with Legos

It turned cold in December and there were blizzard conditions on the 11th.

Sunday afternoon was the regular time to talk to the girls on Skype.

Dale came on the 21st and took us to Rochester the next day. Linda fixed a spaghetti supper and most of their kids were there. The next day I made a big batch of lefse and Linda and Dale helped me. On the 24th I helped Dale make another batch of lefse. It goes fast as everyone seems to like it. Saturday was Christmas day. Linda fixed a big dinner. We opened our gifts and watched movies. The 26th was Dale's 61st birthday. He made another batch of lefse with Bob's help. Dale is getting pretty good at it. The next day Dale took us as far as Owatonna and Paul and Barbara picked us up there to go back home to Madelia.

Bob's cousin Carol Morphew died on the 23rd. Barbara and Paul took Bob to the visitation. I wasn't feeling good.

My right eye was bothering and I thought it might have an eyelash in it. I went to Dr. Pace on the 29th and she said it was a rather bad scratch just below the pupil. I have no idea how I did that.

I should mention that Dale came to see us off and on whenever he was in the area. It was always good to see him.

That ends the year 2010.

Family portrait – November 2010

2011

Suzanne came the afternoon of the 4th and took me to Rochester. We stopped on the way to see Jim Blanshan in the nursing home. Then we went on to Rochester to stay at Bob and Sarah's. They had such a cute and very nice little house. The next day we got up early to make my 7:30 appointment. Bob took Suzanne there and dropped us off. I had blood work done and a CT scan. I saw the doctor at 3:00 p.m. He said nothing had changed except for my hernia getting larger. Bob picked us up again and we left for Madelia. Suzanne left the next day (6th).

Barbara and Paul left on the 4th for Chile. They were going to visit the family of the two boys who stayed with Barbara and Paul as foreign exchange students. They arrived there about noon our time on the 6th.

Sixty-four years ago on the 10th of January we arrived in Norfolk, Nebraska to go to Bible College – and Bob smoked his last cigarette. He always remembered the date.

January 16th we went to a first birthday party for Bryleigh Arkell at the VFW.

Al called on the 18th and told us that Florence was in the hospital. She had fallen and shattered her hip and broke her wrist. For recovery she will go to the same nursing home where Jim is.

I celebrated my birthday by going to the Happy Chef in Mankato. I got 85% off of my meal cost. I had liver and onions, which is one of my favorites. This was on the 26th since you could go any time during January.

We had a nice surprise on the 28th. Carol Hull and Betty Escritt came. I fixed them a nice dinner and used my good dishes. They couldn't stay long.

On my actual birthday Bob took me out to eat for breakfast and gave me a pretty bouquet of flowers. I got lots of phone calls and over 100 birthday wishes on Facebook.

The next day was Sunday and Larry and I rode with Brad and Denise to the Truman church. The Adoration singing group from Crossroads College were there. The President of the College was there too and gave the sermon. They had a fellowship dinner afterward. Polly and Jimmy were singing in it so I got to sit and visit with them during dinner.

Bob and I often went down to the community room for coffee and to visit with the other residents. Sometimes someone would bring rolls or cake.

On Bob's birthday on February 4th we had a party for him at 6:30 in the community room. Dale, Billy and Bobby came. Dale had gotten a barbershop quartet from Mankato to come, which was Bob's favorite music. Bob was really surprised and loved it. They sang both secular and gospel songs. Allen and Barbara Burnham, Merrill Davis and wife from Truman also came.

I heard that my cousin, Lila Colebank, had died and the funeral was February 8th in Trimont. Only two relatives came, her nephew from Loveland, Colorado and I. A number of social workers were there and had arranged the funeral with even a meal afterward. She was very well liked. Her nephew stopped to see me on his way home.

Barbara and Paul got back from Chile. She brought scarves for us.

March 26th Barbara and Paul took us to Rochester for a baby shower for Bobby and Sarah. I had been asked to give a talk on advice about babies.

On April 5th a lady from Human Services who was Lila Colebank's guardian brought me reproduction of a Tiffany lamp that Lila had. Eric told them to give it to me. It is a very beautiful lamp with butterflies and flowers on the shade. I was quite honored that he gave it to me.

We had another cousin get together in North Mankato at the Best Western.

Molly was all excited because she could get the house she wanted in Butterfield.

I went with Barbara and Paul to Forest City, Iowa for a bridal shower for Liz Hanson, Boyd/Blaine's fiancee.

Easter Sunday came on April 24th. Myron Martwick and Callie picked me up for the early breakfast. They asked me to sing for church and I sang "We Shall Rise".

Bethel Lucille was born April 26th weighing 8 pounds 13 ounces and 20 inches long. Bob and Sarah Blanshan are her parents.

Bethel Lucille Blanshan with parents Bob and Sarah

On Saturday Barbara told me not to make dinner on Sunday. The next day was church, May 1st, and there were Steve, Bonnie,

Keren Williams, Irindy, and Anna and Travis Edwards and four kids. What a surprise! I didn't expect to see them at all. They came to see our apartment and then we all went to the Triangle to eat. Then they all went over to Barbara and Paul's to see their house.

Mother's Day was on the 8th that year. As usual my kids gave me a variety of gifts. They are so thoughtful that way. Paul and Barbara took us to T.G.I. Fridays for lunch at noon. I always enjoy eating out. Bob liked to go down to the Triangle and have coffee with the guys. Brenda had given us a $100 dollar gift certificate to the Triangle which we really enjoyed.

Barbara held her annual piano recital in the community room at our apartments. It was nice. She used a keyboard. They all did well with just a few mistakes, which were to be expected.

My cousin Ann in Anchorage Alaska said her husband could no longer walk and needed to be in a nursing home. When they asked him where he wanted to be he said in Fertile, Minnesota. Son Reid and Ann flew down with him. Reid lived in Fertile. After being there a while, Mel said he liked it there. He got more company than when he was in Alaska. Ann and Mel had lived in Fertile for a while when her folks were still alive. Ann went back up to Alaska. She had to do the finishing up of things up there.

On May 27th Dale picked us up and we went to stay with Bob and Sarah in Rochester again. Liz Hanson and Boyd (Blaine) Eser were getting married the next day at a camp near Stewartville, followed by a reception. Boyd was still in the Army. He was home about 10 days and then was going to Korea.

On June 9th Bob bought a scooter from Phil McCabe. It had belonged to Marilyn Carstenson and she had died. He paid $500. for it.

Bob fell in the bathroom on June 17th. Barbara and Paul came and helped him get up. He seemed to be okay – no broken bones.

We had a surprise visit from Bob's cousin (Auntie Alta's daughter) Beverly Bares Hines and her husband and son came from Oklahoma. We hadn't seen them for years and enjoyed the visit.

Our annual Blanshan reunion was on July 16th. We had it in the park in Madelia. Kim and Tim Wussow had their camper parked in the park. Quite a few came in spite of hot and humid weather.

We got word that Emily and her good friend Billy Ingalls were in a very bad accident. Her friend was killed in the rollover and Emily had a badly broken arm.

Barbara and Paul had visitors from Illinois on Saturday, July 9th. It was Merna and Leland Vandeveer and daughters Pam (and her husband) and Shelly and five kids. We went over to see them too.

The Madelia VFW notified us that they were giving each veteran one hundred dollars worth of groceries. Bob had to pick it up at the VFW. There were really nice things in there. That was the first and only time that happened.

After moving into the apartments I had a lot of things I needed to do something with so I decided to have a rummage sale. Four daughters (Nancy, Suzanne, Rebecca and Barbara) a daughter-in-law (Linda) three granddaughters, and four great grandchildren were there to help me. I had been pricing things for a long time. We set it up in the 3-car garage of Brenda's. It was a lot of work. Nancy brought things to sell, mostly new things. Barbara had her own sale in her garage next door. She had a lot of linens left from her antique shop. Barbara made $700, Nancy $400 and I made $230, which was good for me because I had all small stuff. The girls took care of what was left as I was not physically able to do much. All in all we considered it to be a successful sale.

Barbara and Paul left for Texas on July 28th to help Brenda fix her house that got all flooded from a broken water pipe. A plumber (Paul) was needed.

The Garden City Fair was on so we went on Senior Citizens Day and got a free meal put on by the Pork Association. The Blue Ox Jazz Babies were playing. They were a small group of older men who were very good. We got tired in three hours and had to go home.

On August 8th I was scheduled for eye surgery on my right eye by Dr. Gavin from Mankato. It turned out well.

Chris Allen was our nurse since moving in the apartments and Molly was still our home health aide. Bob went to St. James for his doctor visits. Amy is taking nurse's training in Ohio.

Our 64th anniversary was on the 20th of August. We didn't celebrate much. On the 28th the kids surprised us with a party. We had no clue they were going to do it. Dale put on a program. Barbara and Paul brought pizza from Jakes Pizza in St. James, (Bob's favorite) plus cake and ice cream. The kids had written songs too. Brenda was able to see and hear it on Skype. It was her idea.

Brenda moved to Scotland for her job. Nancy went over to help her look for a place to live.

I had cataract surgery on my left eye September 12th. It went okay except this one was thicker than the one in my right eye and he had to pull harder. My eye hurt for the rest of the day.

The Younger Brothers celebration was on September 17 and 18th. Dale gave a talk on the stage up town and later at the Historical Society. We went to hear him at both places. At the Museum he talked and showed slides about the bank robbery at Northfield by the Younger Brothers.

In October we got word that my nephew Jim Colebank, in Port Angeles, Washington fell off a ladder and broke four ribs, two vertebrae and partially collapsed a lung.

Barbara's neighbor Pearl Peyton moved into the apartments next door to us. She was a heavy smoker and the smoke would come into our apartment through the outlets and make me cough. I reported it to the manager as this was supposed to be a smoke-free building but they said they couldn't do anything unless they caught her in the act. They sent the janitor to put something inside the outlets to keep it out. It helped some but not enough.

Brenda announced that she got a ring from Richard. She rented a small castle in Kirkliston, Scotland, a suburb of Edinburgh.

November 3rd was a sad day for us. Barbara had to put down their little dog Molly. She had gotten very thin and was bleeding from the mouth. She was almost 13. She was such a nice little dog, part maltese and part yorkie.

Sterling had the misfortune of cutting the tip of his little finger off at work at Winnebago in Forest City, Iowa. They were able to reattach it.

I usually fed Molly my home health aide after she got done with work. She liked my hamburger soup. I would fix a big kettle full and divide it up and freeze most of it. It was a help for me too as I fixed it with the vegetables I was allowed to have.

We heard that grandson Aaron Hinrichs up near Shevlin bought a Harley Davidson motor cycle. I'm sure he will enjoy that.

Aaron with his niece Joely

Brenda, Richard and Evelyn arrived on November 20th for Thanksgiving. They stayed at Barbara and Paul's. We had some nice visits. We all left for Rochester on the 23rd. We were having our Thanksgiving celebration at the Senior Center there. We had a large group including Jane, Jeff, Mark and his girlfriend from Joplin, Missouri, Fred and Liddy and young Fred from New York, Jeannie and boyfriend, Joci Eser from Alaska, Lois Hill and boyfriend Stu and Kathy (Hill) and Gene Jackel and Dwight Hill plus many other relatives. There was plenty of good food. The girls enjoyed the nice big kitchen to work in. We continued our celebration the next day with a baby shower for Bethel (Bob and Sarah's) and lots of music and other entertainment. We were staying with Bob and Sarah. We left on Saturday, stopping in Owatonna to see Bob's brother Jim in the nursing home there.

About a week later Rebecca put on Facebook that her granddaughter Joely had fallen off of a toy and broke both bones in her left arm and would have to have surgery. It seems like there has to be a few broken bones before we get them grown up.

I got the flu December 10th. By Wednesday I was feeling worse so Bob took me to Urgent Care. They gave me an antibiotic and prednisone. That night I had a bad asthma attack. I was coughing a lot so I started using my nebulizer. By Sunday Bob got sick too but didn't have the lingering cough. Later Barbara brought a humidifier which seemed to help a lot.

On the 23rd I got a big surprise. They brought me a power chair. I thought I had been turned down but there it was! I was very happy to get it as I am sure I will really need it later on. It took all forenoon for explanations and paper signing.

Christmas was on a Sunday. The preacher Allen Burnham was sick so Brad gave a little sermon before he left to preach in New Ulm. I had to play the organ by myself as Denise wasn't there. I had forgotten to bring my reading glasses which I needed to play the organ with. I somehow got through it.

Rod came and picked Larry and us up and took us out to Mindy and Neil's for dinner. Mindy had fixed a big very good dinner. They gave us gifts too. They were living in Lewisville. They had a nice big house there.

Brenda was now living in Scotland. Barbara and Paul left on January 10th to go and visit her.

The stork was busy on January 16th. He brought Ashlyn Joann to Mindy and Neil Arkell and a little boy named Gavin to Renata and Greg Selzer.

Barbara and Brenda called from the Lake District in England where the Colebanks came from. They also visited the place called Holmfirth, where "The Last of the Summer Wine" was filmed. That was a British comedy that I liked that was on PBS. They also drove part of the way into Wales.

Al, Bonnie and Sandy came on the 28th for my birthday and took us to the Home Town Cafe in St. James for my birthday dinner. They have good food there and give generous portions. Their sour cream raisin pie is delicious. That is Bob's favorite pie and I like it too. Dale came and brought pizza on the 30th. Rebecca also came that day and took us out to eat for supper at the Bowling Alley. I got over 100 birthday wishes on Face Book.

Michelle Van Hee from the Madelia newspaper came and interviewed us for an article for Valentine's day for having been married so long. It appeared in the paper February 9th. It was a nice article.

On Sunday February 5th we met Betsy and the boys in Fairmont. They were on their way home from visiting Carrie. We met at Perkins. I got to hold the new baby, Malcolm for the first time.

On February 12th I started feeling sick. I wasn't better by the 16th so Barbara took me to the doctor. They gave me a powerful antibiotic shot and sent me home. The nurse came the next day and she didn't like the way I looked so she made an appointment with the doctor that afternoon. They admitted me into the hospital right away. They gave me oxygen, an IV with prednisone and an antibiotic plus the nebulizer four times per day. It took me a while to get better and I went home from the hospital March 3.

The kids had put Bob in the nursing home as I was too run down to take care of him any longer. He always said he didn't want to be put in a nursing home but that's where he ended up. The girls took turns staying with Bob while I was in the hospital. When they got the paperwork done they took him to the nursing home. Barbara was getting stressed out with all the paperwork. I wasn't home very long when I began to cough more and not feel good. Nurse Chris Allen thought I should see the doctor again. She made an appointment right away that day. He put me right back in the hospital again. They put me back on prednisone and Lividen again. When I got better they sent me to the nursing home to recover. That was on the 12th. Paul had already brought my recliner and TV before I got there. Of course Bob was very happy to have me there but I had to have a separate room.

Blaine (Boyd) was going to go to Afghanistan on the 14th of May. They sent him to Korea instead. Amy passed her big test in her nursing course.

Barbara and Paul came and took Bob to church. He was very happy about that. He took me for a ride outside in the wheelchair on the 23rd because it was so nice. They sent me home on the 26th. I sure hated to leave Bob there. We both cried when I left. I had our car so I went and visited Bob every day.

Clara Lovisa made her appearance on April 6th. She weighed 7 lbs. 13 oz. She is making her home with Drew and Samantha Olafson.

Baby Clara with Grandma Suzanne and Grandma Janelle

Amy called to say she had been asked to speak for her graduation from nursing.

When we rented the apartments we rented two so we would have enough room. They made a door between them. When Bob wasn't coming back I could only have one apartment so they filled in the door again.

I don't know how many of the kids were in on it but Nancy ordered a large new computer desk. Paul put it together which was no easy task. It has drawers and shelves and is very tall and is a dark brown. I like it very much.

Paul took me to Rochester for my annual checkup. Dale met us in Owatonna and took me the rest of the way. We stopped at Winn and Betsy's for breakfast. Dale took me to the clinic and I had blood tests and a CT scan that afternoon. He took me to Bobby and Sarah's to stay overnight. The next day Dale took me to the Gonda Building to see Dr. Husmann. While we were waiting to see him we saw a piano player in the Gonda lobby. We sang hymns with him. We had to wait three hours to see the doctor – I guess he had an emergency to take care of. He said there was no sign of cancer and everything looked okay. He can't do anything for the rupture by my stoma. Radiation had ruined

272

the muscles there and there would be nothing to fasten to. Dale had to leave to do a program in Mason City so Barbara and Paul came and got me. I waited for them to come in the Senior Center building where Linda was working,

The nursing home was quarantined so I couldn't go and see Bob. Paul picked him up and brought him to church. Paul picked up Bob and me and took us over to Barbara and Paul's that afternoon. Albert and Bonnie, Sandy, Kim, Shandy, Maria and Pam were there and brought some Jake's pizza and Kim had made a sour cream raisin pie (both favorites of Bob's). She also brought a pecan pie. Bob enjoyed the visit.

Paul had an angiogram on May 7th. They told him he had a bad valve and needed three to five bypasses.

On May 10th Mindy and Neil invited us for supper. Neil picked us up and took us to their house. Bob had trouble getting into the van for the first time. She had spaghetti which was one of Bob's favorite foods.

Mother's Day was Sunday the 13th. I picked up Larry and Bob for church. I stayed and ate dinner with Bob at the nursing home. I got phone calls from Dale, Amy, Suzanne and Brenda and Lois Zimmerman. Brenda and Richard sent a big bouquet of flowers and a pound and a half of assorted fudge from the flower shop. Paul brought a bouquet of flowers too. Barbara gave me a corsage. Nancy came later in the day. We had a meal of pork chops together and then she went over to Barbara's. I had some unexpected visitors too from North Mankato. Viola's daughter Carolyn and her two daughters, Christy and Cara and Cara's two little girls. What a nice surprise! I certainly had a good Mother's Day!

The Thrift Store had a nice used spinet piano. I decided to buy it as my other one was gone. It looked very good and was in tune. I asked to put it in the community room and they okayed it.

Barbara had her piano recital at the Baptist church on Saturday May 19th. They had two good pianos there. It was very nice.

Paul had his heart operation on May 24th in Rochester. He came through it ok, but had trouble coming out of the anesthetic.

We went with Suzanne and Jon to Rochester for Billy's graduation party at Dale and Linda's. We went to see Paul in the hospital. He was partly out of it. Suzanne and Jon went and picked up Bob so he could ride in the vets wagon in the Memorial Day parade. He loved to do that. He was very patriotic. We went to the program at the Elementary School and then to the cemetery and looked at graves. We had dinner with Bob at the home. Jon and Suzanne played violin and piano while we were waiting for our food. The people really liked that.

I was doing a lot of coughing again. The nurse (Chris Allen) came Thursday May 31, and when she listened to my chest she made an appointment right away that afternoon with the doctor. Dr. Bacon ordered an x-ray and blood test. She called later to say I had pneumonia again. She put me on prednisone, an antibiotic and an allergy pill. I didn't sleep all night for coughing. The nurse checked on me at 8:00 a.m. the next morning. She called the "Take Me There" car to take me to the hospital. I was in Room 2. They gave me steroids and antibiotics (Zithromycin, I think.) They also gave me extra water pills. I had lots of company and phone calls. I didn't get to go home from the hospital until June 11th. The nurse ordered a hospital bed for me. They brought it on June 15th.

Driving the car made me nervous so I sold it to Dale. Dale, Peggy and Polly came and got it.

On Monday June 18th I started having pain in my stomach. Amy took me to emergency that night at 11:00 p.m. They gave me three enemas and a shot for pain and sent me home. The next day I woke up with steady pain again. By this time I was vomiting because the blockage was making everything back up. I went to the hospital again and they put a tube down into my stomach and called the ambulance. The ambulance is like riding in the back of a pickup. They rushed me to Rochester. Dale, Peggy and Polly were waiting for me at the emergency door. This was the Joseph wing of St. Mary's hospital. (Room 2).

Dale stayed with me all night. They put a lot of needles in me and put some dye down my tube and then x-rayed. They came back and told me the dye had gone all the way through, which was good news. They had me swallow a lot of water with a laxative in it which worked right away. They gave me liquids at first and then solid food. Rebecca came down and I rode with her home.

Time for the Blanshan reunion again. We had it in Madelia at Watona Park in the blue shelter. They took me down in a wheelchair. I was able to stay about three hours. They went and got Bob and brought him to the reunion too. There were more people than expected (40 to 50). The weather was nice so we all had a good time.

July 5th through 8th was the Blanshan/Petersen/Williamson Reunion. It was held at Ironside Christian Camp. It was a wonderful place to have it. Meals were furnished which was good because we got to visit instead of cooking and doing dishes. I had a room with air conditioning. We celebrated Alvin's 91st birthday and 25th anniversary Friday night. Afterward we had cookies and ice cream. The next day Rod went and got Bob so he could visit too. He lasted a few hours. Saturday night, the 7th, we had a jam session. Lots of singing and playing of instruments. There were many talented people in the bunch. Jon sang, Suzanne played, Dale led singing and sang in a quartet. On Sunday we had a church service in the dining room. We went out to Dale and Linda's for dinner and then left after dinner.

The extended Blanshan clan at BPW 2012

Brenda took me to the eye doctor on July 10th. They ordered new glasses which would be there in about a week.

Nadine Colebank Olson's daughter Marynda had not seen her father for years. He was in the nursing home. She wanted to see him but was afraid as she didn't know what to say, so I went with her. He seemed to realize who she was and thought she was very pretty. Her father was John Morgan.

On Saturday August 18th we celebrated our 65th wedding anniversary at the Luther Memorial Nursing Home. I wore the white dress that Barbara and Nancy had gotten for me for our 40th anniversary – I also wore it for our 50th and 60th wedding anniversaries. They gave me a corsage of yellow roses. I also got a bouquet of yellow roses from Brenda and Richard. Brenda sent a pretty bouquet for Bob's room. They had the program on Skype for Brenda and Amy. Jon was the emcee. Barbara, Rebecca and Suzanne sang the anniversary song Rebecca wrote for our 50th anniversary. Rebecca and Ellie sang and Ellie played her cello. Suzanne played "Prayer Perfect" on her violin. Little Warner Beach recited the Pledge of Allegiance and did very well. It was all a beautiful program. We had cake and ice cream afterward. Bob's sister Sandy came and also Gillian and her two children. Three of our kids were there and two grandchildren and two great grandchildren. There were some people from town there plus all the nursing home people, of course. This was the last anniversary we had together. I am glad we had a celebration.

I was feeling tired so much of the time and decided to see a heart doctor in Mankato. Dr. Wong did a lot of tests and said my heart was out of rhythm. He said I could have it zapped and put back in rhythm or just let it go. I decided to just let it go as I had several friends do it and it didn't last very long and had to be done again. Dr. Wong thought that was the best thing.

On Thursday Rod and Amy took me to the plane in Minneapolis to go to Houston for Brenda's wedding. Rod had gotten me a ticket with his frequent flyer miles. We rented a car and got rooms at Best Western. On the 19th we went with Brenda to get her hair fixed which took a long time. The groom's supper was that night at Monument Inn. We had a large variety of seafood. The wedding was on Saturday the 20th at the Sacred Heart Church at 1:00. Brenda looked very pretty and Richard looked nice too. It was a short ceremony but very nice. Jon did a wonderful job singing the Lord's Prayer. The girls sang several songs. One was "Devoted." A priest friend of Richard's did the ceremony.

After the service we went to a barbeque place and ate. Then we went to Richard's sister Janice's house where Richard and his siblings were raised, ate some more and sang some songs. Then we went back to the motel for pizza with Jon and Suzanne. Richard seemed to have a nice family. We went to a non-instrumental church on Sunday and visited with Brenda and Richard in the afternoon at Richard's house. We left for home the next day.

On November 9th Nancy picked me up and we headed for Bemidji, stopping at Kimball on the way to visit Mandy and Steve.

We went to Steve and Bonnie's and stayed overnight. Nancy, Suzanne and I sang a song ("The Savior is Waiting") accompanied by Jon. They had a fellowship dinner and it was wonderful to be able to visit with old friends again. That afternoon we went to Suzanne and Jon's concert at the High School. It was very good. We left for home the next day.

I was busy making a quilt for Brenda and Richard as a wedding gift. The pattern was "Crown of Thorns." I got it done just in time as Brenda and Richard arrived on the 19th. Paul brought a Christmas tree for me and Brenda and Evelyn helped trim it. Brenda had bought some ornaments for it in Mankato.

On the 21st we went to Rochester for our Thanksgiving celebration. We were holding it at the Senior Center again. Some of us stayed at the Koehler Hotel and Evelyn and I had a room together. The next day was Thanksgiving. We had a good crowd including Dwight and Vivian Hill, Kathy and Gene Jackel and Stu and Lois Main. Later we had a baby shower for Drew and Sam.

Sam's baby shower

The next day we had a wedding shower for Richard and Brenda. I gave them the quilt. I think they liked it. We left on Saturday. I rode home with Amy and Rod.

We had a surprise visit from Bonnie and Steve Williams. They had been on a trip out east to see Martha and Derek and family in North Carolina.

We spent Christmas with Mindy and Neil and family in Lewisville. Rod picked up Bob and I and took us there. Neil brought me home. That night I got a bad pain in my stomach. Amy took me to Urgent Care. They admitted me to the hospital, put a tube down my throat and pumped my stomach. That relieved the pain. It got better after that and they let me go home on the 29th. I probably ate something I shouldn't have and it caused a partial obstruction of the bowel.

Bob was getting increasingly hard to handle. He still loved to go to church though. Sometimes he didn't want to go to his room.

2013

I talked to Bob on the phone and he thought they were coming after him that night. He said I may never see him again. It was so real to him. He constantly thought someone was after him. He told me he loved me. The next day he told Amy that he guessed the ones that were after him may have gone on to the Cities. It was so hard to hear him like that.

I started having a bad pain in my pelvis and Barbara and Paul took me to the doctor. They x-rayed and found the front of my pelvis is disintegrating from the radiation I had 13 years ago. The radiation doesn't stop but keeps eating away. They gave me pain pills. It eased up after about a week. Meanwhile I had been coughing for quite a while. It got worse and Barbara and Paul took me to the doctor and she put me right in the hospital. They thought it was viral bronchitis. They treated me with various things. I went in on the 22nd and went home on the 27th.

They took me to Barbara's. I had the room downstairs where my Grandma used to sleep. This was when I began to sleep in my recliner so I could breathe better. It also helped my asthma. Prednisone helped a lot but I couldn't stay on it too long. I was very weak and it was a slow recovery. Paul was a wonderful help in bringing my stuff over to their place. The computer desk was very large and had to be taken apart in the middle. I never heard him complain. I spent my 87th birthday in my recliner. I got lots of calls, gifts and flowers.

Our good friend and Bob's cousin, Muriel Auringer, died and her funeral was January 26th. Albert, Bonnie, Pam and Sandy came to see Bob after the funeral and then came to Barbara and Paul's to see us too.

Barbara's good friend Shari Kilmer brought her little dog Jewel every day for Barbara to dog sit. She was the best little dog. No bother at all. She liked to sit on my lap.

Amy's daughter Joci got married to Kyle Brownlee of Alaska on Valentine's Day. The ceremony was held at the Madelia Church of Christ and Amy's husband Rod performed it. The reception was held at the VFW in Madelia. I couldn't attend the wedding because I wasn't feeling well and Kyle and Joci made a special trip over to the house to show me how they were dressed. That was very nice of them.

Joci and Kyle and wedding party

The next day I didn't feel good at all – very weak and washed out. Barbara noticed my heart was racing (170) so they took me to Urgent Care. They gave me medication which got it down to 80 by evening. I was in the hospital overnight. Amy had to give me shots in the stomach twice a day. They said my thyroid had gone crazy which was the reason for the fibrillation. They made an appointment with a heart doctor, Dr. Wong. He said to go on with treatments as before and see how it goes. They also put me on Warfarin to thin my blood.

On February 23rd I had another bowel obstruction. They were able to get it fixed without surgery. I was in such a weakened condition that they sent me to the nursing home to recover. I was in the hospital the 23rd through the 27th, then went to the nursing home on the 28th. Bob was glad to have me there. Amy was working there as a nurse so I got to see her too. They had me doing therapy. I will always remember that therapist telling me "If you don't keep doing these exercises I can guarantee you will be back in the nursing home in 6 months. I got home from the nursing home on March 20th.

I had been playing the organ for church up until the time I got sick. I won't be playing again. I will miss it.

I got real good care at Barbara's. She made sure I did everything right. Molly was coming four hours per week and Nurse Christina was coming once per week.

I never really got rid of my cough and it got worse again in April. Barbara took me to the doctor again. She gave me a shot and prescribed prednisone. It was some kind of bronchitis again. This had certainly been a bad winter for me. Barbara said I was run down from taking care of Bob. That could be – Bob had fallen quite a few times and was hallucinating more.

Barbara was giving piano lessons. The piano was on the other side of my wall. We usually shut the door and kept the dogs with me as they were a distraction for the kids. I didn't mind listening to the kids learn. Her recital was Saturday, May 11th at the Baptist Church. Nancy, Crystal and her two children came for it.

The next day was Mother's Day. We had a service at home as the weather wasn't very good. Rod and Neil went and got Bob and brought him here for an hour. The girls gave me a Kindle which I thought was too expensive a gift.

Nancy gave her little black poodle Bailey to Barbara because she made Dennis nervous. She got along okay with Jewel, Shari's dog. Both of them liked to sit on my lap.

Ruby Shellum died. She lived next door to my Grandma's house for many years. Brenda bought her house and we lived in it before we went to the apartments. Her funeral was May 29th but I didn't feel up to going.

Joci had her first baby on June 13th. They named him Jackson. They live in Juneau, Alaska. Nancy's Crystal had a girl on June 23rd and named her Charlotte Esther. She is their third one.

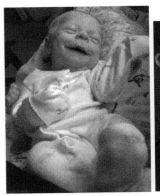 

Jackson Brownlee and Selah Egland with little sister Charlotte

I was quite an avid reader and read three or four books every two weeks. I had a library lady (volunteer) who came every two weeks and brought new books and picked up the ones I had read.

Barbara was working at the flower shop quite a bit. Paul sometimes delivered flowers for them.

On July 19th Bob was sitting in his wheelchair when he decided to get up. When he got up, he fell. The nurse saw him fall but couldn't get there fast enough to stop him. He fell so hard his head bounced. The floors are cement. They told him he would have to go to the hospital and he said "Oh no," and that was the last thing he ever said. He was bleeding from his ear and seemed to have broken his shoulder and other places. He was in

284

excruciating pain so they kept him sedated at the hospital in Madelia.

The next day the doctor told me he would not be going back to the nursing home and he would pass away in a matter of days. Barbara was busy notifying everyone. Rebecca, Suzanne, Jon, Gillian, Sandy, Garry, Betsy and Winn and boys, Roger and Carrie and children, and Mindy and Neil and kids came. We sang hymns for him in his room. The nurses stood outside the door and listened. The next day I sang "I Must Have the Savior with Me" which was his favorite song he liked to hear me sing. Polly stayed all night with him.

saying goodbye

On the 23rd he died in the forenoon before I got there. Suzanne and Rebecca were with him. Al and Bonnie got there just as he was dying. Brenda came but didn't get there in time to tell him goodbye.

The funeral was on Saturday the 27th. I think all our families were there. I was surprised at the amount of people who came. There were around 250 people. The program was very nice. Dale led the service, and Bob's brother Albert sang as well as Suzanne's husband Jon. Our kids sang "Dusty Road" at the end. Bobby carried Bob's ashes at the head of the procession since he was his namesake. Nancy made the dinner. She had everything all organized so it went smoothly. I got a number of calls from friends. Nancy and Brenda helped me write out thank you notes. We had been married 65 years and 11 months. I was prepared for his death since it seemed like he died when his dementia got bad. He was not happy in the nursing home and his quality of life wasn't good any more. I miss him very much as we enjoyed doing things together. But what's done is done and life must go on.

Bob's urn

I was torn between which church to go to—Madelia or New Ulm. I tried to alternate, favoring the Sundays they were having a pot luck dinner. Every Sunday in New Ulm we would go out to eat after church and quite a few of the church members would go along. Barbara was playing the piano for church in New Ulm and Amy leading the song service in Madelia. Madelia has always been a favorite since I was baptized there, married there, and Bob was ordained there. We held Davie's funeral there, our 25th wedding anniversary, our fiftieth anniversary, and our 80th birthday celebration. Bob preached there 3 years, I played the piano and organ for a number of years, and Bob's funeral was there. I hope my funeral can be there too. I have Bob's ashes with me so when I die we can be buried together in Minneopa Cemetery near Mankato.

The Blanshan Reunion was held at Watona Park in Madelia on September 7th.

On September 14th we went to Lois Hill and Stu Main's wedding. Jon played the piano and guitar and the girls sang (minus Rebecca and Brenda). It was a nice wedding. Nancy catered the meal.

On October 2nd Wendell Barr and wife from Cattaraugus, New York stopped to see us. He is a cousin of Bob's on his mother's side. He has done a lot of genealogy on the Barrs. They came from Ireland. Wendell was a Major in the army and knows a lot of people in Washington, D.C. He gave us some of his history. We called Glen Hruska to come and visit with him too since he is also a cousin.

Madelia is supposed to be the pheasant capital of the U.S. They had a big banquet at the VFW for the opening of the season. That was on October 10th. The Governor of Minnesota attended. I guess he likes to hunt too.

On October 14th Molly and I took a walk over to Brenda's house next door where we used to live to have a last look at the house before the lady who bought it moves in. We don't need the house anymore for extra beds at Thanksgiving time because we are now having Thanksgiving in Rochester.

Shari has been a good friend of the family for many years. She was always bringing us stuff she thought we might need or could use. She found some nice antiques for Barbara. She loved to cook and was always bringing something for our meal and cooking it. One of her specialties was potato salad – of course we loved that, and we also loved her rice pudding.

Little Eden June Blanshan entered our world on October 17th. She makes her home with Bob and Sarah Blanshan and sister Bethel.

On November 10th I started having a lot of pain in my right knee. Barbara took me to the doctor the next day. She poked around in my knee to see if there was water on the knee, but there wasn't so she put a shot of cortisone in. The x-ray showed a lot of arthritis. My knee got much better after that.

Brenda, Richard and Evelyn came on the 24th for Thanksgiving. It was always nice when they came early so we would have a chance to visit. I had an appointment at the clinic in Rochester on Wednesday so we left in the forenoon. At the clinic I had my blood work done and a CT scan. We were done by 4:15 p.m. so we went on to the Senior Center where we were having our Thanksgiving celebration. We had supper there. Richard and Brenda took Evelyn and I to the Koehler Inn where we would be staying. The next day was Thanksgiving. The girls worked in the kitchen to prepare it. There were plenty of tables and chairs for us. In the afternoon we had a surprise party for Rod's birthday.

Brenda's husband Richard and James Lyon destroying the turkey

That night we had a birthday party for Dwight Hill. On Friday we had a baby shower for Joci. A few more new people came. Jon and Billy took me to the recording studio at the Bible College and they recorded my song "I Must have the Savior with Me" plus a little talk about my childhood days. They were putting it on a CD along with other musical pieces by the kids. On Saturday Brenda, Richard and Evelyn left as well as the others. I think Rene and Niecey Docherty and family were there from Lincoln, Nebraska. We went over to Dale and Linda's for the night. I was very tired so I didn't go to church on Sunday. We got up early Monday morning and went to the clinic to see Dr. Husmann to get the results of my tests. He said the tests were all good with not much change. He saw some small fractures on the lower pelvis and the hernia was bigger. We (Barbara, Paul and I) left then and went home. The dogs were overjoyed to see us.

On December 15th we had a Christmas program instead of church. I sang "No Room at the Inn" with the Omnichord. The auto harp got too heavy for me to handle so I switched to the Omnichord. I wondered if this was the last time I would be able to sing solos as my breath was getting shorter and my voice not as clear. I thought it must be ok yet as they kept asking me to sing. The program was followed by a fellowship dinner which I always enjoyed. I guess I have always enjoyed food just like my mother.

Barbara celebrated her 65th birthday by working at the flower shop. Dale came as he was asked to speak at the church here in Madelia the next day.

On Christmas Eve we opened our gifts. I was surprised at all the nice gifts I got including a big jewelry chest. It had eight drawers in it and the sides opened out so you could hang necklaces in there. This was from all the kids except Nancy and she gave me a tape recorder. I thought I would never have enough jewelry to fill it but by the time I put my mother's jewelry in there plus mine it was full. It's a beautiful piece of furniture. I was very happy to get a tape recorder too so I could sit in my chair and listen.

Barbara had Paul's daughter Chris and family for dinner the next day. I had been sick all night and still didn't feel good on Christmas day so I stayed in my room all day.

Brenda and Richard left for Scotland on the 31st. I think they will have a lot of visits from the relatives while they are there. I would like to go there myself.

2014

The winter of '13 and '14 was cold and snowy. In fact, the Governor called for all schools in the state to close on one day. There were other local school closings off and on too plus a number of blizzards. The length of the below zero weather caused the ground to freeze deeper than usual and many people's pipes froze outside their houses. Molly's froze and she didn't get it fixed for a while and had to get water from the neighbors. It was expensive to have it thawed out too. We were lucky as ours didn't freeze. The pipes in the New Ulm Church froze up.

I heard that Dale fell down the stairs and dislocated and injured a finger. He immediately put it back in place himself. That sounds like something Grandpa Blanshan would do. Grandpa took some of his kids to the doctor to have their tonsils out and had his done first so he could show them it wouldn't hurt. He had no anesthetic at all. He also pulled some of his own teeth. Bob remembered his Dad doing that.

We had visits quite often from the kids. I gave Suzanne my copier as I no longer had room for it in my room. She took it to school and found lots of uses for it in her classroom. I'm glad it went somewhere where it will be used.

Barbara had her piano recital at the Baptist Church on Saturday, May 10th. Nancy and Crystal and three kids came. It was very nice as usual. Ellie played "Solfigietto." The next day was Mother's Day and I was treated royally as usual. They put a nice tablecloth on the dining room table. They also used my good dishes (Royal Albert Country Roses). My favorite foods were served: Kentucky Fried Chicken, potato salad, string beans and a jello dessert. We were joined for dinner by Brad and Denise Kuebler and Shari. All that attention made me feel good. The other children called me. We had all gone to church in New Ulm that morning and Nancy played the piano and the girls played violin and cello. I always enjoy watching my kids perform and feel proud. I wonder if other parents feel that way.

Kathy and Gene Jackel and Lois came on Saturday the 17th of May. Kathy and Lois are daughters of Dwight and Marilyn Hill. Kathy had told me she had some cards for me. When she brought them in it wasn't just a few cards but a whole big box full of an assortment of cards. I send out a lot of cards so that was a blessing to me. God always supplies me with cards when I need them. I guess you could call it a card ministry. I like to do it. Our drug store was closing and had a lot of bargains. I was able to get quite a few good cards there too.

Paul and Barbara are working on the house. They tore all the wallpaper off the dining, living room and hall walls. That was a big job. Paul put a new wood ceiling in the living room. It looks really good. It was hard for him to put his arms up to work on it. They were going to paint all the walls.

Suzanne, Renata and boys came on Saturday May 24th. Suzanne played the violin and sang with Renata for church the next day in New Ulm. They sounded great. They had to leave Monday.

Another new arrival in May -- Lilliana Eser. Proud parents were Boyd and Liz Eser. That makes another great grandchild. They brought her to see me when she was just a week old. She looked so tiny and cute.

Polly also came that weekend and helped me sort out all those cards from Kathy. She took me to church, Sunday School and fellowship dinner. She left about 6:00 p.m. that evening. Before she left Amy, Rod, Mindy, Neil and 3 children came. She got to see the new baby the day before. Joci and Jackson from Alaska were here also.

Betty Boomgarden, a good friend from church picked me up off and on and we went to the Triangle for breakfast. I have always enjoyed going out for breakfast, I don't know why.

Another new baby came this month too. Drew and Sam were the happy parents of another girl, Halle Elise, on June 6th.

We left on June 13th and got to Rebecca's around 6:30. Wayne had steaks all ready for us. We all went to the little town of Leonard for breakfast the next morning. They always serve good food. Suzanne came at noon. We all went to Bemidji to witness the wedding of Keren Williams and Benjamin Pope. Both are such really nice kids. I'm sure they will make a success of their marriage. We got to see many old friends there including Alvin and Jean Petersen, and Richard and Thelma Snell and their family.

The next day being Sunday we all went to church in Bemidji. It was good to visit with old friends again. They had a fellowship dinner that made it easier to visit. Their new building is very practical for serving meals. I understand the ladies of the church had something to do with the planning of it. Richard Snell preached. We left for home after the fellowship dinner.

I attended a party in St. Peter for Bob's sister Sandy who turned 75. Quite a few were there. I didn't know a lot of them. Sandy's kids were all there so it was nice to see them.

Nancy brought my sister Vickie's daughter Alathia from Scotland here on Thursday July 10th. She seemed to really enjoy visiting with her cousins. While she was here she made us a Jamaican meal of salt fish and ackee, also rice and peas (red beans). We love Jamaican food. Nancy, Barbara and Alathia sang "Great is thy Faithfulness" in church in New Ulm the next day. Nancy and Alathia had to leave on Tuesday July 15th. Alathia needed to go back to Lincoln, Nebraska to visit her daughter Niecey and family and son Douglas. I really hated to see her go as I see her so seldom.

Al and Bonnie came on July 24th to take me out for a birthday dinner. The weather could not be depended on in January so Al and Bonnie decided to wait until summer which was fine with me. Barbara and Paul went along and we went to the Home Cafe in St. James. I had their rice hamburger hot dish. It was really good and such a generous portion. I took it home and had another meal out of it. Al and Bonnie were surprised at the low prices and good food. They make the best sour cream raisin pie too.

Peggy was planning to marry Travis Jorde. They had a bridal shower for her in Rochester on August 2nd and we went over for that. They were married September 6th out at Winn and Betsy's farm home near Byron. It was an outdoor wedding and it was a nice day for it. They had the reception in the barn which worked out real well. I think most of the kids were there. Brenda and Richard flew up from Houston. I barely got a quilt finished for them in time for the wedding.

Peggy Blanshan/Travis Jorde wedding

September turned out to be a bad month for deaths. My cousin Grace Colebank Anderson died; also our good preacher friend Richard Snell and Bob's nephew Harold's wife Linda. They will be missed. Also little Bailey the dog died too. Barbara took her to the vet to have her teeth cleaned because they were bleeding. They gave her too much anesthetic and she died. I felt very bad at first but then realized she didn't have to suffer. She was old and soon may have developed something painful to deal with.

We went to Linda Schultz's funeral in Sleepy Eye on October 2nd. Barbara played the keyboard, Amy sang, Dale preached and they all sang "Dusty Roads" at the end. Adam Schultz's mother -in-law collapsed at the cemetery and had to call the ambulance. I think it turned out to be a stroke.

On October 6th Home Care notified me that Molly would no longer be coming. I was very upset as I had had her for 6 and a half years with no problem. They wouldn't give me a reason. Barbara called them later and asked why and they said they couldn't afford to pay her mileage. They had others working for them who also had to drive quite far, however. Molly applied for work elsewhere and got a good job in Trimont, Minnesota. I missed her very much.

All this while Larry Davis, our good friend from way back, was coming over quite often to play Skip Bo with me and stayed long enough to get lunch. I think he was very lonely after his wife died. I did enjoy playing games with him though.

Our close neighbor Shirley Karou decided to move to an apartment near the nursing home. We missed her dropping in to visit off and on and the home-made ice cream she brought us. She also shared cookies, banana bread and other baked goods.

The church in Madelia always has a Thanksgiving dinner on the Wednesday a week before Thanksgiving. They had a program with someone from each family contributing something. I sang "Father We Thank Thee for the Night" with my Omnichord. Every time I sang I wondered if it would be my last because my voice was getting hoarser.

Brenda, Richard and Evelyn arrived Sunday November 23rd to be here for Thanksgiving. On the 26th we headed for Rochester. I had appointments at the Mayo Clinic for tests that afternoon. After that we went over to the Senior Center. We stayed at Gary Cradic's for the night since they had a recliner I could sleep in. Thanksgiving was very enjoyable with all the good food, etc. Dwight and Vivian Hill, Kathy and Gene Jackel and Lois and Stu Main were there. We had over 90 people. Bob and I didn't realize what we started when we got married.

Thanksgiving bingo

The next day we had a baby shower for Boyd and Liz's Lili and Jeannie's Bennett. Again we had lots of music. We went to Dale and Linda's on Saturday and spent the day there. We went to church with them the next day and joined them for their family dinner afterward.

The next day was Monday December 1st and I had an appointment with Dr. Husmann to get the results of the tests. He said everything was about the same which was good news. We stopped to see Bob's brother Jim in the nursing home in Owatonna on the way home.

On Sunday the 21st Dale was asked to preach in Madelia. He also sang "O Holy Night" accompanied on the piano by Mindy. Amy led the singing. Nolan played "Jingle Bells" on the piano. It was quite a family affair. We went to the Bowling Alley for dinner afterward. It was Barbara's 66th birthday. Paul didn't go because he was sick.

Nancy and Dennis came to be with us for Christmas. Bonnie and her three kids also came from Ohio. Dennis read the Christmas story that evening and we got to each open one present. Brad Kuebler stopped by. Barbara had Santa Claus come for the kids. She made her usual oyster stew for supper. The next day we opened the rest of our presents and had a very nice dinner. Barbara made ham loaf. Paul's daughter Chris and her husband and son Isaac came for dinner plus Brad and Denise Kuebler. On December 31st Barbara and Paul took Bonnie and kids to the airport to go home. It was really nice to have them here.

2015

January started out with a lot of below zero weather and a blizzard. My 89th birthday was celebrated quietly. Barbara made breakfast for me and oyster stew. Amy took me to New Ulm at noon to eat at the Pizza Ranch and Dale met us there and ate with us. Then Amy took me somewhere to get a pedicure, which I had never had before in my life. I enjoyed it though. When I got home a lady came and gave me a massage. I hadn't had that before either but it felt good.

In February I discovered I had shingles. The painful sores circled my body from front to back just above my waist. About all the doctor could do was give me pain pills plus a drug called gabapentin that helped me relax. It was supposed to be healing for the nerves, too. The shingles lasted about six weeks and I didn't feel good most of the time.

Amanda Fenske is now my home health aide. She is Nate Fenske's wife. Nate's mother is a Colebank. She is okay but I miss my Molly.

Harvey, Mary and baby Terry

Bob's brother Harvey died of lung cancer on April 1st. The funeral was on Monday the 6th at St. Joseph the Worker Catholic Church in Mankato. Amy, Dale, Barbara and Paul, Suzanne and Jon and I represented our family. He was buried in the new part of Minneopa Cemetery.

I got a letter from Dale Colebank's wife Loita saying that Dale had died. Dale was the second son of my mother's twin sister out in Oregon. He and Vickie were in the same grade in country school. He was very talented in music. He played the piano, guitar and other instruments. Loita sang.

Mother's Day was on Sunday May 10th. The Friday before that I got a very big surprise – Nancy came and brought Brenda. I had no idea she was coming. She brought a huge bouquet of flowers.

Saturday was Barbara's piano recital. Nancy and Brenda were a big help in getting ready for it. I believe it was at the Church of Christ this time. On Sunday we went to New Ulm for church. They took me out to eat at the Green Mill in the Holiday Inn. I had 4 daughters there. Brenda left on Monday and stopped at Crystal's before going on the plane home.

Bob's niece, Pam, had developed Alzheimer's. Bob's sister Sandy brought her over to visit. Pam had a Bible cover with her that her mother had made. It was coming apart. They thought maybe Barbara could fix it. It proved to be a little harder than they thought. Pam seemed to enjoy herself.

Rebecca arrived in her brand new white car—a Ford Fusion. She brought Joely along. On Friday June 5th, she took us for a ride to visit the graves of my parents and grandparents and sister. The next day we went to Walnut Grove to see the place where Laura Ingalls Wilder lived.

Amy and Rod were remodeling their house, gutting the downstairs and making a lot of changes. Paul liked to go over and help. He was able to work on the dry wall. The retired Baptist preacher who lived across the block behind us took Paul over to

Rod's. He was very good to Paul and came over and visited him quite often, usually bringing doughnuts or rolls.

On Thursday June 18th we got word that Bob's good friend, Dwight Hill had died suddenly. The funeral was in Cedar Falls, Iowa. The funeral was in a big beautiful Methodist Church.

This was the year for the Blanshan/Petersen/Williamson reunion that is held every three years. It was held in the same camp as last year on June 25th to 28th. Barbara and Paul brought my recliner and they put it in Evelyn and Brenda's room. Joe, Dale and Brenda came and sang for me that night. It was a little walk to the dining room so they found a wheelchair to push me around in. We had such a great time reminiscing about old times. We also had a music fest. There was so much talent in the group it was fun singing. We had services at the camp on Sunday and then left for home. There were 135 or more people who came.

Bob's nephew Harold's son Jason was planning to get married. He and Diette asked Nancy to do the catering. The wedding took place at the Catholic Church in St. George, Minnesota. The reception was in New Ulm at the bowling alley. It was prettily decorated including white covers on all the chairs.

The 18th of July was the date of the Blanshan reunion held in Watona Park in Madelia again. There were quite a few there including Albert and Bonnie, Harvey's son Jay, Florence, Bruce and Marsha and three grandchildren, Mickey, Sandy, and Pam, Kim and Teresa and our children and grandchildren who were able to come. We had a good time visiting with those who hadn't been there before.

On July 25th and 26th my Uncle Royal's grandson Kenneth Colebank and his daughter Nina and fiancé came from Boone, Iowa to visit us. We had never met them before and were so glad they came. Uncle Royal grew up in the house we were living in. We also showed them the farm where Uncle Royal had been born and the cemetery where Royal's parents were buried. They seemed like real nice people.

Grandson Boyd (Blaine) Eser graduated from the Police Academy in August. I think he was the only close relative in police work at that time. Bob had been a police officer in West Concord and Lake Crystal. Albert's son Alan was in police work then too I believe.

My eye doctor wanted me to go to the retina clinic in Mankato because the macular degeneration had gotten worse in my right eye. Amy took me there on August 24th. They said my left eye had the dry kind and my right eye the wet kind and gave me an injection in my right eye. They didn't get it numbed good and it really hurt. I really didn't want to do it again. Everyone I talked to that had had the shot said it didn't hurt but mine sure did.

Grandparent's Day was September 13th. I had put that on Facebook. Some wondered if I was hinting – ha ha. I guess I kind of was. I do love to get cards. I got quite a few and on Grandparent's Day Peggy, Travis, Caitlin and Joel came and brought seven cards. That was a surprise. It pays to advertise I guess.

We attended Jimmy and Marissa's wedding on October 16th. It was a very nice wedding and reception held in the Hope Summit Christian Church in Rochester. Brenda, Suzanne and Jon, Nancy and Mandy and Crystal and Amy were there. We stayed again at Gary Cradic's because they have a recliner I can sleep in. It was very nice of them to let us stay there.

Maurine Hage, the woman who played the piano for our wedding, was killed in a car accident. We attended her funeral on October 17th in North Mankato at a mortuary there. She had died several weeks before so the body wasn't there. It was more of a celebration of life. I think Bob's brother Jim was the only one left of our wedding party, and he was in the nursing home.

I got another eye injection on October 26th. I told them it wasn't getting numbed and they waited a little longer after putting the stuff in but it didn't make much difference – it still hurt.

Another great grand baby arrived on November 17th. Loretta Jo Lynn Brownlee was born and delivered by her Grandma Amy. Amy was thrilled to do that. Proud parents were Kyle and Joci Brownlee in Juneau, Alaska.

Brenda, Richard and Evelyn arrived November 21st. They stayed with us and Evelyn slept in my room on the bed. Since I was sleeping in my recliner I didn't use the bed. I thought she was brave to do that. She said I didn't snore. On the 25th we went to Rochester for our Thanksgiving celebration. We stayed at Cradic's again and were thankful for their hospitality. We had our dinner at the Senior Center again. We had varied entertainment including a surprise "pre-90th birthday" celebration for me. We also played bingo and had a tea party in which we each brought our own tea cup and saucer. Then we had our usual music and singing. We ended our celebration on Saturday. We went to church where Dale and Linda go the next day. Linda fed us a delicious dinner before we left for home.

Amy took me to Rochester for my annual checkup on December 7th. I had a CT scan and blood work. We had supper with Dale at the Country Kitchen and then went to the Comfort Inn for the night. The next day I had an appointment with Dr. Husmann to tell me the results of the tests. He said everything was the same except one kidney was swollen and the spot where the intestine narrowed was swollen. He wanted to see me in six months.

One morning we discovered four chickens wandering around our house. One flew into the back yard and the dogs got it. Barbara called the police and they took the chicken (it was still alive). We hoped he would notify whoever they belonged to and tell them to keep them home. We found out they belonged to a neighbor (Mexican). They didn't keep them in and they got down to one chicken. Maybe someone wanted a chicken dinner.

Barbara had her piano recital at the nursing home on December 13th. I think they enjoy seeing the kids perform.

My cousin Ann and her husband moved from their home in Alaska to the nursing home in Fertile, Minnesota. Ann was interviewed as one of three couples in the home who had been married more than 65 years. Mel died shortly after this and Ann was in very poor health weighing only 80 pounds. Ann and I were double cousins and we were like sisters.

Our dear friend Alvin Petersen died December 19th. Now I am the only one left of the original six of the Blanshan/Williamson/Petersen group. Alvin's funeral was December 28th in Tilden, Nebraska. Barbara, Dale and Nancy were able to attend.

Nancy and Dennis came for Christmas. Brad Kuebler brought a turkey that he had deep fried and it was very good. Crystal and her three children came the next day. Dale also came as he was asked to preach in Madelia the next day.

2016

My sister-in-law Joyce called and said her husband Chet had died. They didn't have a funeral. He was cremated.

It was time for another eye injection. I dreaded that. I had the shot on January 11th. They still didn't get it numbed. I was to come back in April. I was glad I got a little time in between shots.

My cousin Ann died January 12th. I was unable to go as it was in Fertile. Suzanne and Jon went and provided the music. I am losing so many cousins. The kids in Uncle John and Aunt Clara's family are all gone now except Martha Ruth who lives in Louisiana. Clarence is the only one left in Uncle George's family. All of Aunt Mary's are gone. I think two boys are left in my mother's twin sister Esther's family and I think there are three left of my mother's half-brother Jack's family. Many are gone on my Dad's side of the family, too.

My big day came – my 90th birthday! I am surprised I made it this far since I was so sick with the cancer and was left with a lot of damage. They had a nice celebration for me at the Church of Christ in Madelia on Saturday the 28th. The girls had decorated and Nancy prepared the lunch. About 150 people came. Brenda, Richard and Evelyn came. Rebecca, Wayne, Aaron and Joely, Crystal, Mark and children, Joci and two children, Nancy, Mandy and two of her children, Boyd, Liz and Lili, Jon and Suzanne, Dale and Bonnie. Bonnie, Barbara and Paul's daughter, came from Ohio. The big surprises were Aaron, Sterling and Bonnie coming. The girls sang "You are a Wonderful Mother", the same song I sang for my mother on her 90th birthday. I had one Madelia classmate there and that was Donna (Biiser) Fisk. I hadn't seen her for years. She lives in Truman, Minnesota. The kids got me a nice recliner. Bonnie gave me flowers and I got a wrist corsage from cousin Dana Larkin in Virginia Beach, Virginia whom I have never met. I got one card with $90 in it and I have no idea who it was from. I got many other gifts too and lots of cards. I was very happy with the event.

On February 2nd we had a blizzard all day. Ten inches of blowing snow. Bonnie couldn't leave because of the storm. That night there was a terrible fire uptown about 2:00 a.m. Firefighters were hampered by the storm. Firetrucks tried to get there but couldn't unless a plow went ahead of them. Eight businesses burned down. Almost a whole block on the north side of Main Street – the flower shop where Barbara worked included. About 38 people were suddenly out of work. They are not sure how it got started, but there was an explosion. It may have been a gas leak – they said there was gas in the soil behind the buildings. Five days later we had blizzard conditions again.

My new recliner didn't fit my body just right; the seat was too long. We went back to the same store in Mankato and I sat in a whole bunch of chairs but none were exactly what I wanted. The last one I looked at was more expensive than the chair I had so I wasn't sure about looking at that one. I sat in it and it was just right. It rocked, swiveled and had an electric control. It was also leather which was good for me in case I spilled on it. Barbara asked how much more money he would have to have. He thought a little and then said we could have it for the same price. How nice of him to do that.

Jon had the main part in the play "Fiddler on the Roof." It was put on by the middle school in Moorhead, but they needed an adult for that part. I decided to try to make the trip. Nancy came to go with us and we left on February 3rd. The play was the next night. Jon was Tevje and had a whole lot of lines to learn. He did a really good job on that and sang some numbers too. His mother came to hear him too. We left on Sunday after visiting Renata's church, Triumph Lutheran. Renata had a solo part in the singing. She has a beautiful voice.

On Sunday March 20th Barbara, Paul and I went to Truman to attend the Easter Cantata at the church there. Barbara sang in it. They had lunch afterward. Before we went to that we stopped at a 90th birthday celebration for one of my classmates, Donna (Biisser) Fisk. We started corresponding after that.

Betsy called and said I might be able to get in Madonna Meadows assisted living home in Rochester. Barbara and Paul were in Rochester for the weekend and went and checked it out. She said it was really nice.

Duane and Katie came April 3rd. It is good for Duane to visit with his dad while Paul is still able to visit. Katie ordered the cutest little iron for me on line. It is a steam iron and light weight and easy for me to handle. Duane and Katie left on the 9th.

Had to have another shot in my eye at the retina clinic in Mankato on April 11th. They still didn't get my eye numbed.

Mother's Day was on May 8th. I had been admitted on May 6th for stomach pain. I got to come home from the hospital in the afternoon. I got lot of nice gifts, flowers and telephone calls.

The next day Barbara took me to Rochester to see my room in Madonna Meadows. It looked like a really nice place. The room was not very big but was very nice.

Barbara had what was to be her last piano recital at the Church of Christ at 2:00 p.m. Saturday, May 14th.

The day finally came that I was to move to Madonna Meadows – May 19th. Brad Kuebler offered to drive his truck over. I was so glad to hear that since we didn't have any one else to do it. He had a covered truck so we got it all loaded up on the 18th. We left about 11:00 a.m. the next day. Dale, Jimmy and Betsy were waiting to help us unload on the Rochester end. Barbara had it all figured out how the room could be arranged to best advantage, so everything was put in its place and looked good. I just had the smaller stuff to put away. I had accepted this change in my life so it didn't bother me to move although I hated to leave my grandma's house. I was actually looking forward to moving. I soon found out the food was very good and there were plenty of activities and entertainment.

Someone from Dale's family picked me up for church. The church is called Hope Summit Christian Church. I like to go to the first service and then go to a senior class during the second service. The preacher's wife is Joe Petersen's daughter. Later Cradics offered to come and get me for church. Gary also teaches the senior class.

They picked a primary doctor for me – Dr. Mauritz Binder. He is from Germany and very nice.

Suzanne came and stayed a few days. I think she wanted to see what it was like. She thought it was just like staying in a hotel. The building here is very nice. They have decorated it beautifully and the furniture is good quality. The outside is nice too. It is all made of brick and has some columns in front and some inside.

There are flowers that bloom in the summer. We have some wildlife too. We see deer quite often out in back. Sometimes they come up to one of the residences window and look in. There are also wild turkeys, rabbits, squirrels and birds. There is a courtyard in back that is nice for picnics etc.

Cael Franklin Eser made his entrance into this world on June 22nd. His parents are Boyd and Liz Eser. This was their second child.

Boyd and Liz Eser with Lili and Cael

I was asked if I wanted to be in an ad on TV for this place. Another lady from our section, Edna Meyer from West Concord, was asked too. They did one shot where it was just us two sitting in front of a fireplace conversing. I was in several group shots too. It has been on TV off and on since.

Dale came on June 27th and did a program on the flag. It was very good. One of the residents who is a veteran said it should be shown in every school.

Rod and Amy came on July 17th and brought my power chair. I was really glad to get it because now I could just take that whenever I had to go very far for an activity. I planned to keep walking to my meals three times a day so I wouldn't lose my ability to walk. It was funny some of the remarks I got about my chair. One lady said "You must be rich to have a chair like that." Another said something like "Here she comes with her fancy chair." When I got to checking I realized it was the top of the line model of the Jazzy chairs. I can't thank Amy and Rod enough for bringing it to Madonna Meadows. Rod put in new batteries and made sure it was working right. When I needed to go on one of the outings I just took my chair. The shuttle has a lift on it so I didn't even have to get out of the chair.

Another thing nice about being at Madonna Meadows is that when you need to go to the doctor they will take you there and then you ask for a wheelchair and an escort and the escort takes you right to the doctor. When you are ready the escort will take you back to the lobby and call the shuttle to come.

On August 18th I went to the Gonda Building to have my eye injection. I told them about my eye being hard to deaden so they waited longer after putting the solution in, plus put in extra solution. I helped a little bit but not much. They didn't tell me how my eye was doing or anything. I got a letter in the mail saying when my next appointment was.

I was very shocked when I got word that my niece Wendy (Warren and Joyce's daughter) had died. They said she just quit eating. She had never been very well. Bob's cousin in Lake George, Minnesota died on July 23rd. We had visited them a number of times. I am at the age now that all my cousins and friends around my age and passing away.

On a happier note, Bob and Sarah and family were planning to come over Labor Day instead of Christmas as they usually do because Sarah was expecting about the first week in December and they didn't want her to travel at that time. They were living in Louisiana. Polly and Isaac were planning to get married but not yet. They wanted Bob to perform the ceremony. So someone got the idea, why not get married on Labor Day while Bob and Sarah were here? So new plans were made and it took some scrambling about to get everything ready on short notice. They were going to have an outdoor wedding at Winn and Betsy's.

Things were going fine until just as Bob was getting started on the ceremony there was a lot of rumbling and down came the rain. He was able to finish the part where he pronounced them man and wife. Everyone ran for a building. The garage was full and other out buildings. They somehow got the tables in place and we had a nice lunch prepared by Nancy. It went off quite well considering the problems. It will be a wedding to remember. The next day they opened their gifts at Dale and Linda's. They got a lot of nice things. Linda fed us a brunch. Bob took me home and came in and visited a while. I enjoyed that.

Grandparent's Day came along again on September 11th. I got one dozen yellow roses from Polly and Isaac, a gift card from Bonnie, a pink flowering plant from Betsy and quite a few cards.

My annual checkup with Dr. Husmann turned out well. He said some things even looked better than last time. Good news to hear.

I was getting very hungry for liver and onions, one of my favorite meals, so when Nancy came to visit she took me to a place called Grandma's Kitchen. They served liver and onions and the helpings were really generous. I shouldn't have eaten it all but I did. It was so good. I was so full I couldn't eat supper. That has filled me up on liver and onions for a long time.

The election was the big thing this year. Everyone was surprised that Trump won. I thought, "Maybe we'll see some changes now." I voted by absentee ballot, the first time I had done that. We didn't dare discuss politics in the dining room. We wanted to all stay friends.

I had to have an eye injection again on November 15th. I told the nurse I would like to try a different anesthetic as the other one didn't work but she said no. She had them wait longer before they did the shot but it still hurt. Maybe I can convince them next time.

Thanksgiving time was approaching. Brenda, Richard and Evelyn arrived on the 19th. Brenda came and put my jewelry pins on a piece of red velvet and hung it up on the door. I let any of the relatives who wanted a pin to help themselves. Carrie's foster boy, Joel, who was five years old was especially interested in them. He took a long time trying to decide what he wanted. He finally decided on two little frogs. He wanted them pinned on his shirt right away.

Nancy brought me a Christmas tree that was about four feet high. Brenda, Evelyn and Matt helped to trim it and put lights on it.

 Linda's mother died and the funeral was in our church. Bobby did the sermon, Dale emceed, four granddaughters sang (Dale and Linda's girls). Gary Cradic said the closing prayer.

We had a little New Year's party at the home on New Year's Eve. We had snacks and sparkling grape juice. We also played bingo and I won twice.

2017

New Year's Day came on Sunday. Cradics picked me up for church and I went with Dale to their house for dinner. He brought me home again about 5:00 p.m.

I had written to nephew Jim Colebank about the picture my parents had in their bedroom. My mother gave it to Warren. He wrote back and said he had it and took a nice big picture of it and sent me. Dale got it framed. I was very glad to get it. I wanted to put a picture of it in this book.

On Saturday mornings I always had a joint call on the computer with my daughters and any grandkids who were available. Brenda started it. It was great to be able to visit that way and see their faces. We usually had about six on the call. I looked forward to these visits.

My heart was acting up so I went to a heart specialist, Dr. Gruber. She put me on Lanoxin. I had taken that for a spell I had around 1978. It helped me at that time. This time I didn't feel good and my heart was still giving me trouble, so I went back to the doctor. They did a bunch of tests and decided to take the Lanoxin away. Later they increased my water pills. The swelling went down and my heart got better right away. I guess the fluid was pressing on my heart and making it fibrillate. They also had me get a strong pair of compression hose which were very expensive. I had to be weighed every day to watch for any sudden loss or gain. Brenda bought me a scale which showed even the tenths of a pound. It was digital.

On Saturday, January 28th the kids put on a birthday party for my 91st birthday. Quite a few people came. Al, Bonnie, Florence and Garry came, plus Barbara, Dale, Nancy and Suzanne. The next day on Sunday Amy and Rod, Ellie, Larry Davis, Mindy, Neil and family and Sterling came. They couldn't come yesterday so they came on Sunday and took me out to eat at Pizza Ranch in Stewartville. Barbara and Paul also came and some people from church so there were quite a few. Suzanne brought a beautiful cake from Fargo and it was very good too. The party on the 28th was held in the chapel since there is the most room there. Dale led a sing-a-long that they seemed to really enjoy. One lady remarked "That's the best birthday party I ever went to!" I got a lot of cards and gifts of money. Evelyn in Florida sent a beautiful bouquet of red roses and baby's breath.

On Valentine's Day Barbara and Paul brought me a beautiful bouquet of apricot colored roses. Betsy and Winn came and brought a huge bouquet of yellow roses, white daisies and other small flowers from Brenda and Richard.

In March they had a "Find the Shamrock" contest. The clue was "It is high and low and loud and quiet." I thought about that that night and wondered if it could be the piano in the chapel. So the next day I looked around the piano and there it was on the back of the piano behind the curtain. The shamrock was made out of paper. For a prize I got a shamrock necklace, a bag of Werthers candy and they took my picture and put it up on the bulletin board.

Jon's orchestra went to Hawaii in March. They performed on the deck of the U.S.S. Missouri, at the Mall and at Pearl Harbor. Suzanne went along as a chaperone and said it was quite impressive.

One of Suzanne's pupils entered a contest where they had to write an essay about why they liked their teacher. She wrote about Suzanne and won the contest. It was put on by Barnes and Noble.

Dale came and put on a program on Ireland for St. Patrick's Day. We had a party with punch and candy. A lot of us wore something green. Dale's programs are very interesting. He does a lot of research on them. He shows pictures, tells stories and does some music with his guitar.

On March 25th Rebecca came and we had a get-together for her in the Colonial Room. There were 10 of us. We had a nice visit.

I coughed all winter. The doctor thought it was fluid pressing on my lungs. I think some of was allergies too.

They came and asked me if I would like to be on Palliative Care. It sounded like a good program to me. They had to see if I qualified first. I guess they thought I did because they put me on the program. I have a nurse practitioner come once a month or whenever I need her. She is very very thorough and can prescribe medicines. The doctor will come once a month and check things out. I don't have to go to the doctor's office very often. I like it as I feel I am getting very good care. My next move will be the nursing home.

Nancy came and brought me an early Mother's Day present – she had made a beautiful quilt. I didn't know she had so much talent in that direction. It was in dark tones and very pretty.

Mother's Day came on May 14th. Amy, Rod, Mindy, Neil, Nolan, Bryleigh, Ashlyn, Joci, Jackson, Loretta, Barbara, and Paul (I believe Ellie was along too) all came and took me to a Chinese restaurant called Ocean Star for lunch. Afterward we went to Dale and Linda's and visited. I received many nice gifts, flowers and money. I feel so blessed to have such nice children and grandchildren. It must be very lonely for those who grow old with no children to look out for them.

On May 19th I had a surprise visit from my old home health aide from Madelia, Molly Solheid. I was so glad to see her.

On June 3rd Suzanne came and took me, Barbara, Paul and Evelyn to Madelia for Ellie's graduation from high school reception. It was held at a building on the golf course that worked out very well. She is my youngest grandchild and the last one of them to graduate from high school.

Another great-grandchild was born on June 3rd. Carrie and Roger had a baby girl named Thea. They also have two foster children that they want to adopt, a baby named Elijah and a five-year-old named Joel. They also have three other children: Caitlyn, Joel and Eaven.

On June 10th I had pain in my stomach all night which got unbearable by 5:00 a.m. I pressed on my life line and they called the ambulance and took me to St. Mary's. They immediately put a hose down my throat and pumped my stomach. I had vomited just before getting on the ambulance but they still did it. Then they gave me a very powerful laxative that really worked violently and fast. It did the trick though and unblocked the bowel blockage. They also did a bunch of tests – a CT scan, EKG and x-ray. They gave me pain medication and put in an IV. I went home on Tuesday. Nancy was here and was a big help to me because I was weak for a couple of days.

Amy had a serious operation on June 21st. She was out of commission for a while. I also got word that my sister-in-law,

Joyce had fallen. Her blood count was way too low. She consented to go home and stay with daughter Lynda for a while.

Bobby and family from Louisiana arrived late on July 4th. They would normally come at Christmas time but Sarah is expecting about then so they had to come earlier. The following Sunday Linda and Dale had a dinner after church and all their kids were there and all their grandkids except the two oldest. Bobby, Sarah and three children came to see me on Tuesday. They left the next day.

Once a month we have a food outing. We will either take the shuttle to the restaurant or we will order what we want and our activity directors will go and get it and we will eat it on tables set up in the chapel. The chapel is used for many activities.

Once every summer we have a family picnic here and invite family members. They serve a nice supper and have live music. Fourteen members of my family came – more than any of the others. We had to have it inside this year because of rain.

Several things happened close together in August. My first great grandchild to get married (Grayden and Morgan) got married and Linda's dad died. Polly was expecting her first child at this time too. As it turned out Linda was able to go to her Dad's funeral in Wisconsin and be present at little Ruth Ann's birth. Ruth Ann came a week late so Polly was also able to go to the funeral. Ruth Ann Miller was born September 3rd.

Polly and Ruth Ann

Bob's brother Jim died on September 16th. The funeral was on the 23rd. Jon and Suzanne came and took me to the funeral. It was at the Redeemer Lutheran Church in Owatonna, Minnesota.

Each year Madonna Meadows does a video ad for the local TV station. Last year I was asked to be in it. I was again this year only this time I got paid $25.00.

On October 15th I got a surprise when I went to church. When I came out of first service there was Lois Williamson Zimmerman. She was here visiting Barbara and Paul. We all went to Dale and Linda's after church. Barbara brought Lois over to my apartment later and we had a good visit. Lois lives in Oklahoma.

On October 18th and 19th I had my yearly checkup at the Clinic. I had a CT scan, blood work, etc. Dr. Husmann was very pleased with the results. He said things looked better than the last time.

I surprised myself on October 26th by going with a group on the shuttle to Kasson, Minnesota where they were having lutefisk meals. It was so crowded we had to wait in line to get a table even though it was at St. John's Lutheran church, which is a large church. They were well organized and things went quite smoothly. They served over a thousand people who came from many different towns in the region. The lutefisk was good but I liked the lefse better -- the lefse was very good.

My granddaughter Emily from Leonard, Minnesota had her second baby on October 29th. It was a boy and she named him Weston Wayne. She also has a daughter named Joely.

I am still having to have an injection in my right eye for macular degeneration every three months. October 31st was that time again. I dread the shots because they have trouble getting my eye numbed. It has improved my eyesight in that eye though.

Thanksgiving came around again. Barbara, Dale, Nancy, Suzanne, Amy and Brenda came early and we had lunch together in a dining room here. The girls all stayed except Barbara. We wrapped gifts for prizes for bingo on Thanksgiving. On Wednesday the 22nd I had a lot of visitors including Mandy and girls; Crystal and two children; and Suzanne, Drew and Sam and two girls. It was so nice to have them come.

The 23rd was Thanksgiving. We held it in the Hope Summit Church since we had 99 people in attendance. I was amazed at how smoothly and organized everything was, thanks to my kids. We had a wonderful dinner and played bingo in the afternoon. The next day Brenda and Evelyn picked me up and we went back to the church, where they held a baby shower for Polly. Jane and Jeff gave a presentation about the work they plan to do in Barbados when they leave in February. After dinner we had music, mostly singing Christmas carols accompanied by piano, violin and guitars.

The next day was Saturday and I wanted some of them to come and put on a program for the residents here. Many had already left but those who were still here came and put on a nice program. We had violin and piano music, songs by children, grandchildren and great grandchildren. Some of the great grands showed off what they had learned in piano lessons. Little Cael toddled about in the audience – not causing any problems – and the residents got a big kick out of him.

About this time Amy's friend Dale Leighton had been approved for a heart transplant. He could not have it done unless he had someone to help him. Amy offered to do that and put her life on hold for weeks to help him out. He came through it well. He got a young heart so I hope it works out well for him.

I decided I would send out Christmas cards as I may not feel like it next year. I sent out about 100 and got about 55 back. I enjoy getting something I can hold in my hand. I got lots of e-mail wishes but although it is nice it isn't like getting cards. This is one way I keep in touch with my relatives and friends. I send out a lot birthday cards too. It is something I enjoy doing. I especially like to get cards that have family pictures on them. That way I can keep track of them and see how they are growing.

The stomach flu made its appearance on the 23rd and we went on lock-down for nearly a week. We had to stay in our rooms and meals were brought to us. Only a few got it. I didn't get it. We were on lockdown on Christmas so I didn't go anywhere. We had a nice meal here.

New Year's Eve came on Sunday. I didn't go to church because of the below-zero weather. We celebrated here with playing bingo and a snack.

2018

My oxygen level was going down and my a-fib moments increased so they decided I need to have oxygen at night. The first night I used it I didn't sleep well but the next night I slept much better. It helps a lot.

My kids held a celebration here for my 92nd birthday. Suzanne and Brenda did most of the preparing. Suzanne brought a cake from Fargo again. Brenda brought two bouquets of flowers. One was huge with roses and a lot of other kinds of flowers and the other was an azalea made to look like a little trellis just covered with rose colored flowers. Jon provided background music. I really enjoyed it. There were five of my children there – Barbara, Dale, Rebecca, Suzanne and Brenda. I was really surprised when Brenda walked in. I had no idea she was coming.

This looks like a good place to end this. I don't know how much time I have left now. I feel I have lived a good life. I have been happy in spite of troubles and trials. God has helped me through them all.

My prayer is that all of my descendants will be Christians and follow the Lord.

My Side of the Family – Health Information

Great Grandpa John Milton MacIndoo

He wasn't very tall. He was in several battles in the Civil War. He had dysentery when he was discharged, and it bothered him the rest of his life. They finally gave him a small pension for it, though it wasn't much. He had a short upper lip and always wore a mustache to cover it up.

Great Grandma Elizabeth Cunningham MacIndoo

She was a really good singer from the time she was little, and they used to put money in her apron to get her to sing when they'd have camp meetings. She was opinionated – the baby of the family.

Grandpa L.S. Colebank

Born in 1852, he remembered when Abraham Lincoln was president. L S was not very tall, I suppose about 5'10", average for men at that time. He had brown eyes. He had a tenor voice and was a good singer. I think he had dark hair, which thinned as he grew older. He had a large growth on the right side of his face by his eye (he called it a "wen"). He died from cancer. It started on his lip where he held his pipe. He lived to be 93(?). He had many siblings (10 or 15), including a twin brother and sister, Joseph and Josephine. His dad was married twice, and he was from his dad's first family. He had a brother that lived to be over 100. I remember him saying he went to "singing school." He had somewhat of an eastern accent, and his favorite expression was "beats all!" He wanted to become a Christian when he was 18, so they broke a hole in the ice and baptized him, and he said he never caught a cold from it. He was a member of the Church of Christ for his whole life.

Grandma Martha Colebank

She was average height and had blue eyes and golden hair (as did Marty, her namesake). She had attached earlobes. She only finished 5th grade but did a lot of reading and was very intelligent. She got married on her 15th birthday. Her husband was a lot older than her, maybe about 29 when they got married. He was a good man and religious, and he owned 40 acres; so her folks thought that was a good deal. She said she didn't know what her parents were thinking to let her get married so young. She had 11 kids. She had typhoid fever when she was middle-aged. There was a family having trouble with typhoid fever and she went over to help them and got typhoid fever herself. They told her she wouldn't live very long because it affected her heart. She lived to be 93 and died of old age. She had big, varicose veins on her legs – big as a pencil. Her favorite expression was "Land sakes alive!" She was a member of the Church of Christ all her life, though I don't remember her saying anything about when she was baptized.

Nils Nasman

Grandpa Nils was Swedish and had blue eyes. He came to the United States when he was 18, and he brought his 15-year-old brother. He died of TB when he was in his early 30s. They were farming in Watonwan County. He lived in the hotel in Madelia for about a year before he died because he didn't want the family to get TB.

Anna Greta Nasman

She was very religious. She worked for a school teacher in Sweden, and she valued education highly. She made sure all her daughters got high school educations. There were no school buses, so she had to take them with horse and buggy to St. James and find a place for them to stay for the week and send food with them to last a week. She'd go get them for the weekend. She was so determined her girls weren't going to be without an education like her (when her husband died, she didn't have any special talents to support herself). She had blue eyes as well. She died of a stroke when I was about 3 (1929).

Lester Colebank

He was born in 1894. When he was a baby, he was so thin that a relative told his mother that she better have his picture taken because she didn't think he'd live. He was the only child of 11 to have a baby picture. He grew to be 6'3" and healthy. I don't know why he was so thin.

He was fussy about his dress-up clothes. He did all the measurements when he sent for a new suit. He wanted to be sure it fit just right. He always looked good in his suit. He had long fingers and long arms, and he had long, narrow feet, a size 12 shoe. He had grayish-blue eyes. He had ulcers, and they got so bad that his stomach got full of adhesions, and he didn't have much space for food. That's how he got thin. He weighed 190 pounds for years, though he ate well. He graduated from 8th grade, which was good for back then. He was a worrier but didn't say much about it at the time. He had a nervous breakdown when I was 11 and he was around 43. He was in the mental hospital in Fergus Falls, MN, for 6 months. He was a farmer, and he loved farming. He didn't want to quit when he got older (in his early 70's), but he couldn't keep it up any longer. He was a good carpenter too. The first thing he built was a barn, because that was necessary to have. Then he built a chicken house. And then he built a house for Mother. I was 14 years old when he started building that. He didn't want to go into debt, so he paid for things as he went along. He had his own teeth when he died, and had only lost one or two of them. And they were good teeth. He also never went bald, never had a hearing aid, and didn't get glasses until he was in his sixties. He had a tenor voice and was a good singer. He played the guitar and the harmonica. He loved music and made sure his kids heard music. He was an Army ambulance truck driver in WWI. While in the Army, he helped chase the infamous Mexican Bandit Pancho Villa.

Linda Nasman Colebank

Linda was a fraternal twin to Esther. Esther was the chunkier baby. Linda was her dad's favorite and Esther was her mother's favorite. Her dad called Linda his little Linnie, but unfortunately he died when the twins were just one and a half years old. Her mother remarried, and sadly Linda's step-father was physically abusive of the children, boxing them in the ears, pulling them by the hair, etc. Linda's mother was so afraid of her new husband that she had Linda stay with a neighbor for several months. Unfortunately the neighbor's 15 year old son tried to sexually molest Linda, but she fought back and got away from him. She ran to the boy's mother and explained what happened. The mother gave her boy a tongue-lashing in German and it never happened again.

Linda was 5'8" and had thick, brown hair that gradually turned white before she died (it was still thick then). She had blue eyes. She had a pigeon breast and narrow shoulders with wide hips and wide feet. She had slight curvature of the spine. She had no hair on her legs or under her arms. She was a pretty lady. She taught at a country school for eight years. She could play simple tunes on the piano, but I never saw her do it much. She could ride a horse. When she was a kid, they had to herd their cows and used horses to do it. She didn't ride anymore after she was married. She had a car before she was married, which was very unusual in those days. The only reason she got a car was because Uncle Jack bought one and wanted to sell it so that he could go to college. So he wanted her to buy the car from him. She said, "Well, I can't drive," but he offered to teach her. He took her out in the field and drove around until she got the hang of it.

Linda loved to eat and liked all foods. She took good care of herself and took vitamins. High blood pressure was an issue in later years, but was managed by medication. Her twin died of a stroke caused by high blood pressure around the age of 69. When Linda was 93 – of sound mind and fairly good health - she broke her hip when coming down the stairs backwards as she always did for safety, but missed the last step. She went down really hard. They had to put a rod into the bone next to her hip – a major operation. Unfortunately, the anesthetic affected her mind. She was never the same after that. But she was fairly healthy and lived to be 100 and died of old age. My folks both attended the Baptist Church in Madelia.

A little more about Esther – her hips were very wide and she had very large babies (12 lbs!) She was converted to be a Jehovah Witness by her husband. Aunt Esther was funny! Both Linda and Esther gave humorous monologues at PTA meetings. Aunt Esther and brother Victor were always playing pranks and doing funny things. Aunt Esther was ill during her freshman year of high school and had to repeat it and doing so got behind her twin, Linda. She tried to take two years in one in her junior year and as a result had a nervous breakdown. My mother helped her through it by going on long walks and letting her talk. As far as I know she never had any more trouble like that the rest of her life.

June Esther Colebank Blanshan

My skin tone was white when I was born rather than the usual, reddish baby skin. I walked at 14 months old. They didn't encourage babies to walk early back then because they thought you would end up bow-legged. My blood type is O-. I sucked my thumb until I was about a year and a half old, when my mom decided that I was going to quit. She put mittens on my hands at night, and I cried for the first night. By the third night, I came and held up my hands to have the mittens put on (I just thought it was part of the bedtime routine). I have attached earlobes, like my Grandma Colebank. I have a slight pigeon breast like my mother. I grew to 5'7" and had brown hair and brown eyes. I wore a size 6 ½ shoe when I got married, but as I carried children, they spread out more; and I ended up with a size 9 foot. I was thin most of my life, though I have Grandma's wide hips. I also had slight curvature of the spine, I think because my right leg is shorter than the other. I also have a geographic tongue which I inherited from my mother.

Skin: I also had eczema on my head as a baby. My mother took me to the doctor, and he said not to use water on it, to just clean my head with oil. She did, and I never had it again.

Barbara, Dale, Rebecca, Nancy and Suzanne all had scarlet fever somewhere around 1958 or 1959 (before Davey) and I got it as well. The children didn't seem much affected by it, but I was very sick. It was the worst sore throat I've ever had, and my skin peeled afterward, probably from the fever. The doctors told me to use Jergens lotion on my skin.

Lungs: I had double pneumonia when I was 37 or 38 (I hemorrhaged). I coughed so much and thought I was allergic to the cat, until I started coughing up blood. It scared me because I thought it was TB, but when I called the doctor, he had me come in for an x-ray and found out it was pneumonia. He told me to go to bed and stay there for 3 weeks. I kept one of the older children home from school each day to help with Davey and Amy. We lived in Lake Crystal at the time.

Breaks: I broke my wrist around 1956 (I think I was expecting Suzanne at the time). We were crossing a one-way bridge near Tilden, and there was a car parked in the middle of it. We started across in our vehicle, which had just had the brakes fixed the day before, and hit him head-on; otherwise, we would have gone off the bridge into the water. I had my hand on the door handle, and my hand got bent clear back. The doctor said I broke it in 7 places, and I had the cast on for 8 weeks. Nancy was in diapers then, and I had the hardest time getting her diapers on.

Teeth: I had to get false teeth in my thirties (upper plate) because my fillings kept falling out. I think my teeth were poor, and I seemed to lose more teeth each time I had a child – perhaps the babies were requiring the calcium. The lower plate I got later (perhaps in my 70's), after having a partial for a while.

Personality: I sang and played several instruments (piano, organ, auto harp, and Omnichord), and played piano and organ in church for years. I taught Sunday school and ladies' classes all of my married life. In my later life I entertained seniors by playing and singing. I could have started earlier if I hadn't been so shy. I started being really shy around age 5 or 6. We lived in the country and didn't see much of other people.

Other:

I gave birth to eight children (6 girls and 2 boys), one (Davey) with Down Syndrome.

I had the usual childhood diseases, 3 kinds of measles, whooping cough and small pox. I had scarlet fever after I was married.

When I was 14 and in the 8th grade, I had tularemia (rabbit fever) from a wood tick. I was sick in bed for a month with big sores on my face.

We spent four years in Jamaica as missionaries, 1975-1976, and 1980-1981. While there I had a parasite (one that gets in your blood and travels between your organs) and took some medicine for it. I also started to get shingles while in Jamaica, and went to an old, English doctor, who gave me a strong shot of some vitamin, and it went away. I had shingles again when I was close to 90 years old, and it was much worse that time (it probably stuck around for about 3 months).

Heart: I have always had an irregular heartbeat. Upon returning from Jamaica in the late 1970's I had an episode with my heart. I think my heart was tired, and I appeared to have an A-fib episode. Bob took me to the doctor and the doctor said I had congestive heart failure, and gave me a heart pill and told me to rest every afternoon, and to sleep sitting up. So I did, and went back after a year, and at my one year check-up was told everything was okay. They did an angiogram and concluded I may have had an infection in the lining around my heart. In 1993 we moved to Colorado, but the altitude had an adverse effect on my heart, so we had to move to a lower altitude again. In 2014 my heart started fibrillating again.

Cancer: In 1999 Bob had an upper respiratory infection (UTI) and was passing blood in his urine. Then I appeared to have the same issue. However, when the doctor checked he said no, it was not a UTI. The doctor had me see a gynecologist immediately, and she said "oh my – we've got a problem, get your things in order and tell your daughters to have a pap smear." I was diagnosed with cervical cancer. She made an appointment with a doctor at Fairview Hospital, but had to wait a month for the appointment. I received a rigorous combination of chemotherapy and radiation. The pain was very bad.

Bob's Side of the Family

Chester Ralph Blanshan

He was quite tall and big. I remember he had a high voice. He died not long after we were married. He used to make lawn ornaments out of wood and sold them. I think he had a variety of jobs during his life.

Elvina Belle Buck Blanshan

She was married twice. Chester was her second marriage, and they lived in Mankato. She had a little boy when she married him, and Chester didn't like him because he was another man's kid. The boy left home when he was pretty young.

Ralph Jay Blanshan

He was about 6'3". It seemed like he was taller than all the boys. He had big hands and was very tough physically. He had his tonsils out when he was growing up and didn't even have an anesthetic. The boys were going to have theirs out, and he did that to show them it didn't hurt (though I think they had a little numbing for theirs). He also pulled some of his own teeth. He was a very hard worker. He did a lot of digging and laying tile. He liked to sing, and he had Jew's harp. He liked hunting and fishing. He loved watching Westerns on TV.

Edith Pearl Barr Blanshan

She had very dark brown eyes and curly hair which turned white when she was thirty. So I never knew her without white hair. She was born in St. Peter. She was short. She had 8 children, several miscarriages, and one crib death. Bob remembered that. He was 5 years old at the time. It was a boy named Dwayne. She never liked to tell anybody goodbye and always liked to sneak out when she left. At church she didn't want to shake hands with anyone and would go out the back way to avoid it. If she got mad at you, she usually stayed mad. She loved to crochet and did a beautiful job of it. She could take something crocheted and look at it and copy it. She could also sew, though she didn't do any quilting. She did about every craft that came along, including macramé and ceramics. She always got Christmas presents for everybody. She always belonged to the Church of Christ.

Robert Chester Blanshan

When he was born, people noticed he had big hands. He also had large feet (eventually a size 13 wide) with high arches. He didn't walk until he was 17 months old (his mom thought he was too lazy). He had A Negative blood type. He was hyper and couldn't sit still in school. He got poor grades (even though he was very smart) because he couldn't concentrate. He was 6'1" with dark hair that had a tendency to curl when it was long. He had blue eyes. Memorizing came easy to him. His mother said that when his sister Donna would bring something home to memorize, he'd listen to her recite it, and he'd have it all memorized before she would, just from listening to her. He sucked his thumb. He didn't want to go to kindergarten because they were supposed to take a little rest in class, and he didn't want to because he was afraid he'd suck his thumb and they'd make fun of him. So Grandma gave Donna the mat and told her to take off running while she held him back. So she got the mat to the teacher, and he was so worried about the thumb-sucking that he put the mat down behind the piano to rest on. He was a chain-smoker by the time he was 19, when I met him, but quit when he went to Bible college. I told him I wouldn't marry anybody that smoked. He was in the Navy and had his first epileptic episode while there (a grand mal seizure), so they sent him to a hospital in Illinois because they thought he had a brain tumor. He had to wait because there were a lot of people in front of him in line. He got tired of waiting and asked for a discharge. He went home and continued having grand mal seizures (his sister Donna said it scared her to death when he'd have one), and his parents took him to the Mayo Clinic in Rochester. They did a spinal tap, and as far as I could find out, they drained a tumor somewhere in his head. It didn't leave any scarring, so I'm not sure exactly where it was. He never had another seizure after that. I wrote to the clinic here to ask them what they had done, and they wrote back and said as far as they knew, that's all they did. They said I could write to St. Mary's for the medical records, but I never did. (His mother and brother claim that he had a tumor.) He seemed to be accident prone and a bit awkward in movement. He was always ending up in a predicament of some sort. He liked to hunt and fish, but he liked animals, especially dogs. He enjoyed most sports, especially football. He had a nice tenor singing voice. He liked preaching in small churches, and as a result he always had to work on the side as well. Some of his other occupations included school bus driver, juvenile probation officer, house and barn painter, policeman, and others. While we were living in Jamaica, he got dengue fever (from a mosquito), and he was very sick with that. It presented like a bad case of the flu, and then it would get better, and then come back again. This went on for about 3 months.

General Info

The Blanshans had tempers.

A member of the Blanshan family was born with three breasts; one did not develop. The Colebanks were thrifty.

Great-Grandkid's Birthdays

1. Bradley Lamm 11-17- 95

2. Grayden Lyon 4-5- 97

3. Matthew Randolph 12-11- 97

4. Benjamin Lyon 11-5- 99

5. Madison Rowland 1-29- 00

6. Josiah Rowland 4-8- 01

7. Corey Randolph 8-25- 01

8. Caitlyn Howard 5-9- 02

9. Grace Rowland 6-23- 03

10. Joel Howard 3-24- 04

11. Hannah Randolph 10-4- 04

12. Evan Rowland 1-17- 06

13. Natalie Rose Marcella Beach 3-28- 07

14. Nolan Arkell 9-30- 07

15. Joely Jane Olson 11-1- 07

16. Oliver Egland 8-18- 08

17. Gunnar Selzer 12-26- 08

18. Eavan Howard 1-29- 09

19. Warner Beach 10-6- 09

20. Bryleigh Arkell 1-18- 10

21. Shepherd Cradic 4-29- 10

22. Selah Egland 9-10- 10

23. Bethel Blanshan 4-26- 11

24. Malcolm Cradic 12-16- 11

25. Ashlyn Arkell 1-16- 12

26. Gavin Selzer 1-16- 12

27. Clara Olafson 4-6- 12

28. Jackson Brownlee 6-13- 13

29. Charlotte Egland 6-23- 13

30. Eden Blanshan 10-18- 13

31. Angus Cradic 12-3- 13

32. Bennett Garrison 2-5- 14

33. Lilianna Eser 5-27- 14

34. Halle Olafson 6-6- 14

35. Loretta Brownlee 11-17- 15

36. Silas Blanshan 2-28- 16

37. Elijah Howard 5-7- 16

38. Cael Franklin Eser 6-22- 16

39. Boone David Jorde 12-8- 16

40. Malachi Matthew Blanshan 12-11- 16

41. Thea Corinne Howard 6-2-17

42. Ruth Ann Miller 9-3-17

43. Weston Wayne Hinrichs 10-29-17

44. Greta Ruth Arkell 9-13-18

WHO'S WHO

June and Bob Blanshan's kids – Barbara Lamm, Dale Blanshan, Rebecca Colebank, Nancy Erickson, Suzanne Larson, Davie Blanshan, Amy Davis, Brenda Blanshan (Prochazka)

Barbara's Family – Husband Paul Lamm, Chris Wilder, Duane (Katie) Lamm, Bonnie (Blaine) Randolph

Dale's Family – Wife Linda, Jessica (James) Lyon, Betsy (Winn) Cradic, Carrie (Roger) Howard, Bob (Sarah) Blanshan, Polly (Isaac) Miller, Peggy (Travis) Jorde, Jeannie Garrison Blanshan, Jimmy (Marissa) Blanshan, Billy Blanshan

Rebecca's Family – Husband Wayne Hinrichs, Aaron Hinrichs, Gillian (Craig)Beach, Emily Hinrichs.

Nancy's Family – Husband Dennis Erickson, Mandy (Steve) Rowland, Crystal (Mark) Egland

Suzanne's Family – Husband Jon Larson, Renata (Greg) Selzer, Drew (Samantha) Olafson

Amy's Family – Husband Rod Davis, Mindy (Neil) Arkell, Joci (Kyle) Brownlee, Boyd (Liz) Eser, Sterling (Molly) Eser, Eliana Davis

Brenda's Family – Husband Richard Prochazka

June's parents – Lester and Linda Victoria Nasman Colebank

June's siblings – Warren Colebank and Victoria Hintz

Bob's parents – Ralph and Fern Blanshan

Bob's siblings – Donna Yokiel, Jim Blanshan, Harvey Blanshan, Garry Blanshan, Al Blanshan, Sandy Mulvehill

DAD'S POEMS

Barbara
(To Barbara on her 40th birthday)

How swiftly by the years do fly – to make us older you
and I
It seems not so very long ago – we took our friends to
the window to show
Our first born and pointed with pride
To the cutest baby they had inside
The nursery in her little bed
Not much hair upon her head
No it seems not so long ago
You played with dolls
And dressed them so
Then off to school and the years flew by
Elementary and Jr. High
After high school years you said goodbye
To home and went out to try
Your wings to see if you could fly
Then came your home and nursery
As you began your family
You watched them grow up and now you sigh
How quickly by the years do fly
As you know they'll soon be gone
To establish for themselves a home
And with this information
There is at least this consolation
Life begins at forty, or so they say
So this really is your natal day

Nancy

("For Nancy on her 50th birthday")

It was the 3rd of November in 54
We had two daughters, about to add one more
I had hoped for a son but knew it was chancy
And sure enough we called it Nancy
As a baby Nancy sure was a beaut
Mama especially thought her button nose was so cute
She tried the drug scene before she was two
Had her stomach pumped before she was through
Nancy was good at saying things her own way
Going to the park on a picnic, if she had her say
Was just going on a parknic
And then she didn't ask mom to make a sandwich for me
It was "put peanut butter on bread and bend it" you see
Nancy grew up and the time came to leave
So off to college she went very ???
To some young girls that might be menacing
She took it in stride and called it "Dennising"
She did volunteer work at jobs some wouldn't have done
Cleaning kennels at the dog pound for one
She kind of went to the dogs with dog shows and
training daily
With Charlie, Brigita, Benson, Cody and Bailey
Nancy doesn't look as old as the calendars show
But if she is that old she's sure a nifty fifty

Suzanne

("For Suzanne on her 40th birthday")

It was in 1956, in Nebraska, in Tilden
We added to our number of children
There were three daughters so a son was planned
But we kept the baby and named it Suzanne
She was kind of cute so I figured one day

We would get the boys in some other way
So we settled for girls and my thinking was right
Several boys succumbed with hardly a fight
Growing up can be hard and soon Suzanne learned
If you play with fire you just might get burned
She looked pretty bad, but it wasn't long
Till you could hardly tell there was anything wrong
Then came the days of the scratching of strings
And the screeching and sawing that learning brings
For into her life a viola came
From then on it was never the same
Screek and scratch was now the rule
Quiet only in bed or when at school
But 'ere long pretty sounds came out of the thing
For Suzanne soon learned to really handle those strings
She played the viola at school and went from there
To Minnesota All-State Orchestra – first chair
Then on to college with music still the theme
When all at once Curt appeared on the scene
Handsome he was, a real head turner
Music was pushed to the back burner
He could truck, and fly, he also could farm
And I guess he could really turn on the charm
He crooned, she swooned, and had it so bad
Couldn't even wait to be married by Dad
Marriage for them proved to be a sonata (music again)
For there was Drew, but first Renata
Now you are 40 and your life is begun
But don't let them fool you, it's really half done
It's what you do with the part that remains
That will determine whether it was loss or gain

To Amy On Her Fortieth
(January 26, 2002)

How quickly by the years do fly
To make us older, you and I
From nine pounds to – oops, I better not say
The years sped by quickly until today
Many memories could be called to mind
And sorting them out, somewhere we'll find
A baby who came because of her brother
We didn't want to quit with him, we wanted another.
When some things come, it's best not to know
Until it happens, and it was Amy Jo.
Two things pleased you, one was to eat
The other when someone was rubbing your feet.
You could talk your little sister into wanting to do
Whatever it was you wanted her to,
Like going ahead of you up the stair
To see if it was safe for you up there
The promise of money for tickling your toes,
How much you owe her the Lord only knows
Then quite quickly came a change in toys
From playing with dolls you found out there were boys.
Well, the years have passed quickly away
There was much sunshine, but some rainy days.
With 5 sisters and 2 brothers, one waiting up there,
With parents who love you and good friends galore,
With a husband and 5 children, how could you ask for a
whole lot more?
Besides this a lot of talents were given to you
And a good sense of humor to help you get through
Times like this when you wanted to cry
"I'm getting older and about to die!"
But older ones say, "You're just getting started,
Life begins at forty so why heavy hearted?
So drag out that humor and not your regretter
Say "I'm not just getting older, I'm getting better!"
So, here's to forty! Take it and shove it!
I'm just getting started and I'm gonna love it!

Dale

("To Dale on his 40th birthday")

40 years, it's been a while since you came to bring us joy
We both were very happy when told "It's a boy"
As parents we were very proud
A daughter and a son
A girl for Mom and a boy for me
But there were more to come and come and come
A chubby boy called Smiley, full of giggles and of glee
We wondered if he would turn out to be a prodigy
We never dreamed on your first day of school
Just how long it would be
How many years would go by
Ere you got your last degree
You grew and grew to 6' 2"
We thought that you would stop there
But no, you had to keep it up till
You grew right through your hair
'Twas said you wore tennis shoes to run from girls who
came to play
But the tennis shoe went flat when Linda came your way
You learned in school that by the rule one and one made two
But experience is a teacher too, that there are
exceptions to that rule
For marriage has a little trick
Of changing that arithmetic
And 2 plus 2 makes 4 or more
Events combine to make time fly
And age us as the years go by
And we're not so young and sporty
But for you there's hope
So don't you mope
They say life begins at forty

Rebecca

(To Rebecca on her 40th birthday)

40 years have come and gone
Since God sent you into our home
So like a doll with 10 fingers and toes
A little bundle we called Rose
Though it doesn't seem that could be so
The evidence will let us know
Too much water under the bridge has passed
And 40 years have gone so fast
Of evidences there are 3
Aaron, Gillian and Emily
And now with them almost grown
We know just how much time has flown
Sometimes the road's a little rough
And we want to cry out "enough!"
Sometimes we fail to understand
And veer off into sinking sand
But we keep on going and eventually find
We have what we need for peace of mind
A family to love and treasures galore
Just how much there is in store
As more time passes it will reveal
What is to come but for now we feel
Thankful that God had chose
To give us our Rebecca Rose

Brenda

(To Brenda on her 40th birthday)

How quickly by the years do fly
To make us older you and I
The year was 1968
January 11th was the date
The nurse told me I had a son

But of a son's characteristics you had none
There was something about you right from the start
And you soon worked your way right into our hearts
The siblings worked with you and soon you were able
At 7 months of age to walk under the table
Well they couldn't leave well enough alone
But they taught you to talk and this set the tone
The word became flesh and we called her Brenda by name
And the world you live in was never the same
Hubert Humphrey was known as a great talker too
But he couldn't hold a candle to you
Traveling, every word on every sign was read
And the Gettysburg Address bounced around in our head
Every state, capital, and every President were
mentioned by name
And even each word on the dash board was also fair game.
Not very interested in boys until 6 college men
Moved in right next door, it was different then
A spark of interest raised its head
But she soon was more interested in her work instead
FMC helped you continue with more and more learning
Degrees from UCF and Rice helped increase your earning
You have served the Lord through years 2 score
By helping your fellow man and what's more
You have lived a life in God's appointed way
And continue to do so to this very day
Not only do I, and your mother too, wish you a happy
birthday today.
And pray the Lord be with you all of your way.
Whenever, wherever, God leads in the years left to you
May your Father in heaven love you as we do.

June

When I was young and in my prime
I saw this girl and said – she's going to be mine

She just doesn't know it yet

So I went up to her and took her hand
And said you're the fairest in all the land
Will you be mine – and she just said "you bet"

Well there's been some hard times and some tears
And a lot of good times thru the years
And we thank God for the day we met

We don't know what's in store
And of time just how much more
But we've had 64 and we're all set

To keep going on through all weather
It doesn't matter while we're together
We'll take every one we're going to get.

PHOTO GALLERY

June, 2 and Warren, 6

Henry Jr., June, Warren
and Maynard in 1929

June and Warren

345

June, Linda, Vickie

Babies June and cousin John Colebank in 1926

Martha and L S Colebank, Clara and Lizzie in 1886

The new frame house Lester built in Woodside Township 1941

347

Linda and Lester with June and baby Vickie around 1931

Colebank family 1943

Farewell gathering at Lengby Lake before Uncle Rob and Aunt Esther left for Oregon

Threshing in Woodside Township in 1940

Norma and Larry Davis with Mark, Doug and Cheryl Martwick

Aaseng family: L to R: Donna, Carolyn, Viola holding Debbie, Belvin and Doug (Viola is June's cousin)

June's niece Elizabeth Jane Robertson, husband Jeff, daughters
Marcy and Rhonda and son Mark

Dress-up day in Lincoln – L to R: Barbara, Nancy,
Rebecca, Suzanne, Dale.

John Colebank kids plus Warren and June in 1932
with Grandparents L S and Martha Colebank

June's double cousin Ann and her husband Mel Hagen in 2002

June age 10   Granddaughter Crystal in 2009

Granddaughter Carrie 2009

Cousins Crystal, Mindy, Gillian, Emily and Ellie

Bob's brother Al and wife Bonnie 2018

Blanshan siblings 2009

June by the back steps of
the Colebank house

Rebecca and Aaron 1974

Four generations: Dale holding his son Bob, Bob, and Ralph

Bob and Clarence Thomas 1998

Great-granddaughters Natalie Beach and Joely Olson - 2010

L to R: Linda, Lester, John and Clara. Brothers Lester and John married sisters Linda and Clara

Warren and family's dog and cat

Dale in Abraham Lincoln garb and Brenda

Paul, Barbara, Chris, Bonnie and Duane 1975

Blanshan family in 1986 (Barbara missing)

Blanshan siblings singing "You Are A Wonderful Mother" at June's 90th birthday party January 2016

Dale and granddaughter Eavan Thanksgiving 2009

June and sister Vickie

Bob and June opening wedding presents

Rebecca, Dale and Barbara about 1951

The Blanshan family in Lincoln, Nebraska: Barbara, June, Bob,
Rebecca, Dale, Nancy and Suzanne in front

Blanshan family about 1954

Linda, Lester and grandkids Barbara and Dale in early 1950

Blanshan family about 1974

Vickie and Jamaican students

Lester and Linda at their Madelia farm in front of their new Rambler

Lester picking corn on farm near Madelia

Madelia farm in winter

Lester and very tall beans

Blanshan family at Rebecca's graduation party in 1969

Paul, Barbara and Chris 1969

Barbara about 1967

Dale, Baby Jessica and Linda in 1978

Vickie

Fred, Vickie, Alathia and Jane Hintz

Suzanne and friend Beth at graduation

Suzanne's 5th birthday in 1961

Barbara and daughter Bonnie in 1995

Nancy, Baby Mandy and Dennis

Williamson family: Jerri and Dale in back; Tom, Marsha, Kim and Lois.
The Williamson family members were lifelong friends of the Blanshan
family.

Bob's parents, Fern and Slim Blanshan

Hill Family: Marilyn, Dwight, Mary, Judy, Doug. Bob and June met Marilyn and Dwight in Madelia and continued their friendships until Marilyn and Dwight passed away.

The Alvin and Ruth Petersen family: Back row, L to R: George, Joe, Myrna, Tim and Alvin. Middle: Bonnie, Ruth. Front: Ruth, John, Ellen, Romona. Bob Blanshan and family members were lifelong friends of the Petersens and spent a lot of time at the Petersen farm near Tilden, Nebraska.

The Blanshan family loved to spend the 4th of July here at Petersen's.

Firewood sawing bee at Woodside farm; Lester on far left

Lester in U.S. Army, Texas, 1918

June's Grandparents: Swedish immigrants Nils Person Nasman and Anna Greta Nelson's wedding photo July 8, 1888.

Linda Nasman Colebank, right, and her twin Esther Nasman Colebank. They married cousins.

LS and Martha Colebank's 50th anniversary photo
outside Colebank house in Madelia

Lester and Linda Colebank 50th anniversary photo
outside Colebank house in Madelia

Boyd, Mindy and Jeannie - Thanksgiving at Dale's
house in Brainerd 1989

Granddaughter Gillian and her daughter Natalie - Thanksgiving 2011

Rebecca's 3rd birthday

Brenda and Amy – winter of 1968

Bob in the Navy during WWII

Bob, year unknown

Bob with Barbara and Dale – winter 1950

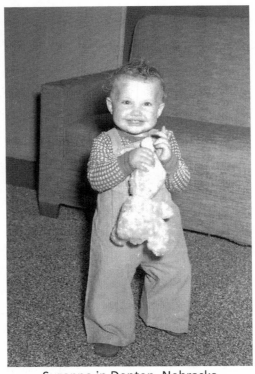

Suzanne in Denton, Nebraska

Warren holding Jim, wife Joyce and June on main
street in Madelia in 1946

Blanshan family in 1955: Barbara, Bob, June, Dale
Nancy, Rebecca, Suzanne in front.

All the Blanshan girls in 1968: Rebecca holding Penny, Amy, Suzanne, Nancy, Barbara holding Brenda.

Amy about 1965

Jessica in 2018

Polly in 2009

Mandy in 2009

Boyd 2009

Aaron 2009

Jimmy 2009

Billy 2016

Betsy and Winn 2009

Thanksgiving play in Brainerd 1988
Back row, L to R: Carrie, Gillian, Jessica. Front: Renata, Betsy, Emily.

June and Betsy making Thanksgiving lefse in 2001

Peggy 2009

Renata 2016

Eliana

Sterling and nephew Jackson 2014

Amy and Mindy

Joci

Gillian 2018

Duane and Katie – 2013

Emily and Weston 2018

Drew 2009

June and Bob, year unknown

Barbara and June at Thanksgiving 2011

Bob and son Malachi in 2018

Lester and Linda Colebank family

L to R: Barbara, Suzanne, Dale, Bob, Amy, Rebecca, June, Brenda, Nancy at Thanksgiving 2009

June's grandparents Martha McIndoo Colebank and L S Colebank

Made in the USA
Middletown, DE
30 September 2018